Chasing Dreams in Lefkas

By

Diane Griffith

Eloquent Books
New York, New York

Eloquent Books
An imprint of AEG Publishing Group
845 Third Avenue, 6th Floor - 6016
New York, NY 10022
www.eloquentbooks.com

ISBN: 978-1-60693-047-2
SKU: 1-60693-047-8

Printed in the United States of America

Book Design: Roger Hayes

Dedication

For my talented son Jamie, who I am extremely proud of, my caring mother, Eleanor and our friends, Maureen and Cliff, with love and gratitude.

Table of Contents

Prologue

Shortly before the author's husband turned fifty, Tony became the victim of his company's downsizing and was let go from his IT managerial position. As a result, Diane and Tony had hit rock bottom and had nowhere but up to turn. That's when Diane had an idea that would both relieve Tony's increasing depression and help the couple earn a living. They decided to sell Tony's precious Mercedes car, bought an 18-year-old VW camper van and traveled to the small Greek island of Lefkas, which they had visited the year before.

With the old VW packed full of video equipment, they set off on the adventure of a lifetime. On the island, they started recording the beautiful scenery and wonderful people they encountered. Using a portable generator in the sweltering heat of the VW, they edited the videos to show them on a television above the sink in their van. The very first night that they showed one of their videos, the open door of the van was facing a cobbled street where the showing caused quite a sensation in the sleepy little bay of Agios Nikitas. After that, it looked as if Diane's idea might just work.

From Agios Nikitas they traveled all around Lefkas filming and editing videos. They had a variety of experiences ranging from humorous to disastrous, but some were astonishingly wonderful. Through all their encounters, they developed many new friendships that will never be forgotten, many of which were with children. In response to the challenging yet rewarding experiences, Diane decided to share her memories with other dreamers who haven't had the same opportunity. If she had not written this book, she would have always looked back and wondered why she hadn't. Now, follow them on their journey and find out if they found the secret of true happiness. Or were they merely chasing dreams?

Chapter 1

"We've made it!" we shouted joyfully, as we drove across the noisy metal bridge and then along the causeway into Lefkas town. We wanted to yell, "We're here!" to the distant purple mountains and embrace the whole place in our arms.

There is nothing spectacular or touristy about Lefkas town. But the waterfront of bright fishing boats and yachts of various nationalities Tony found extremely exciting.

We viewed with awe the numerous beautiful yachts moored along the large colorful harbor: A mass of tall, proud, white masts against the blue sky. We remembered looking at them longingly the year before. Tony shook his head in disbelief. "Everything looks exactly the same!" He paused, gazing at the sights around him. "It's amazing! I can't believe that we're actually here!"

"Look," I interrupted, "there's the cafe where we sat with Lynne and Paul and the kids."

We had become holiday friends the previous year and sent them a copy of our holiday video featuring their children: Kate, a confident dark haired nine year old and Chris, two years younger and slightly autistic, with fair hair like his mother. Lynne had telephoned me one rainy evening in October to tell me how thrilled they were to receive the video.

The rickety, red plastic chairs were scattered about the pavement just as they had been then. Old men were standing around in groups talking. Sometimes they were shouting at each other, as though they were having the most awful argument, but they were in fact merely amiably discussing some minor incident. Greek conversations sometimes sound like arguments.

In the centre of the square was a railed garden of ill-kept geraniums and stunted palms. In the background stood the fortress of St. Mavra, with grey stone sloping walls that were covered in brown moss. This enclosed a lagoon, where the ruins of Peratia (Griva's Castle) stood. It was a constant reminder of more turbulent bygone times.

There seemed to be a ceaseless confusion, between the crowds of people and surge of traffic. Occasionally a donkey loaded with packages and bunches of brilliant flowers slowly picked its precarious way through the hurly-burly of the street. There was the intermittent hammering of a pneumatic drill and the dust and blare of passing traffic.

Our old VW looked appropriate and fitting as it made its way through the noisy streets, along with many other VW's. However, most of them were old and battered and none had English number-plates! All the cars, trucks, taxis and buses had worry beads hanging on their windscreens, just as we had! It made us feel at home.

Tony remembered the way to the little fishing village and bay of Agios Nikitas, so we headed through the cluttered streets. There was the usual hold up at the precarious traffic lights and the usual clamor of noise, as horns of different sounds blasted out constantly, even just to say "Hello" to a passer by, while a policeman stood in the middle of the street blowing his whistle relentlessly.

Music blasted from every dusty vehicle with a background of loud chatter and intermittent call of friendly greeting, while everyone, from young streetwise children to extremely old-looking women dressed in long black clothes, dodged in and out of the noisy traffic. The crowded pavements were lined with market stalls of fruit and vegetables and fish stalls that could be smelt before they were seen!

Young men loaded big boxes and cartons into trucks and old men sat at roadside café-bars sipping ouzo and water or drinking tiny cups of Greek coffee as they rattled their worry beads or car keys, their craggy weathered faces occasionally breaking into broad smiles showing gold teeth. In their dark eyes lurked a rebellious glint when frequently there was a loud verbal sparring that Greeks seem to enjoy. But mainly they just chattered the hours away and presumably solved the problems of the world.

We headed out of town. It was a straight road lined with trees and occasional smallholdings, with the words "Rooms to let" scrawled on makeshift signposts along the way.

We passed through dense olive groves with black netting bundled under the trees. Hens ran about scratching at the dusty, dry earth, where some cockerels strutted assertively. We passed a few tethered donkeys standing sleepily under trees and goats in small enclosures, chewing at heaps of leaves.

The old VW chugged along steadily, climbing the steep hill. The road was rough; on our left were rocks that appeared to be burning gold, against the high blue sky.

At the top, where the road curved, we parked and got out, emerging into the scorching sun.

I took a photograph of Tony by the side of the van.

This was the view that we remembered; it looked even more beautiful than we recalled.

"The last time we saw this view it was from the coach taking us home!" Tony was speaking wistfully.

Behind us was the view of Lefkas town, the impressive harbor, with the causeway, bridge and the old castle remains, all surrounded by brilliant, blue sea.

We looked down dreamily at the blue-green depths. To the right of the view lay the bay of "Yiro" which means "round." It was a long, sweeping promontory of white sand and shades of turquoise sea, following the curve inland again to hillsides covered with pine and olive trees.

∞∞

Then, as we drove around the corner, we saw a great expanse of yellow stone, bleached by the scorching sun, our hearts were beating faster!

We were quite overcome with emotion and excitement when at last we saw the village of Agios Nikitas.

"There it is!" We both uttered the words on a simultaneous sigh! It looked so beautiful, nestling at the foot of steep green mountain sides and sparkling blue sea. The sun was reflecting on the white buildings and irregular terracotta roofs. It seemed to be shining in the liquid shimmer of the sun, like a pearl that had been dropped in the middle of a mass of different shades of green and blue.

We parked on the side of the road, in the shade of huge white rock and turned the noisy engine off. There was only the sound of crickets, as we sat for some minutes without saying anything. We wanted to always remember this vivid impression and keep it in a secret corner of our hearts. We both felt the same tremendous joy. What had been a dream for so long had suddenly become reality.

"Well, here we are at last!" Tony put his arm around my shoulders.

Then he turned the key in the ignition, the engine jumped back to life again. We drove along the rugged coastal road until we reached the top of the cobbled street, which led steeply down past a few tavernas and finally opened into a small bay. We had longed so very much to see this again. We parked the VW and got out into the full glare of the sun. It was such a strange feeling! Our old van had brought us from our driveway at home, all the way here! It seemed unbelievable! I thought it looked tired, but curiously proud.

I patted its metal front, hot from the sun, but dusty from the journey, while quietly whispering, "Thank you!"

Then with trembling legs and a sense of increasing anticipation we began walking down the cobbled street wanting to savor every sight and sound.

It was all too much to take in, we were simply drifting along happily, enchanted by the feeling of something wonderful!

As we came to the Poseidon, a young lad came hurtling down the steps almost bumping into us. It was fat Yani. He looked up, his dark features braking into a huge grin. Then suddenly he was hugging both of us saying, "Yiasas!" (Hello)

We were surprised that he remembered us! Turning briefly he called up the steps to his younger brother and Demetrious somewhat more cautiously, came strolling down muttering.   "Yia!" although reticent, he too evidently remembered us.

We were walking carefully on the shiny cobbles, unaware of the fact that fat Yani was to become our 'very best friend'.

An old lady, wearing the traditional long brown dress and shawl walked past whispering words of acknowledgement. I smiled at her and saw her old eyes twinkle. Then she walked on, shaking her head in a rather bemused way. Little did we know then, that she was to become our most dedicated video fan?

We entered Nikos' Mini market, a small dusty shop, through a tunnel of beach accessories, with everything from T-shirts, to rusty racks of out of date post cards and dusty bottles of sun cream.

I picked a loaf, some eggs and a bottle of water, and then I walked to the check out at the doorway. I handed a thousand drachma note to the tall young man who had a very large hooked nose.

"I... remember... you!" He was one of the few people in the village, who spoke Basic English. He raised his hand in emphasis with an expression of surprise. "You were ... here last year."

"Yes, but this time we came all the way by road," I laughed. "It took us four days."

He shook his head emitting a low, whistling sound, and then with a smile that was also in his dark eyes he spoke softly.

"Welcome! Welcome to Agios Nikitas!" It was at that moment that we felt the long hard journey had been worthwhile!

We walked on to the end of the street and stood motionless gazing at the pretty little bay of shingle and sand. It was just how we remembered it and had visualized it over and over again, during the dreary cold miserable months at home, which seemed in another world now. I felt a little tingling thrill running down my spine.

The same few fishing boats were bobbing almost silently on incredibly clear turquoise sea and we listened again to the sound of the gently lapping waves caressing the shingle. Greek music was floating from the "Captain's Corner" and my heart did a somersault!

I suppose that how magical a paradise really is, depends on how you perceive it. But this little place had not yet been violated by the modern world, so in it's lost ness, it had somehow been blessed with solitude.

11

We sat down on the old wooden seat that we had sat at so often the year before, overlooking the bay, absorbing our surroundings: Breathing in the smell of sand and sea. It was mid afternoon; the sun was blazing down on the ochre colored cliffs beside us. It was all so beautiful!

It was the focal point of the village, everyone sat there for a time it seemed, to be at one with the environment.

Old men shuffled there every evening and young men strutted, with an acceptable degree of arrogance that was actually rather appealing. They all tinkered with either worry beads or keys, as they talked about football, politics and women.

Sometimes elderly women in peasant dress and shawl would exchange a few words, as they hobbled by. At other times attractive girls, with hair the color of a ravens' wing, would walk up to join in the friendly banter. They had a certain self-confidence and casual air, that gave an impression that was very hard to describe, but was particularly typical of their culture.

I wondered how old this seat was. It must have been there a very long time, yet no one had vandalized it, or indeed none of the walls or buildings had been defaced.

I felt that somehow we had stepped into a different world. A world without aggression!

The sun was beginning to sink behind the pine-clad mountain and in the distance we could hear the sound of cockerels calling at different scattered destinations. We watched some local teenagers begin to prepare a game of volley ball, using two tall wild pampas canes and a piece of string across the beach, which they noisily, but good naturedly, put together. Then along with the younger children of the village they began their nightly game, amid much laughing and shouting. "Ella...Ella 'tho!" (Come... Come here!)

I loved listening to the children. I had thirsted to hear Greek language spoken naturally, instead of from my Linguaphone cassettes.

Eventually, we became aware of the sound of gravel underfoot, a few old men were shuffling about, while eyeing us shiftily, so we realized that it was time we vacated the seat!

We walked around the corner and sat on white plastic chairs at a white plastic table at the "Captain's Corner," where we could continue to watch the children playing.

After a few minutes Zak came out to take our order. Tony spoke some of the small amount of Greek that he knew.

"Theo beeres parakalo!" (Two beers, please)

"My friends! My friends!" Zak called smiling broadly.

He brought us two large glass tankards of draught beer, something Tony had been longing for! Then dragging a chair over to our table he sat down looking at me curiously and remembering that I spoke some Greek, he asked when we had arrived, as he had not heard of any English tourists arriving at Agios Nikitas. Most of the holiday companies were taking tourists to the larger resorts of Nidri and Vassiliki, on the other side of the island.

I explained to him that we had not come with a holiday company, but had traveled by VW camper. He was completely enthralled and demanded to know which way we had come, how long it had taken and how much it had cost...

I tried to tell him as best as I could, but he spoke so quickly that I had trouble understanding everything he said. Tony told me to tell him about the reason why we had come. So again I took a deep breath and surged ahead with my Greek explanation. I did not know the word for "redundant," so this brought the attention of some nearby locals who then joined in the conversation. Zak was most impressed with the idea of a video of Lefkas featuring Agios Nikitas and insisted that we film him and his bar. Tony I were overjoyed that they all seemed so ecstatic about our idea.

A couple of pints later I asked if anyone knew of a room that we could rent.

"Iro"s rooms opposite the Poseidon," Zak said pointing up the street.

So reluctantly we said, "Yiasas." (This means hello and goodbye.)

It was under a large tree that we found Iro, sitting chattering and smoking, with her sister and an old man, around a large wooden table covered with a red and white plastic table-cloth. I asked for Iro, whereupon she slowly stood up and walked towards me. She was dressed in a black jumper and skirt with hair that had been dyed black, although there was a noticeable white parting.

"Angliki?" (English?) She smiled showing dark circles under her tired eyes.

"Ne." (Yes.) I replied before continuing in Greek. "We would like a room, a cheap one!"

This made her laugh and putting her arm around my shoulders she gave me a hug. We followed her up some concrete steps to a landing, then opening a faded blue door she showed us a clean though basic room.

It contained twin beds, two bedside tables a small table and two chairs, which, she pointed out we could put outside on the small balcony if we chose. There was a shared bathroom completely tiled in sparkling white and in the passage, was a battered old communal fridge that droned away continuously and looked as though it desperately needed defrosting. The door would not close. Iro's brow lifted and in a subdued voice she made some apologetic comment closing her eyes to emphasize how exhausted she was. Then she let her voice sink even lower as she added that we could bring our own food in if we wished. So we agreed to pay the equivalent of about £9 a night. This was, in fact, the only place where we could park the van, as there was an open area next to her untidy garden.

When I explained our plans to her, at first her brow furrowed in puzzlement. I emphasized that we hoped to stay for three months if we could sell the videos.

Taking a deep breath, she told us to park the van in the street opposite the Poseidon during the evening and show the video to passers-by as the street was wide enough at this part. We explained that we were a bit worried that children might damage the generator, or someone might fall over it.

"No problem!" She was using the only English that she knew. She told us to put it in her garden behind the wall. It would be out of the way there. She seemed to want our project to work just as much as we did! She began talking excitedly about our plans to her sister and the old man who listened intently. Everything seemed to be working out well for us.

Our room was at the back of the building so was thankfully always in the shade. Alongside our balcony a narrow path forked, one way led across the rugged headland to a beautiful white sandy beach called Milos. The other led into a thicket, so this would give me the ideal opportunity, while sitting on our balcony, to direct people the right way and to casually mention our videos!

It was Wednesday 24th. June 1992 when we put our case in the room looking forward to a good night's sleep in a real bed! We both had a long shower and as we were getting ready to go for a meal we could hear the bouzouki music coming from the Poseidon.

"They are still playing the same tape!" Tony threw his head back and laughed.

Just then we heard the tune, 'Zorbas Dance' and we both immediately thought of young Chris, who although locked in his own little world, loved this tune so much!

Lynne had told me that it was only when he saw our video that he talked about the holiday for the first time. It was as if the music had unlocked a window in his mind.

"They're playing Chris' song!" I was looking into Tony's eyes.

"I wonder if we'll ever see them again." He replied thoughtfully knowing that it was Chris who had given us the idea to do this venture in the first place.

It was a bizarre feeling walking along the street again with the same local people acknowledging us with, "Yiasas," and the same children, who had grown slightly, smiling at us, also the same bars, playing the same music as they had done the previous year.

"It seems funny without Lynne and Paul and the kids around!" Tony seemed saddened to a certain extent.

"Yes it does!" I also felt a bit moved.

Suddenly he grabbed my arm pointing to the Poseidon steps

"There's Chris!" he shouted. I looked and was astounded! He was standing with Thanai, the pretty little seven-year old daughter of the owners of the restaurant.

We walked up to him and I spoke gently to him. "Hello Chris, do you remember us? Can you take us to your mummy and daddy?" There was a dazed look in his eyes for a second; then his face brightened and he ran up the steps beneath the twisted hanging vines.

Lynne and Paul were staggered when we walked in with Chris! Lynne opened her mouth and then closed it without uttering one single word.

Then shaking her head she spoke with a gasp.

"I could not believe my eyes! I had just at that moment been telling a couple on the next table about you two! I told them that we met a couple here last year; and they had sent us a lovely video and how delighted we were to get it." She paused momentarily before she continued her voice high with glee. "I said I keep expecting them to walk in through the doorway!" She gave a little laugh. "No sooner had I said the words, when you did!"

It was such a coincidence! They had also arrived that day! But they had left England at 3pm! And arrived 4 hours later: It had taken us 4 days!

We had a sensational and memorable evening. There was so much that we had to tell them. They were shocked to hear from Tony how he had lost his job.

"The bastards waited for me to come back from holiday, to tell me I was redundant. Not only that, but I lost the big pay out that I should have had after twenty four years."

"How come?" Paul looked puzzled.

"The company was taken over and so the terms were changed. Under the original terms I was to receive a months pay for every year I worked, but with the new terms I got one month's pay."

"So," I added, "our comfortable lifestyle abruptly ended and we could either sit and cry about it or do something that we would never have done, so we decided to do this. It was actually because you were so pleased to get the video that gave me the idea."

Lynne's face brightened. "Well I'm glad of that anyway and I do think you will do well. But the situation must have been extremely worrying for you. I realize your need to get away."

Paul was shaking his head in a thoughtful way. They were very interested to hear how we had traveled there and both children were also pleased to see us again. Vassilis was still dancing around balancing all sorts of things on his head. His party trick this year was to pour a glass of water up to the brim while continuing to dance and not spill a drop. He swaggered over to us, a cigarette hanging between his lips, with a smile playing at the corners of his mouth. "Kalos tous! Kalos tous!" The welcome shone sincerely in his dark eyes. Showing very uneven teeth, he was beaming, as he looked at us through the smoke of his cigarette speaking in stilted English. "You… came… here…er… by car?"

He was vastly surprised; and promptly began dancing and singing, with a kind of madness which is typical of many Greeks.

It was a peculiar feeling going to bed without the performance of moving all our belongings! It was also strange to be able to get out of bed without scrambling over each other and go to a proper toilet during the night, instead of hiding discretely behind the van! The 'porta-potti' was quite inaccessible during the night, so it was kept for emergency 'wees'! And it was always our main priority to have a toilet nearby! So this was indeed a luxury!

Although it was still early morning when we walked down the street the sun was strong. The sound of birdsong echoed all around us and within minutes we were contentedly swimming in the beautiful clear sea. The feeling was too marvelous to describe!

After a short while Tony spoke on a sigh, "Who'd have thought that so much could have happened to us in one year."

"Yes indeed, if we had known what we were going back to." Our eyes met and held for some time. A communication passed between us, fully understanding what had been conveyed without the need for words.

We were remembering the terrible day in November 1991 when he came home from his managerial position in a large company in Liverpool. He sat down heavily on our sofa and his expression was one of utter devastation and defeat.

"We will lose everything that I have worked for." His eyes were full of tears. "We can't pay the mortgage, we will have to sell both the house and the car." It had long been his ambition to own a Mercedes car, so on his forty eighth birthday we bought one in a lovely shade of metallic blue. It was his pride and joy.

I had a one year old BMW; we could afford these luxuries, but I knew we couldn't any more.

I looked around our cozy home, together we had strived to achieve a comfortable lifestyle, glad that we had both found happiness after both our former marriages ended in divorce. We were almost forty when we met and we were married three months later. We had bought our house in a neglected condition and now we had it just the way we had dreamed it would look when we bought it seven years ago. It was the home we intended to retire in and it was very important to us.

I put my arm around his slumped shoulders. "We still have each other."

He didn't look up, but continued to stare at the floor without seeing anything. "I feel that I have been cheated."

"How can they do this?"

"**They** can do **anything!**" The muscles in his jaw were pressed tight. He rubbed a trembling hand across his face in an earnest attempt to control the pain of his emotions. Then he reached into his pocket and took out the check with shaking hands.

"Is that all I am worth!"

I couldn't bear to see him so heartbroken and humiliated.

He was approaching fifty; unemployment figures had never been higher in the UK. In addition he had the disadvantage that an injury at birth had left him with very restricted use of his right arm. Whether it was the fact that weaknesses get worse with age, or whether the worry of our predicament had affected it, I don't know. But he had been suffering a lot of pain. Our doctor had arranged for him to see a specialist, but since we no longer had the privilege of private medical care, we expected a long wait.

We put our lovely home on the market and lived as cheaply as possible. We sold the Mercedes; redundancy had brought grim reality.

As the black days passed, each much like the one before it, we began to recollect our holiday on the island of Lefkas. It was especially memorable because I had been happy to realize the fruits of my studying the Greek language.

On the blackest most miserable evenings we tried to escape from the real world by watching our holiday video. At one part, Tony had filmed through the shuttered open window of Zaks' beach side café, The Captain's Corner, as the sun was slowly sinking and everywhere was bathed in mellow, evening light. I had walked to the waters' edge to cool my feet and was unaware that he was filming me. The song, 'It's No Sacrifice' by Elton John was playing which was unusual, as Zak usually played Greek music. When I saw Tony filming, I smiled and waved at him, feeling so content. I returned to our table and with a smile I raised my glass of beer to him. This captured moment in time was one of those special memories that come back to you when you hear a certain song. So much so that whenever we hear that song we both know each other's thoughts. A warm setting sun, blue gently lapping sea and a big glass of cold draught beer: Complete happiness!

The cheerful sunny images magically turned our grey world momentarily brighter. But our future looked very daunting; I felt that I had to think of something to aim for and also to relieve Tony's increasing depression.

Winter passed into spring. One gold and green day we were working in our garden in a relentless effort to involve ourselves in something constructive. I was mowing the lawn; the hover hummed and the continuous low-pitched droning sound sent my thoughts drifting. My mind reflected and contemplated until I eventually recalled how thrilled Lynne had sounded when she had received the video we had sent her. I switched the mower off and walked up to Tony.

"I've thought of something!" I shouted. I was suddenly excited. "I know what we could do!" So the idea had been born...

We had a purpose that we could work at together, a project, a goal, a dream! The dark cloud of gloom that had hung over us for so long was lifting. We began to ease out of our sadness; the healing period had begun.

We enrolled at night school to learn more about video techniques, although it had been Tony's hobby, so he was already quite proficient. I made computer graphic titles in glowing colors which Tony transferred on to a video cassette to take with us.

Then we printed posters to stick on the vans' windows, to advertise our films. We looked through the local papers for a 'work-horse' for this sort of expedition.

The first time we saw our VW camper van it was standing on a road in Liverpool, in torrential rain, begging to go to Greece! From the moment we saw it, it was love at first sight! Tony drove it home while I drove our other car, which we were going to sell behind. When it was parked on our driveway it definitely looked happier, as though it knew that it was to be a very important part of our adventure.

We planned our route, with a map spread on our dining-room table and a bottle of whiskey. Agios Nikitas was to be our eventual destination, although it seemed so terribly far away.

"The journey looks horrendous!" Tony was beginning to panic. "Two hundred miles to London and then another hundred miles down to the sea port of Dover, over to France, then through Germany and into Switzerland."

"Do you think we will be able to sleep in the van, since it will be so packed up with equipment?"

"We can move everything to the front from the back at night." He continued looking more in control. "After Switzerland we'll head right down the leg of Italy and eventually get to Brindisi Port. There we can board a ferry to Ignoumitsa, mainland Greece. From there it is merely 50 miles to Lefkas."

During the day this all seemed very exciting, but as night time approached, it seemed a bit daunting and we'd have another whiskey!

Tony was concerned about the van. "What if it brakes down? I know nothing about engines!" We were both scared, but we were not put off. This was our ambition and we were determined to see it through. We were fortunate to find a doctor who needed to rent a place for three months. This would cover our mortgage.

Journeys usually begin at airports, or railway stations, ours began on our driveway.

Although it was the 18th of June, it was cold and grey, the sky was heavy with dark clouds. The Greek Comboloy, worry beads, brought back from our holiday, looked most inappropriate as we headed away from home towards London.

The journey to Dover was uneventful. But we were aware of a mixture of emotions from nervous apprehension of what lay before us, to growing excitement. As we approached Dover it began to drizzle. We had no heater in the van, so we were cold and uncomfortable. We were bustled onto the ferry at Dover so quickly that no one asked to see the carnet of all the equipment we were carrying. Tony had laboriously made three copies of everything electrical as he had been instructed to do. So we spent the rest of the journey worrying whether we would finish up in some jail accused of smuggling! But we were past the point of no return.

It was raining heavily; the sky looked very somber. The boat cut steadily through the grey sea, but we were off to blue sea and blue sky, so we turned to look for the new horizon.

Within a few minutes of reaching Calais we were heading along the French motorway at a steady 50 m.p.h. as the rain lashed down in torrents. At St. Brice we found a picnic area and spent our first night in the van. We looked at each other in the darkness and the topsy-turviness of the van, feeling rather ill at ease.

Tony looked suddenly confused. "What the hell are we doing?"

"We're having an adventure!" I replied pushing him over onto the bed.

We both lay silent for a moment, looking into each other's faces. Then I saw his eyes crinkle at the corners and he began to laugh. It was a moment to remember. It had been so long since I had seen him happy.

The next morning we were disappointed to find that it was still raining.

Driving through France was easy; the road was quiet and straight.

By early afternoon we had passed into Germany and became aware of the distinctive accents on the radio and we felt an increasing excitement growing inside us. Then as twilight drew I was so looking forward to seeing Lake Lucerne. It was dusk when we reached the lake and it looked so beautiful, that we decided to stay there for our second night.

To our delight the rain had stopped but everywhere was still wet.

Tony re-arranged our belongings, while I fried sausages and heated up some beans as I sang, "By the beautiful lake of Lucerne"...until I banged my head on the roof of the van.

As we had not slept much the previous night we were extremely tired and still very cold. So we settled down for the night still wearing our jeans and sweaters.

"Wrap up well, it is freezing." Tony looked concerned.

I wrapped a woolly scarf around my head: This was not a time for decorum.

The night was black and the cold was the sort that seeped through to your bones. As we lay silently under our flimsy cover, a shiver ran through me.

"This is awful! Are you alright honey?" Tony whispered as he held me close.

"Yes of course, don't worry about me." I began to giggle. "I'm having the time of my life!" Then we both began to laugh. This made us grow warm and before long we were both sound asleep.

We awoke to see the sun rising over the lake. We had admired lakes before, but this, with the snow-capped mountains raising majestically all around it, was something different. The sky was still heavy with dark ominous-looking clouds; also across the still waters the mountains looked dramatic against the grayness of the clouds. And there was a wonderful silence.

As we headed through the countryside we were filled with a brand new feeling. I leaned my head out of the window and took a deep breath. "Ah! Switzerland!" I was feeling the air cool and fresh. Huge rolling mountains surrounded us, their snowy summits reaching the sky, disappearing in a shroud of mist. We could hear the sound of cattle bells as cows grazed in lush green pastures.

We emerged from the ST. Gothard Tunnel, which was about 17km long. The day was bright and for the first time we were able to sit outside to eat.

We found a picnic area with tables and benches.

A stream was rushing by splashing on shiny dark stones. Many waterfalls tumbled down mountainsides in the distance, appearing as little shivers of silver between black rocks.

Birds were singing, proclaiming their happiness to the world and fluttered in the nearby wet branches. One tiny bird smaller than a sparrow fluttered like a leaf and settled on our table. It ruffled its feathers and moved about quickly, looking for crumbs with sharp black eyes.

There was a delicate fragrance of wild flowers of hundreds of brilliant colors. We felt enraptured and strangely intoxicated.

We entered Milan and paid another toll. Italy looked interesting. There were many tall blocks of flats with washing hanging over balconies. The road suddenly became very busy. Traffic sped past. There was a lot of honking of horns and revving of engines and loud blasts of music from passing vehicles.

"I can see the Adriatic coast!" I shouted after some time. It was a thin shimmer of silver in the distance between tall buildings. This lifted our spirits. We could feel the temperature rising. We were now in the swing of things.

"Well navigator, where's the next big name on the map?" Tony asked smiling.

"San Marino." I was following the bright yellow line with my finger.

Our next night was spent behind a service station just off the busy motorway. I felt that our little VW camper van looked so vulnerable beside all the huge trucks and lorries.

Tony was soon snoring, while I lay listening to the sound of large diesel engines. I must have slept for some time because I was suddenly awakened by the headlights of wagon lighting up the van. I glanced at my watch and saw that it was 6.15. I knew that Tony wanted to make an early start so after a short time I woke him gently.

"How about starting off now? We could get some miles behind us before the road gets busy."

He made an inarticulate sound, before he groaned," What time is it?"

"Quarter past six." I was tingling with a sense of adventure.

"Oh! All right!" he was yawning. "But I don't feel as though I've had much sleep."

After moving all our belongings we were soon on the road again, romantically called the autostrada.

Tony yawned again and looked at his watch. "What time did you say it was before?"

"Quarter past six."

"Well how come it's ten past four now?"

We both burst out laughing. I had read the hands the wrong way round. It must have only been half past three.

However we were heading along the highway of the sun and by late afternoon we were nearing Brindisi. I noticed a sign indicating that there was a camp-site nearby so we made our way towards it as we desperately needed a shower and a good night's sleep.

The campsite shop was still open so we were able to buy some fresh food. After a quick fry-up with crusty bread, washed down with some cold beer we showered and were soon fast asleep. The van parked beneath a canopy of bright pink bougainvillea.

We awoke to the delightful sound of birds singing all around us.

We were almost on the last lap of the journey that had looked so very daunting.

Brindisi was intriguing. Big and bustling and the shops looked very sophisticated and expensive. Women strolled around looking proud and chic in gold backless sandals. Children were dressed in lovely bright colors and unusual styles. The main road through the centre of the town was lined with trees, and women with buggies, or shopping bags hurried around. It appeared as though all the young generation traveled on accelerating motorbikes or scooters. Handsome young fellows, with attractive girls, sitting behind them wearing trendy little garments, with the shortest skirts, skidded everywhere. Music pounded from every doorway and often boomed from a ghetto-blaster, accompanying the already conspicuous motorcyclists, in their unrestrained pursuit of pleasure. We sat at a roadside cafe called 'Harry's Bar' I wanted to take a photograph to send to our friend Harry who's ambition it is to have a bar abroad. We ordered two ice creams and one can of orange. The bill was £11.50! "What daylight robbery!" Tony said with dismay.

At 6pm we boarded the vast ship. Then we sat on the deck and gazed at white surf on dark blue sea, churning away behind us in a huge V shape. We had decided to sleep in reclining seats since we couldn't afford a cabin. This was a mistake. The temperature below deck was extremely cold and the seats were far from comfortable. Since it had been so hot when we boarded we were only wearing shorts and T shirts.

We spent the entire night trying to get warm. Eventually we crept into a corridor of cabins and found an air vent where there was some warm air. We lay down together beside it and hoped that nobody would open their door and find us there. The pulsating beat of the engines was deafening and drummed through our bodies making it impossible to sleep.

"Let's go up to the deck again." Tony whispered at around 4pm.

So we watched the sun rise over glimmering sea. It would have been delightful if we hadn't been so bleary-eyed and utterly exhausted.

"Look I can see Greece." Tony said after an hour or so.

In the distance loomed monstrous mountains, covered in pine as far as the eye could see. We could make out incongruous white buildings and stone walls that zigzagged up the hillsides retaining the red fertile soil.

We arrived at Ignoumitsa at 10am. After climbing into our van amid a lot of shouting and whistle blowing we were waved out of the hull of the ship by an angry looking, large man.

There was a lengthy queue at the customs and there was no escaping the scorching heat of the sun. Eventually it was our turn to hand our passports to an extremely hostile looking man in uniform. I spoke in Greek to him, but he was not impressed. He merely indicated to the serial number of our video camera that had been stamped in Tony's passport, on our last holiday. Luckily I had been filming some of our journey with that camera so it was near me. He checked the number, then sternly and rapidly without lifting his head, he waved us away. I wondered if we should tell him about the other new camera, all the equipment and 300 tapes under the seat? But we were so hot, tired and disorientated, that we merely drove off.

We had been traveling for about half an hour, heading towards Preveza when Tony looked worried "What if the police ask us about our equipment when we are showing the film?"

We both contemplated, experiencing our own private panic attack. We knew that video equipment was very expensive in Greece. This was another reason why we thought our idea was so good. We wouldn't be encroaching on the local's livelihood.

After a few moments I replied. "Well I don't think we have done anything wrong. If he had asked us if we had anything else we would have told him."

This decided it. We were in the clear, we hoped!

From then on, it was a wonderful feeling traveling along the coastal road to Parga. We were thrilled to hear Greek music on the radio. I was so delighted.

"I can understand most of the words!" I called feeling so proud.

To the right of us was shimmering endless sea that paled into the pearly distance where it met the sky. A few fishing boats were reflected in the liquid mirror beneath them. On our left were olive trees, old and knarrled and twisted. There were valleys with nothing but craggy rock and crumbling walls, where some sheep and goats wandered about grazing. Occasionally, we saw ancient white-washed churches that people still used. At frequent intervals along the road were the customary rusty metal memorial, with a lighted candle and some flowers inside the glass box on the top. Flowering bushes lined the road and brilliant white houses were scattered at random between the trees, where a sleepy, donkey stood. Everywhere was embraced by the sun.

We were welcomed to a camp-site at Sivotta by a friendly young Greek man. He opened a small shop so that we could buy some more food and was impressed that we had traveled from England. He was also equally impressed that I was so skilled at speaking Greek. This gave me renewed energy.

We sat in the shade of a big tree to eat our supper. The ground beneath us was soft with pine needles. Somewhere in the distance goat bells were ringing. Then the clicking of small hooves and the jingling of bells became louder. To my delight a herd of sheep and goats trotted along the road nearby. The sun was rolling over to the west, the sky was pink and shadows fell bewitchingly between the trees.

By 9pm we were sound asleep and didn't wake until 7.30 the next morning.

After a quick shower we were on our way again. Tony was steering the van along the high, hot road.

"That site only cost us four pounds, whereas the site in Brindisi had cost us more than double." He was impressed.

A few miles on we stopped at a ramshackle garage and Tony searched for his notebook so that he could enter the latest mileage. I remembered putting it on the bumper of the van when we were having our supper. I felt so guilty, because all his carefully logged notes were lost. Tears sprang to my eyes, and I gave him a pleading look.

"Oh! I'm so sorry!"

"Never mind!" He sighed, patting my knee reassuringly. Nothing could spoil our growing excitement now. "We are almost there!" It seemed that he wasn't entirely happy though.

Before us were Parga, Loutsa, Himadi, Kanali and Preveza: And always in the distance was the shimmer of liquid heat.

We had just past Himadi when we spotted a small taverna between the endless olive groves and scattered dwellings among the vineyards.

Tony pulled in to park under a tree, and immediately the whole family came out to welcome us. The father, a bearded middle-aged man stared at our number plate. I could see that he was puzzled, so this gave me another opportunity to try some more Greek Language. He wanted to know if we had come from England. They all listened as I explained as best as I could. His wife dressed in a shabby black dress stood silently smiling at the doorway. Two little boys came running out and one came to our table showing us a small, red, plastic bus.

"Mou arressi to leoforio sou" (I like your bus) I said smiling at him.

This made him chuckle and run off to play with his brother who was kicking a ball beneath the trees.

We ordered bacon and eggs and the man lifted his finger which indicated that we should wait.

The food was delicious, with a big bowl of Greek salad, feta cheese and freshly baked bread. We had two bottles of 'Fanta' orange drinks and the whole lot came to the equivalent of £2.

After we had eaten we continued to sit under the billowing trees, with silvery leaves making a rustling sound above. Tiny black and white birds ducked and dived around us, disappearing into crevices under the eaves. The sound of their merry chirping was mingling with the constant sound of crickets. I was filled with happiness. I was speaking to these friendly people in their own language and Tony loved to listen. Maybe I wasn't saying everything correctly, but we were communicating; and that, to me, was wonderful.

As we got up to leave, an older woman who had been smiling and listening at the open window, came out with a loaf of bread, still hot from the oven, wrapped in some paper napkins. "Yia taxithi sas" ("For your journey")

I offered to pay her, but they all protested. "Ohi!" (No) Then, they all stood at the roadside waving to us until we were out of sight.

It was an incredible feeling driving past Preveza airport that we had flown to, the year before.

Then we were standing on the small ferry that took us across a wide harbor and saved a long drive around. We could see the island of Lefkas which stood beyond this languid blue lagoon. It was an oasis of quietness, except for the steady beating of the engine and the thumping of our excited hearts.

In a very short time we would be at the old metal drawbridge that crosses the small isthmus that separates Lefkas from the mainland.

ഇരCള

My recollections were suddenly interrupted by Tony swimming up to me.

"Wasn't it a hell of an experience getting here?" Shaking the water from his hair, he laughed out loud. "This is all so amazing!"

Evidently we had both been thinking the same thoughts.

"Let's go back to our room and have some breakfast," I replied smiling.

We sat on our balcony drinking coffee and eating eggs, boiled on the cooker in the van and carried carefully up to our room. We had established a space of our own in the fridge and in our room reserved one drawer for tinned food and another for bread, biscuits crisps etc. So now we were much more organized and extremely comfortable!

After we had eaten we decided to go to Lefkas town to stock up with provisions.

We drove into the busy market place and left the van by the side of the harbor. It was extremely hot so we walked in quick short bursts, pausing under the occasional tree that offered glorious shade.

By the time we found the supermarket we were exhausted. Tony spotted a small café bar on the shady side of the street just across the road. So we headed for it. There were wooden chairs with wicker seats and an assortment of rickety tables. A cheerful plump woman served us two bottles of cold "Amstel Beer" while some locals nodded a casual greeting. Tony decided to stay and have another beer, while I did the shopping at the supermarket. After I returned we both walked around the market stalls buying fruit and vegetables.

We had decided that we would have a brief holiday and get acclimatized before we began making the video. Furthermore we found it difficult to concentrate on work when Lynne, Paul and the children were around. Nevertheless we did make a start!

"First of all," Tony said. "We have to have a 'story-board.'"

So we drove around the many places that we intended to include in our film, to see what the best positions would be to film from so that we did not hang around more than necessary in the blazing sun. The following day, having decided on all our best 'takes,' we drove to the drawbridge where Tony began filming.

Inevitably someone would walk past and spoil the shot! So we took four shots of each place, to enable us to choose the best one when we were editing the film.

While Tony drove along the road to Agios Nikitas I filmed through the van window, this would give the film direction and movement, which would add interest. It was a journey everyone who came to Lefkas would recognize.

We still spent time with Lynne, Paul and the children, but they understood that we were there to work. I must admit that we were quite glad when they decided to spend a few days on Kefalonia, another island between Lefkas and Zakinthos. That gave us the chance to really get down to the task of finishing our video.

We were surprised to find that unlike the year before there were not a lot of English people in Agios Nikitas. There were mainly Italians and Greeks, on holiday from the mainland. Lynne and Paul had come 'flight only' and got a taxi from the airport, because they new that the children could play safely in and out of the 'Poseidon,' so giving them some time to themselves. However, we believed that we would have the film ready by the time the British tourists did arrive.

We had completed filming magnificent views, from Lefkas town to Agios Nikitas and we had featured the street, where many of the locals were unaware that they had been caught on film. Liana, a pleasant curvy lady who worked at the car hire office had been extremely amused on finding that we had filmed her. She usually seemed remarkably composed although her two little girls constantly harassed her; pulling at her skirt and fighting for her attention by trying to scream louder that the other. I wondered if this was a ploy to ensure that one didn't hang about to complain about faulty brakes, or any other problem that we would consider drastic, but by their standards were quite acceptable.

We had made our way down the street filming all the tavernas by day causing such excitement amongst the local owners. Finally we filmed the 'Captains Corner' where we took a shot of Zak, smiling proudly while he strutted around looking rather like Danny De Vito. Then, we took a succession of superb shots of the quaint little bay that was so picturesque.

Later on we trekked the footpath over the headland to Milos. This was rather treacherous carrying the tripod, camera, batteries, a bottle of water and some crisps, as there was nowhere to buy refreshments there. We also took a few beach necessities, but these were limited since Tony's arm had been giving him a lot of pain.

Rocks had fallen onto the slip of a path that wound its way through dense pine and past a gigantic cactus, green, fleshy and spiky, monumental against a cloudless blue sky. All the while there was the background noise of crickets and the smell of pine, lavender and dry ochre colored earth.

We climbed further up, emerging from the pleasant shade of the trees passing an ancient ruin near the top. Tiny birds fluttered by screeching surprise at the invasion of their territory, and butterflies of wondrous brilliance danced between myriads of wild flowers. At one place a large tree had fallen across the slippery path, making us scramble over it.

Finally we reached the highest point and standing among the bracken we were panting in the burning air. The view that lay beneath us was sensational!

Tony mopped his brow with the back of his hand. "We really must get a few shots from here."

"Oh! Yes! It was well worth that climb!" I was also sweating and I tried to sit on a rock but found that it was too hot.

When we had taken enough footage we then began our decent. The path sloped downward sharply and the ground had deteriorated to small loose stones. It was extremely difficult to keep a foothold, so before long our already tired limbs were trembling and every muscle ached. My foot slipped beneath me but luckily I collided with the trunk of a small tree, so preventing me from tumbling down the steep embankment.

"Take it easy Di!" Tony looked alarmed. I'm not sure if it was me, or the equipment that he was concerned about!

He had to jump the final part, since it was a sheer drop onto the scorching, white, soft sand. Then I carefully handed the equipment down to him and jumped down myself.

We made secure our belongings, then rushed into the brilliant blue sea and immersed ourselves. It was such a joy to be able to cool our aching bodies and burning heads.

The long beach was almost deserted so there was an absence of footmarks on the even sand. Gulls swooped above us and at one end, on an outcrop of white rock; a lone fisherman cast his line.

Later on we took some close-up shots of the clear water, capturing the sound of gentle splashes as the lapping waves rippled softly on the sand.

₧

The following days' filming was taken on the busy road leading to lively, cosmopolitan Nidri. When we first set eyes on the town, we completely recaptured the excitement that we felt when we saw it the year before.

We filmed the busy harbor-front, with the impressive yachts and the many boats that offered trips to peaceful, beautiful beaches, like Porto Katsiki, that were virtually otherwise inaccessible. Opposite the harbor, on the other side of the street was an interesting assortment of cheerful tavernas and friendly bars. And at the end of the road was a narrow sandy tree lined beach that swept into a curve and a small promontory that led to another similar beach.

The water here was shallow making it perfect for families as well as many water sports. Across the harbor were the little white church of Saint Kiriaki and the house of Mathouri. We were told that this was a popular landmark, but we never exactly found out why! But we filmed it anyway from across the port, because it looked so enchanting!

There was a main road of colorful shops running parallel to the harbor-front. Filming here was particularly difficult. We wanted to capture the bustling atmosphere, so we persevered, dodging the noisy, erratic traffic and the occasional, heavily-laden mule.

The next location was Vassiliki where sail-boarding was exceptionally popular. The valley between high mountains on either side caused ideal wind conditions on the large shallow bay.

At one end was a row of tavernas where you could sit under the sweeping branches that almost reached the water, as you enjoyed a freshly cooked meal or a refreshing drink brought across the busy, narrow street by a light-hearted waiter prancing to Greek music.

Filming here took us all day, as there was an abundance of interesting shots.

We bought some fresh bread, tomatoes and cheese and had a picnic on the beach. Although we were disappointed to find that what we had thought was white sand, was in fact very sharp stones, making it too uncomfortable to sit on.

"Good job we have our chairs with us," I said as I handed one to Tony.

"Let's go for a swim," Tony groaned about half an hour later. "It's so very hot."

When we entered the water I was disheartened. "The sea here is not clear, it's so murky!"

"That's because of the underlying sand. But I suppose it is better for the surfers, especially when they fall into the sea, not to encounter the sharp stones and boulders that are on the shore." We felt that somehow nature had got things the wrong way round.

Even though we were weary from the heat and tired of carrying equipment and it were a constant struggle to find a smooth piece of ground on which to place the tripod to obtain the best angles for our shots, we were happy to be working together; and realizing our ambition!

On the way back to Agios Nikitas, I gave a sigh saying, "We simply have to stop and film some of this wild, spectacular scenery."

The air was heavy with the scent of wild herbs and the ever-present smell of pine. We had climbed so high that there was a slight breeze from the sea making the intense heat just about bearable. The fresh, green, tree-clad mountains sloped gently and were reflected in azure blue sea. From this height we filmed the panoramic views in all their glory, the smaller islands, like Skorpio, the Aristotle Onassis' island and the gulf of Vlychou, all blue and emerald. And Sivota, a unique natural port, where boats and yachts seemed to hang suspended in the still, transparent sea. We looked down on valleys, where hawks circled above. All around was beauty! Even where there was no sea, there was beauty.

There were little mountain villages, swarmed with olive trees and as we drew nearer we were fascinated by the distinctive white-washed houses. The old window-frames and shutters were painted in bright green or pale blue in striking contrast to the white rough stone walls. These were adorned with a profusion of brilliant flowers and climbing plants wound their way up white-washed stone steps and over irregular old craggy roof-tops. Ancient ochre tiled roofs rose in a series of irregular gables interspersed with rambling vines. Crooked poles supported time-worn wooden balconies laden with containers from which fluorescent pink and red geraniums grew. A sleeping cat basked on a hand-made mat at many of the open doorways, where nearby lines of washing hung in the bleaching sun.

In some way these humble little villages seemed to typify all that was Greece! Thousands of stories and thousands of secrets! It was this atmosphere that we wanted to portray in our film. So that when people went home, they could take with them, some of the peace and tranquility and beauties of the island.

Later that day at Zak's bar, a middle-aged couple sat at the next table to ours with their suitcases.

"So you're off home then?" I asked.

"Yes!" They both replied regretfully.

Then the fair-haired woman asked, "How long are you here for?"

"Three months." I answered.

"What?" She looked so surprised.

Then I told them about our video idea and they both seemed very impressed. The man nodded his head thinking, then looking directly from Tony to me he stressed, "I really do think it's a very good idea!" How much will you charge for a video?"

"About 20 pounds," Tony answered. "That's six thousand drachma."

The woman then spoke hesitantly. "Do you think that you could send us a copy when you have completed it?"

"Yes!" We both responded simultaneously.

"Don't send it from here, in case there is a problem, you can post it to us when you are back in the UK." Her husband then added looking thoughtful.

"Yes," his wife agreed. "I would really love to be able to show this place to our family, complete with the friendly atmosphere."

They gave us two £10 notes and their address written on a small piece of paper.

Just as they were leaving, another couple came to join them. Excitedly, they told their friends about our video idea and to our delight they also wanted us to send one to them. They gave us a cheque and their address. Then they all left.

We were overjoyed! We were in business! We had sold not just one, that would have been good enough, but we had sold two. And we hadn't even made the film yet!

We followed the people, who had given us such joy, because they believed in our idea, to the top of the street, where we waved to them until the coach had turned the corner. At that point we exploded into hysterics.

"What did I tell you?" I shouted. "I knew it would work!"

Tony was hardly able to contain his happiness.

"It's just the way we hoped it would be!" He shook his head in disbelief. "This calls for a drink!

All at once we were laughing.

We were still laughing when we resumed our positions at Zak's bar, still in a euphoric daze. It was that time of the day when the beach was quiet and half in the shadow of the purple headland.

It was just the way it had been on the day we had filmed it the year before. There was a warm setting sun, blue sea, white plastic tables and chairs and of course, a pint of cold beer.

We were sitting gazing at the calm, silvery sea reflecting on the changes in our lives. Our world had fallen apart. We had lost the material things of life, but while we were here, we had gained, 'all this!'

At that moment we heard the song, *'It's No Sacrifice'* being played over the speakers. It was the same song that was playing the previous year when Tony filmed me at the water's edge from this little bar, and the memories of that time came flooding back to us.

We felt a cold little shiver run through us, as the tinkling music and the words rang out...

It's two hearts beating... For our hearts were beating so fast...."*We lose direction, no stone unturned...*We were looking at each other in complete understanding as the song continued, "*Cold, cold, heart. Hard done by you... Some things looking better baby... just passing through... And it's No Sacrifice.... No Sacrifice...*

Tony reached for my hand gently squeezing it, his eyes smiling into mine as he whispered along with the song. "*It's no sacrifice... at all.*" To confirm his feelings, he lifted his glass of beer. "Here's to us! Somebody up there likes us after all!"

"It's so good to see you happy," I said reaching out to stroke his cheek tenderly.

It was so lovely being together and feeling cheerful. It was such a warm evening, only the lightest breeze was touching our hair. As daylight gradually slipped away into darkness we stood up to leave. Just then Zak came out of his bar and lifted our camera from the table to take a photograph of us, because we looked so delighted.

Chapter Two

Nightingales sang vociferously as we parked in a clearing of dried weeds and grasses.

We tried to walk with confidence, to give the impression that we knew exactly what we were doing.

Friendly farmers with layers of covering over their heads and bodies greeted us warmly with, "Yass!" Then stood leaning on their sticks, staring at us. I suppose, on reflection, we did look rather odd. Tony was carrying the large camera on his shoulder and the tripod, while I was carrying a bag of spare batteries and other accessories and a large bottle of water. In my other hand I held a clip board.

We filmed the steep winding road that led to Kathisma beach. It was an endless stretch of white sand with incredibly turquoise sea. Sometimes in the gleam of the wide bay waves would begin to form, then as they grew nearer they became bigger, until eventually they broke into sparkling white frothy foam. At one end of the beach there were enormous white-grey rocks worn smooth by the sea. Stretching up the high, purple mountain there were lines of almond trees, interspersed with olive trees and trailing vines.

Kathisma beach was renowned for the most beautiful sunsets. Late in the afternoon the sun shone with blast furnace heat, a huge crimson and orange ball in the sky. The whole beach was exposed to its power; a desert of glistening sand that reached down to the shimmering blue.

Then later the sun's rays reddened the sea, so that two worlds fused together in a blaze of brilliant, fiery splendor. Sea and sky turned slowly from burnished gold, to shades of pink and lilac, then not long afterwards, long probing fingers of light spread out all over the darkening sky.

We waited to capture this magnificent sight on film, although it took two hours of filming to acquire about two minutes that we would use in our production. But it was quite spectacular! We were more than satisfied.

The following day was Sunday 4th July. Tony walked from the bathroom, his hair still wet from his shower. "I am determined to have a break from filming until the evening, when I plan to film Agios Nikitas by night." He was now sitting on our balcony facing me.

"That's fine by me," I replied looking up from my Greek text book. "Let's spend the day on the beach."

In half an hour we were kicking off our sandals and letting our feet sink down into the sand and soft shingle, deliciously warm in the sun. Before us was the sea and we both sat down near the water. We were dreamily thinking of our next 'shoot' while relaxing on our raffia beach mats, listening to the gentle regular swishing of the sea on the shingle, enjoying the feel of the sun on our bodies.

Suddenly we were startled out of our sleepy thoughts by the sound of children's loud excited voices imminently nearby. Two Greek boys were shouting and racing around.

After a few minutes, we felt a shower of sand, as one of them landed along-side of me trying to catch a ball that suddenly whacked Tony's shoulder with a powerful blow. We both looked up, showing our annoyance at the disturbance.

A handsome dark skinned boy of about twelve years old, with laughing brown eyes was smiling down at us.

"Sorry!" He called as Tony gave him his ball. We were surprised when he offered his hand to him in an apologetic manner. The other boy was younger and could have been mistaken for a girl. He was smiling sweetly at us, as he pushed the wet, black curls away from his face, so that they fell in soft coils down to his dark shoulders. Then they moved a little further along the beach, but we were still aware of the pandemonium they were causing as they played in and out of the sea.

Before long the ball came very near us again and the older boy came to retrieve it. I was lying with my feet on the sand and my knees bent up. As he bent down to pick up the ball I saw him slyly looking up my sun-dress.

Then he shouted to the other boy in Greek. **"Eenai prasinos!"** (**They're green!**)

With that, they both burst into laughter. I was amused at the idea that they obviously didn't think for one minute that I could understand them.

I whispered this fact to Tony, who remarked with a scowl, "Cheeky little bugger!" But he couldn't help smiling.

A few minutes later as they were swimming, I heard them singing a little song. I didn't understand much of it, but I did know that every so often the words, 'she wore green knickers' came into it! They were looking shiftily in my direction and laughing.

After a while the older boy came out of the sea shaking the water from his short dark hair. I looked directly at him and spoke in my very best Greek.

"How is the sea today? I hope that it is warmer than it was yesterday!" His mouth dropped open as though he could hardly believe his ears. Then slowly, as though his lips had been gummed together, he replied in Greek.

"The sea is very nice today. And it is warm! But I don't know what it was like yesterday, because I and my family only arrived today, for our holiday."

"I see," I nodded. "Do you always come here for your holiday?"

"Yes," he replied, while a smile began to spread across his handsome face. His dark eyes looked enquiringly into mine, and then with childish curiosity he asked me, "Are you a Cypriot lady?"

"No" I answered.

He looked puzzled; there was softness in his eyes; he looked down quickly, as though he was about to be reprimanded.

"Er...Excuse me, I Er... thought that you were an English lady." He was nodding towards my basket, where an English book lay clearly visible.

"Yes, that's right, **I am**!" I responded, with a nod and a somewhat triumphant smile.

He immediately held out his hand and surprised me by speaking quite good English.

"Hello, Er...my name is Yiorgos Tsetikas, but I like it very much, for you to call me... George... How are you?"

I shook his firm young hand immediately forgetting that I had been annoyed at all.

With that he paused a while, to think in English, before speaking with a strange sincerity for someone so young.

"I am sorry... er... if I offended you...or your husband." He looked towards Tony, making a sudden gesture of apology, bending his body over and lowering his head. "I give you my salutations."

We were not quite sure what he meant, but we smiled anyway.

Thus encouraged he continued. "Er...I was, how you say, having a. bit of...laughing and fun...er. with my brother Fotis, he is nine years old, er... but he does not speak the English, not at all! No. but ...er...we did not mean to be bad!"

"That's okay!" I replied. At that moment he looked relieved and put out his hand to Tony and when Tony took it, he shook it vigorously up and down.

"Thank you, thank you!" he smiled shyly now saying, "Er... It ees a little bit er... funny, yes?"

With that, we all began to laugh, so he went on. "Er I can, sit and speak ...er...some English with you, yes?"

"Yes, of course!" I answered, completely captivated now by his charm.

That was how we first met George! We could never have guessed what a difference he and his family's friendship would make to our stay in Lefkas.

I told George that our little grandson was also called George. He seemed impressed, but confused. "Why, he is not... called Tony? In Greece a child always takes the name of the father's parents: Or er... the grandparents."

So this is why there are so many children in the same family with the same names, we realized. I tried to explain, without going into too much detail that this is not done in England.

All this time, Fotis sat quietly listening and smiling at us, as he played with the white pebbles at the water's edge.

Suddenly, he shouted in a loud voice that didn't match his appearance. "**Mama! Papa!**" And both he and George began waving franticly.

Their parents walked towards us carrying an assortment of beach accessories that they put down on the sand near us. Behind them sauntered a little girl. The parents acknowledged us politely with a smile and a nod of their heads. Then standing side by side, the mother called, "**Yiorgo, Foti, ella pethia mou.**" (**come my boys**) whereupon, they both ran straight to her.

I couldn't help hearing the boys relate the story of how we had become acquainted, since their talking was so loud. I noticed that their parents seemed both amused and slightly annoyed. There was an outcry from their mother. "**Po! Po! Po!**" She was shaking her head from side to side. Slowly she got up and came towards us. She resembled Nana Mouskouri, except that she was quite a lot heavier looking.

"Signomi," (Excuse me) she said, before continuing in Greek because she did not speak any English, "I am sorry that my boys have disturbed you. They are very high spirited because they have been so looking forward to their holiday and we have traveled from Agrinion on the mainland for three hours."

"Endaxi!" (It's alright!) I replied, assuring her that we understood. The little girl had followed her and was eyeing me curiously. I asked what her name was and commented how pretty she was.

"Antigoni," she replied and then she thanked me, "Efharisto."

She told me that Antigoni was almost four years old and then she introduced herself. Her name was Mata and her husband was Demetrious. But when you speak directly to someone you drop the 'ous' or the's' from their name. He was a good-looking man with cropped, silver, curly hair. We introduced ourselves and then we all shook hands, as is particularly customary in Greece. She was astonished that I had taken the trouble to learn the Greek language. Both she and her husband were very proud that Yiorgos spoke English and they were delighted to listen to him having conversations with us. We understood how they felt!

At one point during the afternoon Demetrious spoke quickly to George, who instantly walked over to Tony saying, "Mr. Tony, er... my father, he ask... if you will go to swim with him?"

"With pleasure!" Tony replied.

Demetrious acknowledged with a smile and a nod of his head. I thought the situation was rather comical, because neither man could say one word to each other! So they walked into the water together and swam in silence.

Then, after some time, they came back again and sat down.

The afternoon passed pleasantly and by the end of the day we realized that we had made new friends. After Mata and Demetrious had gathered their belongings together, they called to the boys, who came running quickly. Demetrious jerked his head towards his wife, instantly she turned to us saying that she hoped that they would see us again soon. I agreed that it would be nice if we could meet them again. Then I asked if I could take some photographs of the children, and Mata smiled saying, "Ne, eve veous!" (Yes, of course)

So I took a photograph of George and Fotis, with the blue sea behind them, that matched the blue of the sky.

Then waving to us, they left the beach; Antigony definitely did not want to leave us.

Dusk was still an hour or two away, but the light was becoming dim.

We decided to film the bay at night from a different angle, so we positioned ourselves at the far end of the curve of white smooth rocks. From there, we were looking at the beach and bars, as well as the end of the street, from across the sea. Our initial shots were taken at twilight, when everywhere was deserted and bathed in a fascinating bluish hue. This graduated by degrees, to shades of lilac-blue as the color of the calm sea turned darker.

There was a cocktail bar at one end of the bay, where a balcony jutted out over the sea. People were beginning to gather there, as well as at Zak's bar at the other end. Also little groups were assembling at the end of the street.

One by one lights twinkled on reflecting in the now ink dark sea. Subsequently the whole scene had taken on a completely different appearance! Like a magical theatre performance.

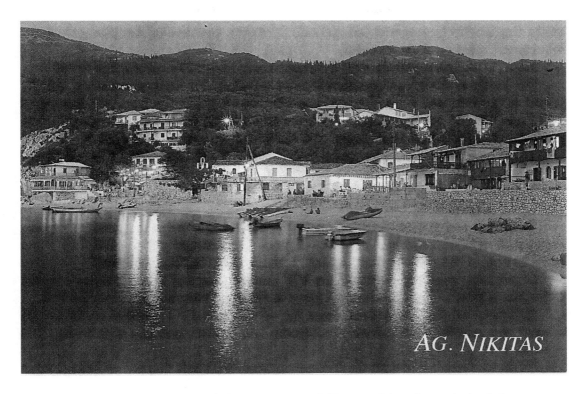

AG. NIKITAS

"Let's move to the end of the street now," Tony said as he switched the camera off.

"Shall we film our next sequence of shots? Working our way up the street the way we planned?" I was helping to move all our equipment. "It will show how different the place looks at night."

"Yes, we'll start at Constantino's fish taverna, after that, The Korali, before gradually getting to the top, finishing at the Poseidon. By the time we get there it will be in full swing with all the kids dancing." Much to our relief, at every place we filmed, we were greeted with smiles and much joviality.

Then we filmed the most respectable eating place, where the standards of hygiene were noticeably higher, 'The Eleni.' The couple who owned this place were both unusually shy for Greeks. He was a pleasant man, but so laid back that sometimes he gave the impression that he was half asleep. His wife was a prim woman who always wore a white hairnet and a clean white apron. Not surprisingly it was her that did all the cooking and most of the hard work.

As planned the last place to be filmed was the Poseidon. By the time we reached there, it was around 10:30pm. and the mood was of unrestrained exuberance! Vassilis was dancing wildly and clapping his hands, with a bottle of 'Metaxa' brandy balanced on his head. The two girls were also dancing, Chrisanthia, the raven-haired seventeen-year-old, was doing cart-wheels, while Thespina, a year younger, but somewhat less attractive, twirled around. However, because of her plumpness, the movements were far from graceful.

As soon as Sylvia saw us with the camera, she began to clear a space for us.

Fat Yani and little Yani, cousins who were called after their grandfather, quickly joined in the dancing, while Demetrious, who was a rather shy boy, not wanting to be left out, tagged on to the end. They were all laughing as they tried to keep in time with the music, which got faster and faster. Everyone was enjoying the fun. Everyone, except Thanai, who stood in a corner quietly observing. She was never one to conform.

We were delighted that we had managed to capture the happy atmosphere of the place, plus it had been a lovely way to bring our video to an end.

When we had folded the tripod away and put the camera in its case, Vassilis swaggered over to us with two bottles of beer. He gestured plainly that they were, compliments of the management, saying, with a wide grin, "No problem!"

On Monday morning we drove the VW passed groups of happy holiday-makers, to Kathisma beach. There we found a place in the open vastness where we parked.

"I'll draw all the curtains and open the windows and side door to try to keep it as cool as possible." I was already extremely hot. The temperature was around 100 degrees!

"First we have to view all the footage and note the shots that we will use. I think this is the best place to park, where we will not be disturbed and the humming of the generator will not disturb anyone else." Tony replied.

He started the generator and we placed the folding table over it, to shelter it from the searing heat of the sun. We began our notes at around 10am. It was extremely uncomfortable, being so hot, but we were committed to our task. At 2.30pm the heat was stifling, Tony looked worried. "I think that the generator might need to cool down. I know that I certainly do!"

We were both sweating profusely when we reached the sea; the walk across the scorching sand had been an added torture. We were so exhausted that we had no breath to speak. However, the sea was so refreshing.

"I feel I am in heaven!" I murmured. It was stimulating, physically and mentally and after some time just lying in its cool embrace we were restored with new energy.

In the shade of our umbrella we ate a huge watermelon, sliced in half. When we had finished Tony got abruptly to his feet saying with a determined, but gentle smile, "Right then, are we ready for work again?"

"Ready and able!" I replied returning his smile.

We continued watching the film and making notes for a long time, until it became quite dark.

Tony stretched his arms, before turning to me.

"I think that we have done enough for today. I believe that we deserve a treat!"

He paused to watch my reaction and smiled when I replied, "That's very kind of you sir!"

It was 10pm when we headed up the steep winding road that led back to Agios Nikitas and our little room. I took myself off to the bathroom, where I stood blissfully in the warm shower, for a long time.

Eventually, we walked across the road to the Poseidon to get something to eat. The taverna was as busy as ever, but we were welcomed warmly. Sylvia asked us to go into the kitchen to choose what we wanted.

Kostas showed us what was still available, with an eccentric kind of enthusiasm, and a cigarette hanging from his mouth.

He was particularly proud of his mousaka.

"Eet ees the best in all of Greece!" he declared with such conviction that we decided to give it a try. It was in fact quite delicious!

Tony asked for two bottles of beer and within a minute, Vassilis placed them on our table, with an exaggerated bow and a grin. "No problem!"

With a wave of his hand he indicated to Kostas, who had put his head out of the kitchen to shout, "**For you! From me!**"

Lynne, Paul and the children had come back from Kefalonia that night.

The following day we gave them a lift to Kathisma.

They spent the day on the beach... and we spent the day in the van! This time we were editing the film in the correct sequence, but since we had to take our friends back to Agios Nikitas, we were forced to pack up at 6pm.

Because of this, we had to spend the following day working in the van at Kathisma, although since we were on our own, we worked until the film was finished.

Happily by late that afternoon we had finished the editing. Also, by early evening, we had added the appropriate music. Tony leaned back on our seat and turned to me saying, "Well, I think we have made a pretty good film there!"

"I think it's great! I feel so proud that we have produced such an excellent film!"

Back at our room, we drank our coffee on our little balcony but I could see that Tony looked decidedly uneasy. When I opened the file of posters to stick on the windows of the van my hands were trembling with excitement. We were both filled with mixed emotions. We thought back to the day when I had placed them in there! It seemed so very long ago! We had been so uncertain of what we were doing, but then our whole lives had been so disrupted that we were insecure and doubtful of everything!

As I descended the steps from our room, I could see Tony standing by the van. He had washed the dust from it using Iro's hose pipe, ready for it to make its debut. So it looked quite respectable again. It was parked in the street outside our apartment block, right opposite the Poseidon.

We were wearing T shirts that we had bought in Liverpool and had the words printed on them. Tony's read, *Your Holiday on Video*, and mine said, *Personalized, Professional Videos by Tony & Di.* We had felt so excited and apprehensive that day.

I walked towards Tony with the posters and a packet of blue-tack in my hands. He looked towards me and beamed saying, "I've put the generator behind the wall."

Realization came suddenly. A new era I thought. The first time we would show the video.

I turned to Tony saying, "This will be such an experience for us, and I can sense that something exciting is going to happen."

"I hope so!" He was smiling, but there was an uncertain look in his eyes.

Before long we were attracting quite a lot of attention in the street as we prepared for our first 'showing.' People stopped to read the printed posters, stuck on all the windows of the van, as they made their way up and down the street. We had only printed them in English, so there were many who were having difficulty reading the poster about having a personalized video made. But everyone understood that we had a video of Lefkas, featuring Agios Nikitas.

We placed the TV on top of the sink, facing out into the street, at the open sliding side door. Tony placed the wooden structure containing the two video players and the mixer on top of our swivel table at the opposite side to the door. Everything fitted in very well. We had decided that it was better for Tony to sit at that side, so that he could operate the equipment, out of the reach of inquisitive children. Also his right arm could be supported on the seat rest. I would sit at the open doorway so that I could speak more easily to people. This was particularly important if they happened to be Greek.

By the time we were seated side by side on our long seat, quite a crowd of eager excited children had gathered all around us. Fat Yani had appointed himself as being in charge and so he stopped all the rest from climbing on the bumper and from trying to look inside. We were quite glad of his help, but we wished that he could have done it a bit more quietly! But that is not the way of the Greeks! So we resigned ourselves to the loud shouting and intermittent screaming from the girls, as fat Yani pulled and pushed them into order. All except Thanai! **Nobody** told her what to do! Still it wasn't too bad if she was the only one that we had to endure standing inside the doorway.

As dusk fell, we switched on! The music began.

There was a sudden silence; all the children's eyes were riveted on the television screen. Then their faces stared in wonder as the words, 'Welcome to Lefkas' appeared. They immediately recognized the town, so there were cries of joy as they stood enthralled. People passing by were drawn to see what all the fuss was about and then they also stood alongside the children, watching with fascination.

Before long there was such a crowd that a squabble broke out amongst the children because someone had stood in front of one of them and spoilt their view! Happily fat Yani soon sorted it out.

Then as the graphic 'Agios Nikitas' appeared, a cry of delight rang out from all the children at once! As the street came into view the atmosphere in the crowd was explosive!

We had chosen Greek music for this part of the video and apparently it was a popular song, because all the children sang along, some swaying in time to the rhythm. So engrossed were they that they were quite oblivious of passers by, who stopped to take photographs of **them**, watching the video! It was amazing to see the sheer happiness and excitement that these children showed about such a simple thing. There was an enchanted feeling in the air that was so typical of this charming little village.

An elegant lady came forward from the crowd holing out her hand, "I'll take one please." She handed me 6 thousand drachmas.

"She wants one!" I whispered to Tony, who was already reaching for a copy out of the box. He beamed back at me, but he began to sweat with excitement.

Then another stout lady pushed her way through the crowd saying, "I'd like to buy a video please!"

I was so excited that my hands were shaking as I took the money.

Tony was sweating quite profusely by this time!

Liana's two little girls were in the crowd. They were moving in time to the music, their black curls bobbing. When suddenly Liana appeared on the video, giggling in a self conscious way, the little girls were so shocked that they yelled out, **"Mama! Mama!"** and their wide eyed surprise made everybody laugh.

The crowd was growing bigger; people were packed as close as possible, from the van, to the other side of the street, right up against the opposite wall. As the different tavernas appeared one by one on the screen, a startled little voice would ring out from the multitude. **"Patera mou**!" (My father!) And other times, **"Mitera mou!"** (My mother)

At this, the crowd would burst out laughing and some local folk shook their heads in bewilderment. There was an elderly woman who seemed to spend her entire life looking after a baby girl, who had just learnt to walk. She was seen every day and at all hours of the night, constantly wandering up and down the street dressed in black with this child. Suddenly she appeared on the screen and the entire crowd, shouted with one voice, **"Oh! Po! Po! Po!"**

An adorable looking imp of around six years, called Constantino, shouted at the top of his voice, **"Yia-Yia mou!" (my Grand-ma!)** Then he abruptly turned and bolted, running as fast as his sturdy brown legs could carry him. His bare feet making slapping sounds on the shiny cobbles. **"YIA-YIA!"** he shouted as he ran inside the fish taverna. Everyone in the crowd turned their heads to watch him, as they all hooted with laughter.

An elderly Greek man was wiping the tears from his face, as he passed me 6 thousand drachma notes, **"Parakalo?"** he simply asked.

Tony's eyebrows rose in surprise. "That's three already!" he gasped. "And we've only been here twenty minutes!"

The video by now was showing the bottom of the street, where it opened onto the sea. At this point everyone caught their breath in wonder, as though they had never seen the bay before!

Then all together, they exhaled audibly in a long deep breath, **"Auraia!" (Wonderful!)**

Even the children gasped totally enchanted, turning to each other murmuring, "Auraia!"

Tony and I were dumbfounded to see such fascination, for a film of a place that was so very familiar to them. Most of them spent every day on the beach, yet they were enthralled.

Suddenly the crowd erupted again into hollers of laughter, as Zak could now be seen on the screen smiling broadly; one young local man clapped his hands together.

"Zachariah! Oh! Po! Po! Po!" he hollered.

Again everyone shrieked with enjoyment!

A red haired lady came from the back of the crowd and spoke in English, "Can I have a video please?"

I gave her a cassette saying, "Do you like it then?" It was a question that seemed quite unnecessary, as she was smiling so much.

"I think it's wonderful!" she answered, as she took the money out of her purse.

By now, Tony needed a towel to dry the sweat from his face; it was running into his eyes and making them smart. Somehow his attack of nerves seemed so funny to me, that I couldn't stop laughing! And the more I laughed, the more he sweated! It was altogether, rather ridiculous.

About half way through, the video featured the little bay turning gradually from day time to dusk and eventually to night-time, with bright lights reflecting in the dark sea. This effect, combined with the sound of a romantic song, caused a hush to fall on the intrigued throng, and they whispered repeatedly, "Auraia!"

It was as though they were looking at flickering pictures in a magic lantern.

Constantino had dragged his granny, who was still clutching the baby, to see the incredible video, soon she too was whispering and sighing with awe.

Then he pulled at my arm, his big dark eyes looked imploringly into mine.

"Parakalo! Yia-Yia mou pali?" he asked. He wanted us to show his grandmother again.

I told him that we would play it again after it had finished. He didn't answer but he smiled up at me and then squatted on the cobbles to watch the rest of the film. With his arms crossed on his bare young chest and his little mouth open, he gazed in childlike wonder!

People were standing above the opposite wall, at the Poseidon watching the film, as well as the commotion in the street below. Suddenly the Poseidon was featured on the screen. Immediately there was uproar from everybody. Thanai, who had been standing staring, riveted to the spot, chewing the ribbon on her plaits with excitement, suddenly sprang out of her trance like state and leapt in the air. She turned to her brother, little Yani, who was equally excited, so that when they scampered away, they collided and stumbled. Then they immediately picked themselves up and ran headlong, leaping up the steps screaming, **"Papa! Mama! Ella! Ella!"**

Fast on their heels followed Demetrious. Whereas, Fat Yani stayed behind to keep his viewing position, but he roared with laughter, while he clapped his hands franticly.

Soon all the staff from the Poseidon was standing on the steps. Vassilis couldn't believe it! He was astounded to see himself prancing about on the screen. His mouth fell open and the crowd pointed at the screen and applauded, all the customers, who were now leaning over the balcony to get a better view, cheered loudly as well.

At the top of the steps Kostas was standing in his long white, none to clean apron. He was shaking his head saying, "Well, well ... What... ees happening?"

The two girls, Chrisanthia and Thespina came down the steps, their leather sandals making clicking sounds, and when they saw themselves dancing on the screen, they were completely overcome with embarrassment! They chuckled self-consciously, hanging their heads hiding their faces in their hands. This made fat Yani holler louder than ever! He was pushing and teasing the two giggling girls.

A middle-aged couple descended the steps, enjoying the interruption of normal proceedings in the street. They hugged the girls, affectionately and slapped Vassilis on his back. Then the man came to the door of the van calling, "I have just **got to** have one of **those** videos!"

"That's **five!** so far!" Tony exclaimed in surprise, lifting a quizzical eyebrow.

"I know!" I answered, "It's unbelievable!" We had only been showing for half an hour. Everyone now had joined in the fun clapping their hands and singing along with the very familiar tunes of bouzouki music as they watched the girls performing.

Soon the boys appeared on the screen, with their clumsy attempts at dancing. At this point fat Yani almost collapsed with shock! Then he exploded into fits of hilarity, as he watched himself, his brother Demetrious, plus his cousin little Yani, trying to master the steps with considerable difficulty, while keeping in time to the music. This added to the continual amusement of the people.

At the closing part of the film, Kostas appeared pointing directly at the camera, saying with a smile, **"Aye! Aye! Aye!"** This gave the impression that he was pointing at the crowd. His action caused outbursts of delight and many impersonations of, "Aye! aye! aye!" from everyone.

Kostas himself by this time looked quite befuddled. He just shook his head from side to side, saying, **"Po! Po! Po!"** While smiling, somewhat bashfully.

Much to our joy, another couple bought the sixth video.

Soon after a tall young man with long blonde hair took a cassette from my trembling hand, saying, "I think you've had a wonderful idea, doing this!"

Tony and I wanted to express our delight but we could only smile and say, "Thank you!" This seemed so insignificant because our hearts were so very full of gratitude!

When the film ended there was a vigorous round of applause.

We were ecstatic to think that we had brought so much happiness to this little fishing village.

There were shouts of, **"Pali!"**(Again!) from many, including little Constantino, who was pushing his granny to the front so that she might see herself better.

Tony re-wound the video, which only took a few minutes, but seemed an eternity, to the waiting throng, who shuffled about discussing the amazing video with endless enthusiasm!

The music started again, so the crowd fell silent. This time most of them knew what was coming, so on this occasion they watched with excited expectation.

Again the road sign of Agios Nikitas appeared and a loud cheer rang out! Again, Liana appeared smiling, while her daughters, who had brought her to see, were screaming with excitement. "**Mama! Mama!**" Liana doubled up and hid her face, as the children pulled at her arms, while they jumped up and down with glee.

So it went on... and by the time the elderly woman with the baby was due to appear, Constantino was on his feet pointing his small finger at the screen, almost touching it. His friends were also jumping with excitement and clapping their hands in eager anticipation, so when she did appear they all erupted into squeals of delight.

His grandmother burst into cackles of laughter; and hiding her face she cried, "Oh! Po! Po! Po!" Making everybody chuckle again!

Constantino's father had left his fish taverna to come and view the video. He handed over the money saying, "**This... I... must have!**"

Then, the more reserved owner of the next taverna, "The Eleni " gave me his money saying quietly, but with sincerity, "Very, very good!"

The owner of "The Korali" and his wife stood waiting until their restaurant was featured. When it appeared, they smiled appreciatively and bought a video saying, "**Auraia!**"

I was surprised when a very old man with a black bandanna wrapped around his grey head, asked for a cassette. I asked him if he had a video player, as he was obviously a local farmer and didn't look as though he was familiar with modern technology!

"Ohi!"(No) He shook his head.

I explained that he needed one to enable him to view the film.

He inhaled deeply and with a great deal of pride, he told me that he wanted to send it to his son in Birmingham, England.

Another couple, who were Dutch, then bought a copy, and then immediately another couple from Germany also bought one.

A large group of people came hastily down the steps leading out of the Poseidon and stood watching. One of the men came towards us. Only the top button of his red, open-necked shirt was fastened and his stomach protruded above his colorful shorts. His broad face met the jowls of his neck and his eyes lay in pouches of flesh and were very bloodshot.

"Well! Now what have we here?" he turned his head quickly in the direction of the crowd, who were all watching him. His chin jerked upwards.

Tony and I both looked at each other slightly alarmed. Was he a trouble maker?

He spoke slowly nodding his head as he did. "You know something? This is the most brilliant thing that I have ever seen!" While handing me the money for a copy he asked, "Whatever gave you this idea?"

If only he knew! But I simply replied, "Oh! We just thought people would like to take some memories home with them, complete with the atmosphere that you can't capture on photographs."

"That's very true, I think it's superb!" He was still bobbing his head as he walked away.

He was soon followed by another man from the same group, saying, "This has been the best night of our holiday!"

"Yes, this has really been an unforgettable night!" A plump woman agreed.

Tony was now ringing out the towel. "We've sold **fifteen**!"

His words were interrupted by a handsome young Italian man who said, "Er...Yes please... I take one?"

We were running out of copies!

Tony thumped his forehead with the palm of his hand, "**I really don't believe this!**" Then he turned towards me saying with a shaky laugh, "You know something Di? I never thought that we would get **this** sort of reaction!"

"Me neither. It's all too wonderful!" Happiness was like a wild thing, leaping about inside me.

The crowd of people were still spellbound in front of the screen and by the end of the video; we had sold the remaining four copies! Another roar of appreciation erupted from the delighted mass as they applauded loudly.

We decided that we would close down for the night and Tony switched the television off. The children were distraught! They pleaded for more, with wails and moans. I did my best to calm them down, assuring them that we would show it again the following night. With this, they were reasonably happy. They began to saunter off to their various homes, talking avidly about the film and relating to the parts that they liked the best, with loud exclamations and bursts of high-pitched laughter. Something new and exciting had happened in their village!

"**This is unbelievable! Four hundred pounds!**" Tony called as he counted the 'takings' of the night, He wiped the sweat from his face, "I've got to have a shower, and then we'll go for something to eat and a drink. **God do I need a drink!**"

We walked into the Poseidon and were greeted with a resounding cheer! Sylvia showed us to a table and Vassilis brought us two bottles of beer. We ordered pork chops with chips and a Greek salad and tsatsiki to wait. The children were all vying with one another for our attention, wrestling in friendly competition. Fat Yani brought the salad and tsatsiki, before Thanai brought a basket of bread, followed by little Yani and Dimitri, who brought two bottles of Amstel beer, and a glass each.

After we had eaten, the children gathered at our table, wanting to know everything about us. We tried to explain in simple terms, before we asked fat Yani to bring us the bill.

He disappeared inside, but came out again immediately followed by his uncle Kostas.

"**What ... you ask for?**" he shouted.

"The bill parakalo?" Tony drew on his hand with his finger.

"**No bill!** You not upset me! You make wonderful video of Poseidon, Yes?"

"Yes!" we replied, "But we must pay for the meal!"

He pretended to scowl. "Why? You must? I... Kostas.. say **NO!**" Then his mock serious expression changed into a wide grin as he pointed towards us laughing. **"Aye! aye! aye!"**

When we were walking down the steps from the restaurant we heard the patter of feet following us and a little voice calling, **"Ella!"** It was Thanai.

She reached out to me, and with her fair head drooped towards her chest she pressed something loosely wrapped in crumpled note paper into my hand.

I opened it to find two little shells and scribbled on the paper in bright red crayon were two kisses. She pointed first to Tony and then to me, and then went down on one knee making a little curtsey before she turned and ran back up the steps.

We understood what she meant, and we gazed after her.

Tony turned to face me. His voice was thick and his words hesitant, "She's ... a funny little madam ... that one!"

We looked at our little gift and in that moment, all our fears and apprehension were gone.

She had portrayed the feelings of everyone.

We knew that this was a token of friendship that had come straight from her heart.

Chapter Three

"Don't plan too far ahead!" Tony warned, as I got more and more carried away with the prospects of making £400 every night. The previous night had been like a Technicolor dream, complete with sound-track from the songs we had put on the video. I felt sure that we had a money-making business.

We were walking down the street to the little bay at Agios Nikitas after making 10 more copies of the video on Kathisma beach, from 10.30am until 4pm, in the baking heat of the van. I was worried that we couldn't keep up with the demand.

Tony carried on, "I can make them as I am showing the film, just as long as we've got a few ready in advance."

Just as we reached the slipway that led on to the sand we heard a voice shouting, **"Mr. Tony! Mr. Tony! Mrs. Diana!"**

George ran up to us shaking our hands saying, "Hello...er...How is you?" He gestured towards his parents, a motion to replace the spoken words. We looked in their direction and found them signaling to us to join them. The merest flicker of annoyance crossed Tony's face, but it was quickly erased. We would have preferred to be on our own, but we walked over to them. Mata told me that they had been in Lefkas town the previous night, but this morning everyone in the village was talking about the video!

George nodded his head and speaking in English stated emphatically, "I want...very, very much...that I see the video!"

Fotis spoke shyly, but his plea was readily apparent in his dark eyes, "Parakalo?"

"Yes of course we will be showing it tonight," I answered with a smile.

Mata explained to me that they did not have a video player because it might interfere with the boys school work. Also video players were so expensive in Greece that not many people had one. So the idea of watching a video was very exciting to them.

After we had all enjoyed swimming and messing about in the lovely refreshing sea, we sat on our towels chatting for some time, but as Tony could only talk to either me or George; his conversation was somewhat limited!

There was a signal from Demetrious, a slight nod of his head; George looked at Tony. "Mr. Tony... my father he asks... you will swim with him, yes?"

I felt quite sorry for Tony, this was becoming a ritual! But I couldn't help smiling as the two men, walked in silence together into the calm crystal sea. They swam so far out that they were almost out of sight, and I was greatly relieved to see them heading back. As they walked out of the water I looked from one to the other, seeing Demetrious stride like some pagan god, his body dark and muscular.

Tony was considerably out of breath. He was gasping, "Very nice! Thank you. Efharisto!"

Demetrious made another slight movement with his head.

Later in our room Tony said, "Christ, I was beginning to panic! I thought he was never going to turn back!"

"Well, just because he went so far out, it didn't mean that you had to."

"I'm not going to let these macho Greeks think I'm a weakling!" he replied giving me a satirical smile.

෨෬

That night as we walked down the steps from our room we immediately became aware of a large crowd of children waiting anxiously around the van. They cheered loudly as we appeared making us feel like celebrities! It was quite difficult to walk between them as each one struggled and wrestled to be nearest to the van.

Tony lifted the generator out of the van, this alone caused much amazement.

"Ti einai?"(What is it?) The little ones asked.

Fat Yiani answered with exaggerated importance, "Einai genitria"(It's a generator)

This brought gasps of, "Auraia!" from all.

We left the curtains drawn across so that we could view the beginning of a copy in privacy, because Tony was a bit worried in case there had been a distortion on the quality of the reproduction, as there had been a 'blip' on the generator at one point during the previous evening. The children fell silent waiting for the show. I looked out of the mesh-covered window to look at their anxious faces; I could see the very old lady who wore the traditional long brown dress and shawl, walking down the street towards the van. When she got closer she must have heard the music that was playing on the video.

She stopped and looking all around her, said, "Pios einai?" (Who's there?) Crossing herself in the Greek orthodox manner she spoke in Greek, "I can hear the heavenly choir of angels!" She continued to look all around, she was breathing fast when she reached our van. It was then that she looked up to the sky saying, "Praise be to the Lord!" After that she continued to shuffle on slowly down the street, still making the sign of the cross.

Satisfied that the copies were good, we finally started the film show again. It was greeted with exactly the same enthusiasm as the night before. They shouted at the same places and then fell silent at the same times, but they were every bit as thrilled as they had been before.

Suddenly a voice that we instantly recognized filled the van. "Hello, How are you?" His hand was there in front of us.

We shook it saying, 'Hello George" Both he and Fotis then stood watching the video, with all the others and they were equally awe-inspired.

At the end, when the crowd cheered loudly, George spoke carefully. "Yes... I like it very, very much!"

He turned and spoke to Fotis, who smiled sweetly at us both and said, in much-practiced English, "Thank you... very... much!"

George spoke again, "My Father... Mother say, you will come tomorrow evening to eat some food with us, Yes?"

I explained that we had to show the film because it was our business; we were not on holiday, but trying to earn some money.

He replied, nodding a very knowing young head. "Yes, of course, I understand. But you can...er... come later when you... finished your business. Yes?"

"Yes!" I replied. What else could I say?

We waved to Fotis, who had been pushed to the back wall by Thanai as she held him in an arm-lock.

We could not understand why no-one had bought a video.

"What the hell's happened?" Tony sighed as he put in another cassette to make yet another copy. "Not **one** bloody video!"

"I can't make it out!" I was equally confused. "By this time last-night we had sold 10!"

Fat Yiani peered inside the van booming, "**Hallo!**"

When we looked out Vassilis was standing holding two bottles of beer for us saying, "Thio bires."(Two beers) He was grinning from ear to ear so we took them gratefully: Tony offered to pay, but he shook his head. "Ohi! Ohi!"

We felt slightly more cheerful, but still bewildered: The children however still shouted, cheered and murmured, "Auraia!" at all the same places.

The old lady in the brown traditional dress came sauntering up the street and paused to see what all the commotion was about. She looked intently and fixedly at the television screen and her old wrinkled face broke into a broad toothless smile as she began to recognize the places on the film, then she cackled with unrestrained laughter at the sight of familiar faces. She shook her enshrouded head in bewilderment and fidgeted restlessly around her face with her long brown woolen shawl, while she looked from side to side to see the effect that the film was having on everyone around her, and giggled at all the merriment.

The film was every bit as impressive to the children, each time they saw it! When it came to the end the second time and we still had not sold one copy, we began to feel a bit silly.

Tony's eyes held mine steadily. "Sod this for a game of soldiers! I'm not the local kid's entertainer!"

I had to admit that I felt the same way, in fact the children, lovely as they were, were beginning to irritate me. It seemed as though they were competing to see who could scream the loudest! And it was a close thing between Thanai and Constantino, until Thanai, not wanting to be beaten at anything, hit him a resounding smack across his head, knocking him over onto the cobbles. He only ever wore swimming trunks, day and night and as he fell, Thanai had pulled at them and exposed his little white bottom. This had infuriated Constantino, who considered crying, but decided against it and belted Thanai instead; much to everyone's delight! But unfortunately this made Thanai scream even more.

"That's done it!" Tony cried pulling the curtain over the screen in an attempt to show the children that he was annoyed. And they got the message. One of Liana's girls asked me quietly if that was all for tonight. I told her that it was. Where-upon she turned to the others making a gesture with her hands, palms upwards shouting in Greek, *"You have spoilt it all now!"* Then she ran into the Car Hire office to her mother, crying, *"It's all **their** fault!"*

₭⌘

"Let's go to Kathisma today and have a day on the beach, instead of a day in the van." Tony was taking our beach towels off the line on the balcony. "I'm afraid I am just not in the mood for a day of George and his family and another bloody 10 mile-out swim with Demetrious." I laughed as I joined him to take our bathing costumes from the line too. He went on, "God knows what tonight's going to be like!"

"Oh! I'm sure it will be alright!" I answered. "After all it will be quite late by the time we get there, so we won't stay long. We'll just have some bread and cheese or something I expect and a little chat; and then we'll leave!"

"It's alright for you, but I can't say a bloody word, I feel a right dope!"

I began to giggle, as the situation did amuse me. Usually we were all chattering away like mad, while Tony sat smiling politely.

At that moment we heard a booming voice, so close that it made us jump. **"HALLO!"** It was fat Yiani, leaning over the edge of steep path alongside our balcony. He was holding a struggling ginger kitten for us to see. Seemingly, this was to join the rest of the family: Vassilis, his wife, and the two teenage girls, fat Yiani and Demetrious, who all slept in a tent. It was free-standing on a newly erected floor of a half-built building, among rubble and large metal containers, close by our room. People on their way to Milos, often remarked about the tent saying, "Does anybody actually sleep in there?" If only they new how **many** and they still worked cheerfully, from daybreak to nighttime, every single day.

₭℞

At Kathisma the sea was unbelievable! It was the color of a kingfisher's wing.

It was pleasantly cooling, but certainly not cold. When we arrived mid-morning, it had been calm and wonderful to lie prostrate in, feeling the warmth of the sun and listening to the gentle swishing of the shingle underneath the sea.

Now, at mid-afternoon waves had built up and huge billowing rolls of turquoise waves rose vigorously up until they broke into massive sparkling white frothy foam. The sound was quite deafening yet compelling to listen to. We sat spellbound only making occasional cries; as yet another massive wave crashed closer sending a ripple of water nearer to us, until we were forced to move further up the beach. Many people had already been caught and were retreating having hysterics, carrying wet towels and clothes. Children were screaming excitedly and daring to stand near the might of the sea, wriggling their bottoms and waving their arms in a defiant manner, only to be sent scurrying and screaming up the beach to avoid another mighty wave.

We decided to pack up and head back. Tony was worried that we would have lost our parking position; the street was always jam-packed with cars, trucks and vans.

Since the road was so very narrow, as well as steep, it was impossible to turn. The Greeks and Italians managed to turn at the bottom of the street, narrowly missing the edge of the path, so avoiding a fall onto the beach. Tony was definitely not going to try that!

We hadn't seen Lynne, Paul and their children for four days, as they had been touring the island taking in as much of the sights as possible, before they went home in two days time.

"We must have a meal with Lynne and Paul tomorrow night," I said as we traveled the steep dusty road back to Agios Nikitas.

"I suppose so, but we really should have another go at selling the videos."

"Oh! We'll have plenty of time when they've gone home."

"Yes I suppose we should enjoy the company while they are here, we are going to be here on our own afterwards."

When we reached the top of the street it was pretty obvious that we had lost our parking place again. One truck had four happy children and a puppy in the back. One little girl was wearing her father's slippers much to their amusement, while a little boy found such delight in a piece of rope.

"Please take a photo of me with these kids?" I pleaded as I picked up the puppy.

After which Tony sighed audibly and looked thoroughly fed up as he pulled into the entrance outside our rooms. Things were beginning to go against us.

"Never mind!" I was trying to sound bright. "Maybe the trucks will move later on, let's have a shower and get ourselves ready for tonight." I knew that the impending meeting with the Tsetikas family was worrying Tony. He was not one for mixing much, except with people that he knew. And he really was at a disadvantage, not being able to speak, or to understand much Greek.

Since we had been unable to show the film, we decided to pass some time at Zak's bar, The Captain's Corner. The Tsetikas' apartment was a little further along the beach over-looking the bay. It was by then 9.00pm. And relatively dark, but we could see Fotis swimming with two other boys. One of them was Constantino; the other was young Demetrious, from the Poseidon.

We heard a booming voice that we recognized to be fat Yiani, as he noisily joined their game, by taking their ball and hurling it wildly yelling, "**Afto einai!**"(**There it is!**)

Constantino yelled back, "**STAMATA!**"(**STOP!**)

"Can't these bloody kids stop shouting?" Tony sighed audibly.

It was at that moment that fat Yiani spotted us, his face breaking into a big grin, as he bellowed, "**Hallo! Hallo!**" He only ever wore either red nylon football shorts, or green ones, with a baggy white T-shirt. Today he wore the green shorts.

Plodding heavily in his flip-flops he came towards our table and spoke to me, "Yeti then thixis to video sto vradi? (Why you not show the video tonight?)

I explained that there was nowhere to park.

He nodded understandingly then gave Tony a resounding thump on his back bellowing, **"Hallo! Tonic!"** Winking at him with dark, laughing eyes, he chortled at his own joke! Then by way of explanation, he lifted an empty 'tonic' bottle from a nearby table waving it in front of Tony. From then on this was the name that fat Yiani called Tony.

Fotis saw us from the sea and waved to us smiling.

It was dark, yet children played with no fear of harm. Liana's little girls, who we had recently learnt their names, the elder aged eight was a small replica of her plump mother called Katrina, the other a dainty pretty child aged five, was called Louisa. They strolled along the beach with Thanai, collecting stones and putting them in blue plastic carrier bags. When they were so full that even Thanai admitted they were too heavy, they called to fat Yiani to come and carry them up the street for them.

There was the usual game of volley-ball going on. And when the ball went in the sea, Fotis, Demetrious and little Constantino would splash through the dark water to retrieve it. There was much fun and exuberant activity. The older children kept a watchful eye on the smaller ones, so that parents could get on with their business without worrying. The younger ones ran freely about, in and out of various tavernas, until all hours, playing simple games. And apart from the odd squabble and fight, which was just as easily forgotten as it was started, they got on well together.

We couldn't help wondering what had gone wrong with our society. These children were so happy! Yet there were no arcades, fair grounds, swing parks, or anything other than the beach. They had no need of money; there was nothing to spend it on, apart from a limited choice of sweets at the little supermarket. Noisy they definitely were, but they meant no real harm or malice!

"Welcome!" George said as he met us at the door. "Please, to go up!" He made a bodily movement indicating towards the white marble stairway, through dark, polished, wood doors. Mata was standing at the top of the stairs to greet us affectionately with open arms and hugs and kisses. Antigony smiled shyly, while she wriggled about on a chair on the balcony next to her father. Demetrious motioned to the two white plastic chairs around a similar table, on which stood two bottles of wine and a bottle of water.

He made a gesture that suggested if we would take wine before our meal.

"Yes please!" We both answered.

We were sitting looking at the dark bay with the lights from the tavernas along the shore. Tony had learnt the word for beautiful, from the children who watched our video, so he ventured to join in the stilted conversation that we were all having.

"Auraia!" he said, indicating to the view, this pleased our guests enormously.

Presently Mata asked if we were ready to eat, I replied that we were, but added that I hoped that she hadn't gone to a lot of trouble.

She dismissed this remark with a wave of her hands, saying, "Ohi! Ohi!" Then she disappeared into the kitchen. We had only expected some little snack.

She appeared again and placed two big bowls of Greek salad covered in black olives on the table. This was followed by two big baskets of hot crusty bread. Then there were two dishes of tsatsiki and a large hot cheese pie. Tony glanced towards me and his expression was one of pleasant surprise. We all settled down to eat; George sitting next to his father and opposite Tony, so that he could interpret between them. We managed to talk, between mouthfuls and the atmosphere was good. I asked if Fotis would be joining us.

"Fotis is like... a little dog, he plays all the time! And he is... outside very, very late! My father... he says that we must buy him a... collar, like a dog!" George replied. At this his parents looked puzzled, so George repeated in Greek what he had told us.

Demetrious smiled and indicated to his own neck with his hands, making sure that we understood the joke.

Suddenly George leaned over the balcony and hollered, "**FOTI! ELLA! PARAKALO?**"

We were surprised the way they continually used this word for please, at the most odd times.

Mata went into the kitchen again, and then we heard the distinct sound of crackling. She came back carrying two enormous plates of freshly cooked fish, of different variety. The aroma was wonderful! One plate had big chunks of crisply coated fish, similar to salmon and the other was of small crisply fried fish that resembled sardines.

Tony and I were both now wide eyed. "This is indeed wonderful!" Tony said.

"Poly kallo!" (Very good) I reiterated. Both fish dishes were equally delicious!

Fotis arrived smiling and dripping wet, so he was handed a large red towel by Antigony. He wrapped the towel around himself, as he joined us at the table, happily stuffing handfuls of fish and bread into his mouth.

Demetrious opened another bottle of wine, so before long we were all very happy and relaxed! And very, very, full!

Presently we said, "Efharisto, ke kalinickta!" (Thank you, and good-night) and as we walked down the steps and onto the boardwalk they all stood waving to us from their balcony, until we had turned the corner of Zak's bar and gone out of sight.

"Well **what** a welcome!" Tony said as we entered our room. "They just couldn't have been kinder to us!"

"No!" I replied, "They really are a nice family, when you get to know them."

As Tony opened our louver doors on the balcony; there came a distinctive cry from nearby, **"HALLO! TONIC!"** We both looked out and saw fat Yiani waving from his tent.

When he saw me, he shouted, **"Kalinickta sas!"**(Goodnight, both of you)

We both smiled and called back, **"Kalinickta Yiani!"**

"I'm looking forward to seeing Lynne, Paul, Kate and little Chris again!" Tony said, "It will be nice to have a normal conversation." Then he began to snigger saying, "Sometimes when I'm with the Tsetikas family, for long, I begin to think that I've lost the use of my voice!"

"But they are friendly," I replied understanding what he meant.

"Oh! They are!" he agreed. "I just wish that I could **speak** to them. It's a bit awkward having to say everything through a twelve year old."

"Mata told me that George had passed a very difficult scholarship; only two boys from the whole school had passed it, to a very exclusive school. He's ever such a clever boy!" I continued, "Not only does he speak English, but French, German and Italian!" I felt that I was getting quite fond of this lad, with his impish grin and dark bright eyes.

"He certainly has charm!" Tony smiled. "And he is **so** polite!"

"What about fat Yiani?" I smiled. "What do you think of **him**?"

"Oh! He certainly is quite a character!" Tony gave a little laugh. "But you can't help liking him, can you?"

"No," I answered. "I rather like **him** too, but they are so **very different.**"

"Oh! God, yes!" Was Tony's happy reply.

⊱⊰

The following day, we were, yet again, unable to park the van in its position. Tony was disappointed and very downhearted. "It's going to be a big problem!" he moaned. "I've never known such a bad parking situation! We are **never** going to be able to show the video now!" He was sitting on the balcony, his head in his hands in despair.

Suddenly we heard, **"Hallo, Tonic!"**

Tony looked up sighing under his breath, **"This,** I could do **without!"** But he smiled just the same and called back, "Yiasu.... Yiani!"

"ELLA!" fat Yiani called, with a flourishing wave, he indicated to Tony go down to him.

"Oh! No! **What** in Gods' name is he on about **now**?"

"I think that you had better go and find out!" I was pulling on my sandals to follow him. When we reached the bottom of the steps, fat Yiani was standing right in the middle of our parking space.

"Here... yes? Video! " He was grinning triumphantly and motioned towards the VW.

"I think he has got our place for us" I said to Tony, who quickly rushed to move the van into it's' position, before someone else took it. Although I don't think many would have liked to argue with fat Yiani!

I asked him if he had got us the space and he replied, "Ve veous!"(Of course!) While he proudly blew on his nails and polished them on his grubby T-shirt.

We had scarcely got the generator out than we were immediately surrounded by the same children, all fighting and arguing as to who was to stand where. Fat Yiani pushed and yelled until there was some semblance of order, but I was already getting a headache so I also yelled, **"STAMATA!"** (STOP!) But to almost no avail. They just continued to make a terrible racket. We tried to ignore them, beginning to show the video, hoping that after a while they would become bored and go away, but that was a hope in vain.

"This is ridiculous!" Tony sighed exasperated. "We've got **no** chance against this lot!"

I tried to appeal to the children again, **"PARAKALO?"**

They looked at me in bewilderment, obviously unaware that they were annoying anyone. This, to them was normal behavior.

Vassilis brought us two beers and smiled at the crowd of children saying, "Very good video ...eh?"

I tried to portray that the children were very noisy by holding my head in my hands.

But he simply nodded in agreement saying, "No Problem!"

"What's the bloody use?" Tony eventually moaned. "We've been here two hours and nobody has even looked at it."

"Hush, there is somebody stopping," I whispered, looking out of the corner of the van window. A young couple, with arms entwined, were standing looking at the TV screen. After a few minutes the lad came nearer and looked inside the van, he was surprised to find Tony and me sitting there. He jumped back and at the same time the girl, equally startled, burst into fits of laughter, before they both walked away doubled up with hysterics.

"Yes, there is somebody operating it!" Tony called sarcastically, before he put his head out of the van and shouted, **"Did you think it was bloody magic?"**

Whereupon the couple burst out laughing again.

"Right, that's done it!" He switched the TV off and slammed the door shut.

I couldn't help smiling; it was so unlike Tony to lose his temper that way.

There was a sudden loud rapping on the window and fat Yani's grinning face pressed against the pane, as he yelled, **"TONIC, HALLO!"**

And Tony answered, **"Yani, piss off!"**

෨෬

We joined Lynne and Paul at the Poseidon but the atmosphere was somewhat strained. I explained that we were getting fed up with the children making so much noise.

Tony said that he felt that people were definitely put off by them. But we were powerless to alter the situation. They understood our feelings and sympathized, but nevertheless were envious of us being able to stay, when they were going home the next morning.

Tony spoke quietly, "Well, I wouldn't mind going home if I had a job to go to!" Then added, "At least you can plan for your next holiday, I'm beginning to feel like the local bloody clown!"

I had noticed that he was rubbing his arm quite a lot, also I could tell by his eyes that he was suffering a great deal of pain of late. All the filming, editing and carrying equipment, after the long drive had taken its toll.

I scribbled a quick letter to my mother and gave it to Lynne together with the reel of film. I had used the last of the film to take photos of Tony and me standing next to the van, with the TV in position, with the posters on the windows, for her to see us in operation. Lynne would post this for me in Manchester, England, omitting the 'international' bit. So hopefully she would get it more successfully.

Sylvia joined us for a final drink with Lynne and Paul, however, on hearing of our failure to sell any videos she suggested, "Why don't you go to Vassiliki, it is the international sail-boarding centre. I think that the training schools would be interested in having videos made, also many young people would like to have a video of themselves wind surfing." We wondered if she was right.

Lynne looked optimistic saying, "Why don't you give it a try?"

Paul agreed that it might be worth thinking about, so by the time we were on our brandies we decided to give it a go.

Paul raised his glass and turned to Tony saying with a grin, "You lucky bastard. It's better than spending the days in traffic jams and a stuffy office."

At any other time I might have agreed with him, but now the bleak expression on Tony's face made me feel slightly worried.

However, this was not the moment to disclose any qualms that I might have had so I smiled, took a deep breath and lifted my chin and said out loud, "Well, I'm sure we'll have a good time anyway."

"At least we will have a break from these screaming kids!" Tony retorted.

›‹

Iro had seemed genuinely sorry to see us leave but understood our reasons and wished us, "Kali tiki!" (Good luck) as she waved to us, and we drove up the street.

"I'm not sorry to leave this God-forsaken street!" Tony said turning to face me.

I knew what he meant. The parking situation was becoming a nightmare. Even getting out of the opening outside our rooms was usually difficult as invariable a truck or car would have parked across the entrance, making it very awkward to maneuver out. And with Tony's restricted arm it was even more of an effort.

As we headed up the street, Tony leaned out of the window and called sarcastically, to no-one in-particular, "Well go on, there's a parking space there now!" Before he had finished speaking, a battered old truck was maneuvering into it.

›‹

We headed across the island to Vassiliki, not sure of what we were actually going to do when we got there.

"I'm sure Sylvia is right!" I assured Tony." We'll probably do really well in Vassiliki."

"I bloody hope so!" was Tony's reply. "We've spent a bit now paying Iro and the meal out last night."

›‹

It was Thursday 16th July. I suddenly thought of our little dog, a Bichon Frise called Sam and wondered if he was missing us, although he was with a very good friend who adored him. We knew that Dixie, our cat would be alright, just as long as she was fed and the doctor, who was staying in our house, had promised to look after her for us.

My thoughts were interrupted by Tony saying, "Isn't that a lovely sight!"

We were driving down the long winding road and in front of us was a huge expanse of open sea dotted with yachts. Then as we turned a bend we saw sail-boards of many brilliant colors. They looked like a mass of butterflies, floating and fluttering in the breeze.

The sun was at its highest and it was incredibly hot when we entered a camp-site and approached a fat sweaty man to enquire about the charge to stay there at night.

"Six thousand Drachmas a night," he replied.

Tony explained, "We don't have a tent, we only want somewhere to park this van."

"Six thousand Drachmas." He merely stated.

Tony stared at him before he turned to me saying, "That's about eighteen pounds!" He gave a snort as he stepped back into the van. "We only wanted the use of the amenities. I didn't want to buy the bloody place!"

To which the man merely shrugged his shoulders and inhaled on his cigarette.

"Well what do we do now?" I asked. "The rooms are all going to be much dearer and anyway its mid-season, they will all be full."

"Let's go for a beer first," Tony sighed. "We'll think of something."

As we sat on the harbor-front, sipping our cold 'Amstel' beers, our minds went back to the time when we were there on holiday and had hired a car. Things had been so different then. We had enjoyed a meal with our drinks and we had a nice apartment to go back to. Now we only had the van and nowhere even to park it.

Suddenly I spotted a red VW parked at the end of the beach alongside another large camper. "Tony, couldn't we go there?" I pointed to the spot." It looks as if someone is staying there already."

"I suppose it wouldn't do any harm to go and take a look." Tony was peering in the direction I was pointing.

It turned out that the red VW had an English number-plate, so this was quite exciting to us. We parked alongside of it and ate some tomatoes and cucumber with bread and tsatsiki at our table, in the shadow of the van, strategically parked to give as much shade as possible.

After a while a slim chap, not young, but not yet middle aged, came strolling along the beach towards us.

"See I've got company," he said, smiling. "Where about in the UK are you from?"

"Near Chester, Merseyside," Tony replied.

"Oh! Beatle country!" he joked.

He told us how he had towed a small boat here with the intention of using it to take water skiers out to pay for his food and beer. But unfortunately the wheel had come off his trailer, on the way and his boat had been badly damaged.

"The wheel overtook me on the Italian motorway!" He gave a little laugh. "I've been trying to repair the engine since I arrived." He indicated to a white wooden upturned boat near the red van." I had to strip the engine right down."

Tony asked," Is it okay to stay here overnight?"

"Yes, I've been here for almost two weeks now," he replied. "And this big van was here when I came. It belongs to a crowd of young Germans, one or two of them stay in it sometimes, but they mainly keep a load of water-sport stuff in it."

We could see a black, rubber dingy tied to a large stone, on the beach nearby and about six sail-boards, with sails. In the van we could see other equipment that looked as if it was used for snorkeling.

"They're not a bad bunch of lads, just a bit noisy at times," he said smiling. "By the way, my name is Eugene."

We introduced ourselves, as it appeared that we were about to be neighbors.

I nudged Tony. "Ask him if there is a loo anywhere near."

He told us that there was one at the taverna directly behind us and that he usually bought a beer or something there, so that he could use it. "Although," he said, "it is always locked at night."

This was not ideal but better than nothing! So, since we did have our porta-potti, we decided to stay there for the night.

We told Eugene about our video idea and he was quite impressed. "You should do very well here," he remarked thoughtfully. "Try the training schools, there is one run by Cosmos right here." He indicated behind the long dry elephant grass to our right. Then he grinned saying, "They are all such posers; they are bound to want a video of themselves."

We hoped that he was right!

Later on that afternoon we saw one of the instructors bustling about outside the 'Cosmos' training school. We waited until he had sat down in the shade, with a bottle of water, before we approached him. As usual Tony hung back and left the initial speaking for me to do!

"Hi!" I said smiling at the slim, sun-tanned young man with rather long untidy blonde hair. "I wonder if you would be interested in having a video made of your training school"

I was stopped short by his curt reply. "No, I don't think so."

"Oh," I stammered. "Well... we just... thought that some of your pupils might like to have a professional video of themselves, all put to music."

"I don't think so." With that remark, he turned away with a dismissing gesture.

I felt humiliated and embarrassed.

"Oh! Okay," I muttered as I retreated back to Tony.

"Why didn't you say something?" I said when we were out of earshot.

"I didn't get a chance!"

"Well *you* should have asked him, instead of *me*," I moaned.

"It wouldn't have made any difference," Tony retorted. "He didn't want to know." Then he added, "He is getting paid to do his job, teaching sail-boarding and that is all he cares about."

"Well, I think he could at least, have said that he would mention our videos!" I must have sounded very disappointed. "What do we do now?"

"Oh! We'll try some other schools."

"You mean **You** will!" I corrected.

"Okay!" he stated flatly. "But I really think that you are better at talking to people than I am."

We deliberated for a long time about what we would say, and how we would say it. Then, in the end, realized that it didn't really matter. They would either agree to try our idea, or not. There was nothing we could do except offer our services.

"But if the instructors won't even tell people, then we should put up posters advertising our videos" I said with renewed enthusiasm. "Let's write some out and stick them on posts and anywhere else that we can." I found some spare paper that we had brought from home and began to write with a bold black felt pen.

That night we walked along the beach feeling like a couple of vandals. We stuck a poster on an occasional large wooden telephone pole. We also stuck one on a couple of walls near the camp-site as discretely as possible and another one near the harbor, on one of the smelly metal rubbish bins. Tony did not think that last one was a good idea! In fact he didn't like the idea of doing it at all, so left it to me! While he kept watch in case anyone saw us. He was very anxious and uneasy, in fact a 'bag of nerves'! But I insisted that we had to try something!

We spent our first night at Vassiliki like a couple of Gypsies, in a clearing at the end of the stony beach, a little way to the right of the shabby beach taverna. We still hadn't seen the owners of the big black camper-van, but we saw Eugene go out for the night, looking very smart. We left the chairs and table outside, so that gave us a bit more room. Tony had also put our case full of clothes on the roof-well and tied it down. We had left ourselves the barest necessities.

At one point during the night some motorbikes came roaring towards us, waking us up from our uneasy sleep. I looked out and saw that there were six men of various ages, two to each motorbike. But they skidded to a stop outside the taverna and they went inside. Later we heard a lot of loud talking and shouting in Greek, but we couldn't tell what they were saying, one seemed to be extremely drunk and another appeared to be angry. But they were probably just having a normal conversation. Then just as the sun was beginning to rise over the valley, two of them seemed to simply disappear behind the feathery bushes, while the other four got back on their bikes and roared back the way that they had come.

We were not able to get back to sleep, so at around 6am we saw Eugene, looking a little the worse for wear, staggering back to his VW.

"I wonder where he's been," Tony remarked. "Still, he's here on his own and he's not bothering anybody."

"Let's have a cup of coffee," I suggested trying to sound cheery.

So we sat outside sipping black coffee and watched the dawn break, while we listened to the twittering of the birds, as they fluttered near us, and hopped about close to our feet.

We were waiting until there were some signs of life at the taverna.

At around 8.30am we noticed a fat, untidy-looking man, with a cigarette hanging out of his mouth, clearing the tables and dragging chairs about as he coughed loudly. We made our way to a table and ordered two cups of coffee, so that we might diplomatically use the loo. We waited a few minutes so that it would not be too obvious.

As I had feared, the toilet was typical of the shoddy, cheap tavernas - the sink was broken, there was no running water and worst of all, the toilet door would not close! This threw me into a panic. I tried to wedge it with one of my flip-flops, but that was not very successful and it was not possible to hold it closed, as it was a considerable distance from the toilet. Directly outside the door were crates of empty bottles and black bin-bags full of rubbish, I could hear footsteps and voices, nearby. As I returned to our table, Tony was looking anxiously towards me.

"Don't ask!" I sighed.

"Well I'm going to have to go. Is it really all that bad?" He was shaking his head from side to side with a sigh.

"Well the only thing in its' favor is that the loo actually does flush, which is something I suppose. But I wouldn't like to guess whether it happens every time or not, maybe I was lucky!"

As he was walking away I added, "You have to wedge the door shut with something."

He looked at me with some concern, so I added, "I used one of my shoes, but it wasn't big enough, maybe yours will be alright though."

I heard him mutter something under his breath.

Returning now to the van, Tony asked, "Well what do you reckon we should do today?" With a chuckle he added, "We've had our worst fears of not having a decent toilet at hand confirmed, what other treats are there in store for us I wonder!"

I had to laugh. The situation was becoming farcical.

He continued, "Shall we have a go at approaching another sail-boarding school and risk being 'knocked back' again! Or what?"

"I really don't know!" I replied. I didn't want to risk that awful humiliation again, yet I felt that we should try to persevere with our idea. I thought for a while then spoke my feelings. "You know Tony, I don't think we should let one rude bloke upset us to the extent that we give up on our whole idea."

He looked at me thoughtfully, before nodding his head in agreement.

I continued, "Blow him! Let's go and try another place, we might get a completely different response."

"Right!" said Tony with renewed determination. "Let's go!"

We stopped the van at the next training school, a little way along the beach and got out. We strolled up to the rows of gleaming white sail-boards, where an attractive, young, sun-tanned woman, who appeared to be an instructor, was fidgeting about as though she was preparing for the first lesson of the day.

This time Tony tried his luck. "Hi! My name is Tony and this is my wife, Diane," he began, "we are here to make professional videos for people..." He was interrupted by a man calling loudly to her and her attention was drawn away. She shouted something back to him, somewhat angrily, we could not quite detect the language, perhaps it was Dutch. She adjusted her blonde pony tail and fluorescent pink head-band, as we heard the man call again. She shook her head in annoyance and strode with long deeply-tanned legs towards where the voice was coming from. As she moved she swayed her shapely bottom in skimpy denim shorts from side to side, while her firm breasts protruded from a tiny white clinging halter-neck top that showed a remarkably narrow, tanned, midriff. Then she turned to us briefly saying, "Excuse me, I am... very busy!"

We were left standing there looking at each other in mutual hopelessness.

After we had got into the van again Tony started the engine saying, "Well, shall we try the next place?

"Might as well, I suppose!" I answered. "What have we got to lose, except our pride?"

"I think we've already lost most of that already!" he replied despondently.

At the next training school a lesson was already in progress, under the sun-shade of another beach-side taverna, called "Alex's."

There was a crowd of attractive girls and equally-appealing lads; in fact it was quite difficult to tell which was which. They were all sitting around, some on the floor and others draped seductively on blue plastic chairs, while others sat straddled, listening in awe to a fair-haired "Adonis" who was sitting on one of the tables cross-legged, wearing bright, yellow and green, floral Bermuda shorts. His expressions were exaggerated, although we could not hear what he was saying, every so often a shrill remark would be followed by hollers of laughter and loud guffaws from the crowd.

"What shall we do now?" Tony asked looking at me for some inspiration.

"We could go there and have something to eat and listen to what's going on. At least we would know what sort of a bloke he is, before we approach him."

"I think I know what sort of a bloke he is!" Tony replied, shaking his head. Then he added, "But you never know, at least he's got them all laughing, so he might be okay."

We got out of the van and walked to an empty table. It was then that we noticed that everyone was watching a small television, with a video player alongside. It had been hidden from our view behind a large sports bag to shade it as much as possible from the sun. Tony looked at me and raised his eyebrows, I acknowledged his interest. Our hopes were lifting.   We ordered the cheapest breakfast, two toasted ham and cheese sandwiches and two bottles of 'Fanta' orange. Then we strained our ears to hear what was going on.

Tony whispered to me, "At least they are using a video for their demonstrations, so we might have a chance here!" I nodded in optimistic anticipation.

After about half an hour the instructor got down from the table stretching his lean but muscular body and thanked everyone for their attention. The group got up and sauntered off in various directions.

This was the moment we had been waiting for.

We looked at each other both feeling apprehensive as we got to our feet and made our way towards the young man who was at that time sitting on a chair with dark sun-glasses hiding his eyes. He had tied his long fair hair with a green band at the nape of his neck and he was beginning to tie the laces on his white trainers. It looked as though he was preparing to go on his sail-board, so there was no time to lose.

"I see you use a video in your training sessions. Tony said.

"Yeah!" he barely looked up.

"Maybe I could be of some help to you," he went on. "I have traveled from England in my VW camper," he nodded towards the van parked near the curb. I noticed that it looked very dusty again, and from the expression on the chaps' face, he was not over impressed.

Tony continued trying to sound confident. "I have brought a lot of video equipment and a generator so that I can make professional videos, editing them in the van..." He hesitated and looked at me for some help.

I joined in, "Yes we have made a film of Lefkas, with music!" I paused to emphasize the point. "It's really good; we caused quite a sensation with it in Agios Nikitas."

He didn't reply, but continued to look at me, although I couldn't tell his expression, as his eyes were completely hidden behind his black glasses.

I carried on talking, "We have been selling copies, by showing the film from the van, but we heard that the sail-board schools at Vassiliki might be interested in having a video made..." I hesitated momentarily, "of whatever... the whole class in action on their boards..."

I glanced at Tony for help, so he took over again. "Yes, or we could do a personalized video for someone if they prefer, anything really!" he ended smiling.

We waited for some response; my heart was pounding so loudly I was sure that he could hear it. I knew that Tony was every bit as anxious as I was. I could see the pulse in his jaw twitching and beads of sweat breaking on his brow.

The young man bent down and began tying first one lace, and then the other.

Tony and I glanced at each other quickly; it was a look of desperation, before Tony ventured to say, "Do you think that some of your pupils or other instructors might be interested?"

I broke in again, "We've been watching the sail-boarders in action and some of them are really amazing!" I smiled as I continued, "It would look terrific on video, with some good music ... some heavy metal, or Eric Clapton!"

He looked up again and slowly got to his feet, towering above me. Tony also had to look up, as this chap was much taller than Tony's five foot ten inches.

Tony then went on to say, "Maybe we could help each other, of course you would be getting a 'cut' on any videos that we sold.... maybe we could work something out?"

At this point he just shook his head slowly from side to side and the corners of his mouth curled down. "No! I don't think so mate!" he drawled in an Australian accent. I am only interested in sail-boarding; I get paid to teach... I don't want to get involved in anything else, like videos." Then he picked up his bag before putting the TV and video into it.

"But you do use a video for your demonstrations!" Tony said hastily.

"Yeah! But this is the stuff I was given man! I just do what I'm told..." He gave a snort as he threw the bag over his shoulder. "At least, I do, some of the time!"

Then turning towards us, he said, "Sorry man! Maybe you should try some of the other schools, maybe they would be interested, but I'm basically just lazy! I'm here to do as little work as possible... and have as much fun as I can!!"

"But you wouldn't have any work, or bother, **we** would just make the videos and cut **you** in!" Tony implored.

"No, I just don't want the hassle man!"

Tony looked distraught. "Look, we'll go **half** with you!" He opened his hands, standing directly in front of this chap. It was a gesture of appeal.

"Sorry man, I'm not interested, but I hope you do okay!" As he turned to go he looked back saying, "Sure sounds like a real neat idea though!"

"Oh! Yeah!" Tony imitated under his breath. "Real neat man!"

"Come on," I urged." We tried our best; it's no good asking these instructors, they are all the same." I didn't know what to say or do. I just sat there for a minute mulling everything over in my mind.

Tony picked up the bill from under the saucer and looked at it.

"2,000 drachmas! That's more than twice as much as other places!" he moaned.

We walked inside to pay, whereupon we were surprised to find that Alex, a fat man with piercing blue eyes spoke with a strong American accent. He told us that he had lived in the States for the last 12 years and that his wife was English. My immediate feelings were that maybe he would help us! So I ventured to tell him of our predicament, but I couldn't tell exactly whether he was smiling, or smirking.

I ended by saying, "You see, if only we could get ourselves known by the holiday-makers, I'm sure some of them would want a video…"

I hesitated and Tony continued, "We were under the impression that there would definitely be a demand here for videos of this sport…"

"If we could advertise ourselves somewhere, so that they could see what we are offering!"

"It sure is difficult!" Alex stated. "Maybe you should come back and see the Scottish girl Annie. She's the Thompson rep, now **she** might be interested in your idea; she's a real smart kid." His smile now was openly scornful; he picked up a cloth and began washing the glass counter, adding by way of ending the conversation, "These are sure hard times for everybody!"

As we were walking out, we passed Alex's new range-rover and his new motorbike parked outside.

"You seem to be doing alright though, especially at those prices!" Tony remarked quietly, Then as we both climbed into the roasting van he muttered, "Thanks for nothing, you robbing bastard!"

We drove a little way almost to the end of the stretch of beach before I said, "Where are we going?"

"Oh! I don't know!" "I just wanted to get away from Alex! Did you see the scornful smile on his fat face when you asked him about us advertising ourselves? Did you?"

"Well, I didn't *ask* him if we could put a poster up in his cafe"

"No. But you didn't need to, it was obvious that was what we were hoping for; he could have offered!" He was parking the van in the shade of a tree. "I bet he heard us talking to that Australian 'prat,' and he knew that we had been waiting all that time. I suppose he was waiting for us to ask him." Slowly, he hung his head in despair. "Won't anybody give us a break?"

I was on the point of bursting into tears now. I felt like a whipped dog as we sat there staring at the groups of happy holiday-makers.

After a few minutes we became uncomfortably hot, it was mid-day, even in the shade the temperature was roasting!

"Let's go for a walk along the harbor," I suggested. "There might be a bit of a breeze from the sea, we can try to think of something else that we can do."

We wandered past the places where we had put our posters the night before, but we were disappointed to find that they had all been torn down. We became even more disheartened, all our hopes and expectations had been dejected. These last

70

encounters had raised some very unsettling emotions and we needed to think of something to help us to come to terms with them.

Suddenly I had an idea, "How about finding this girl Annie, the Thomson rep, we saw the office at the top of the street, we could ask her if she could mention our video idea at her 'welcome party' or something."

"Wouldn't do any harm to try, I suppose," Tony replied.

With that we headed in the direction of the office.

We entered the cool office and found a black-haired, exceptionally pretty, girl speaking Greek both loudly and excitedly on the telephone behind a counter. There was also a fair haired chap of around twenty sitting behind an adjoining counter; his chair was at an angle, rocking backwards and forwards, while one foot was supporting his weight against the edge of the counter. He had a radio cassette alongside of him, which was playing quite loud 'rap' music, while he was reading a magazine.

We both stood in front of him until he eventually looked up saying, "Can I help you?"

"Well we really wanted to speak to Annie, the Thompson rep." Tony said, clearing his throat nervously.

The lad pointed to his badge, which indicated that he was also a Thompson rep. "Will I do?"

In response I launched on our prepared script.

"Well, we were wondering if we could get ourselves known here in Vassiliki, maybe we could be mentioned at the 'welcome party.' You see we make videos. We have traveled from England in a camper, bringing with us a lot of video equipment and our own generator for electricity, so that we can do our editing in the van and show the video from the van on a TV ..." I was interrupted firstly, by the girl on the telephone shrieking with laughter and shouting down the phone something that made her explode into more fits of hilarity and secondly by the other telephone near the lad ringing.

"Excuse me," he said, raising one hand and picking up the phone in the other.

I glanced at Tony, who was trying to look calm and confident; he made the slightest of facial movements to let me know that he would continue when the conversation on the phone was finished. The girl continued to talk exuberantly, while she fell about laughing very loudly attracting the lads' attention.

After a while he said, "Chow!" As he replaced the receiver he looked up at us both saying with a slightly annoyed sigh, "Now where were we?"

This time Tony spoke. "We were telling you that we can put together a professional video, all with music..."

He put his hand up again to stop him. "Ah! Yes, well have you got something to show me?"

Tony looked blankly at him and said, "Well we have made a video of the island and we have been selling copies at Agios Nikitas..."

"Yes, we caused quite a sensation," I broke in," showing it in the street, we sold loads of videos!"

"Is this video commercially packaged?" he asked, rocking on the back legs of his chair.

We looked at him, in a somewhat bewildered way.

Tony replied, "It's a VHS, high quality, tape..."

"No, I mean has it got a proper sleeve, with a picture of the island on?"

"No," Tony answered beginning to tremble. His nerves were getting the better of him. Hurriedly he went on, "That is not the issue; we can make a video of anything that people want! We thought that the sail-boarders would like a video of themselves doing their 'own thing'..."

Again the lads' hand went up and he glanced at the pretty girl, who had finished her lively telephone conversation and was now listening to what we were all saying.

"So, what do you want from me?" His head was on one side and he was chewing the corner of his mouth, as he made a slight jocular movement from side to side with the whole of his body.

Tony replied, "Well we were hoping that you might, as I said, mention us at the 'welcome party'..."

"Sorry, nope!"

This sort of threw us, so I spoke hesitantly, "Well we were only trying to offer holiday-makers an added attraction here!"

"What, for free?" He mused, still wobbling from side to side, again glancing in the girl's direction with a mocking tone in his voice.

"No, of course we would charge for the video," I answered, "But they would be cheap..."

"How cheap?" he grinned. His eyes held a strange expression, a glimpse of something like contempt, just for a moment we were bewildered.

"Well it depends of course on what people want," Tony replied.

This time the lad was smiling quite scornfully. He looked at us both in turn saying, "I mean, what's in it for **me**?"

At this Tony replied, "Well it depends what you want! but I should think... that, we would be happy with ...about a tenner. He added, "that's ten pounds. It's up to you what profit you want to make." Tony gave a small nervous laugh and rubbed his hand across his face. "Of course we intend to cut anyone in who helps, but we haven't got any hard and fast rules yet." He paused momentarily and smiled apprehensively. "I mean we haven't started here yet! We are only putting out some 'feelers'..."

"Sort of looking for some advice," I broke in.

The lad nodded his head with his eyes closed, with his tongue in his cheek.

"Tell you what," he eventually said. "you go and make a video of some 'boarders." He waved his arm in the air in an affected way. "And take it to the 'Tunnel Bar' at the top of the street here, it's where all the 'boarders' hang out and I'll take a look at it, and we'll take it from there."

He must have seen how glad we were to have this ray of hope, because he added quickly with a smirk, "But I'm not promising anything!"

"Thank you," we both said at the same time.

As we were leaving he called out with a note of authority, "You can leave the video with either Rob or Kev, they run the bar.... Have it there by eleven am. tomorrow."

Promptly, he picked up his magazine again and began reading.

We made our way through the crowds of bustling holiday-makers along the busy narrow street, lined with colorful shops full of all sorts of bright beach accessories, rails of brilliant T-shirts and sun dresses and rows of shorts of all types of designs.

"What have I come to?" Tony murmured under his breath. I looked at his troubled face and he summed up the situation. "I'm dependent on a little up-start like him; and the awful thing is, that I actually feel grateful that he has given us a chance!" He shook his head and blew out between clenched teeth, "I used to interview and reject, blokes who were much better by far, than **him**!" We were near the van by this time, and he reached for the keys saying, "Now I feel that this little arrogant sod, is interviewing **me**!"

We climbed into the van and as he started the engine, he ended by saying, "And, what is worse... I feel that he has got me by the balls!"

Chapter Four

"Let's park here on the stony beach where we can film as many sail-boards as possible." Tony was steering the van onto a reasonably clear space.

It was difficult to keep any one particular one in the view-finder for any considerable length of time as they moved so quickly, dodging about jumping over waves and sometimes the owner would fall into the sea, making a not very graceful exit! We knew that nobody would want that on film, so we tried to avoid filming such an occurrence to save on editing time, but it happened so quickly. One second they were there flying through the air, the next they were down!

Tony, not seeing things in color in his view-finder, would call, "Where's he gone?"

"There's a sail at three o'clock, keep with him, he's going well." This was the only way that I could help him to keep track of the brilliant colored sails diving in all directions. When I thought that he was heading for a fall, I would find another and call, "To the left, about ten to ten..." and so on, until we had captured what we believed to be a lot of really good footage.

The sun was scorching, I held a sun umbrella over us both in a vain attempt to keep the burning rays off us, but the sweat was running into Tony's eyes and he was having trouble keeping the view-finder from misting up. People were staring at us, occasionally we were conscious of some loud guffaws which made us feel pretty uncomfortable and embarrassed. But I suppose, on reflection, to say the least, we did look rather peculiar!

We drove the van further along the beach in the opposite direction from where we were camped and parked on a piece of level ground a little way from a beach taverna that we hadn't noticed before. It had been hidden behind some trees. We decided that the generator would not bother anybody here, so we arranged all our equipment and proceeded to view our footage, having drawn the curtains over to block out some of the brilliant sun.

We were pleased with the film and immediately started the editing, having chosen all our best shots, as well as the most impressive sail-boarding techniques. Not being experts ourselves, we could only judge their performance by their speed and by what we thought looked clever. We made a point of getting as many people as possible on the film, since we didn't know who we were filming, we hoped that some of them would recognize themselves when, hopefully, they watched the video at the Tunnel Bar.

Finally we chose some music and decided on some heavy rock! By the time we had finished the film it was nine o'clock at night, and we hadn't eaten since our somewhat expensive toasted sandwich; so we were very hungry. We decided to go for something to eat; But before doing that, we wanted to look at the finished product.

We were watching it on the screen when I became aware of some people at the nearby taverna also trying to view the screen.

I spoke quietly, "Turn the screen out to the doorway of the van, I think they are looking!" Tony turned the TV outward. Before long a young Greek guy came over to our van and stood at the door smiling.

We smiled at him and I asked, "Milatei Anglika?"(You speak English?)

"Ohi," he replied, then surged on with such enthusiasm, that his dark eyes were positively dancing with unrestrained delight. The only thing that we were sure about was that he was very impressed with the video and the music! He swayed from side to side in time to the heavy metal bands, repeatedly gasping, "Auraia!"

"Efharisto!" We both said. We were both exhausted; we just wanted to get to sleep. It had been a long and tiring day. He obviously wanted to see the video again, but I managed to placate him with the word for to-morrow, "avrio!"

This seemed to satisfy him. "Endaxi, efharisto!" Showing sparkling white teeth, he smiled and waved with a circular motion of his hand, before he sauntered away shaking his head. His obvious pleasure reassured us.

The next morning we awoke early, we were so excited at our new prospects.

"I'm sure when they see that video at the Tunnel Bar, they will be really impressed."

"Yes it's a bloody good film that!" Tony smiled agreeing with me. He was feeling very pleased with himself. "It was damned difficult to do though, in that heat, especially with all those people watching us!" There was amusement in his voice now, "We must have looked a right pair of silly beggars!"

"Yes I expect we did!" I laughed too. "I don't think there was any need for you to wear those big earphones."

"I thought they made me look professional!"

"No! They made you look daft!"

"They were a bloody nuisance, I couldn't hear a thing!"

"No wonder you were shouting your head off!" I giggled and we both fell about laughing. We were in such high spirits for the first time in the last few days.

୨୦ଔ

Things had taken a turn for the better. Tony was singing as he shaved, standing outside in the fast decreasing shadow of the van.

The door of the big black camper opened and a young skinny lad with straggly long hair emerged, he looked at us with watery pale blue eyes that were heavy from sleep: and he spoke with a German accent. "Good morning."

"Good morning," we both replied. At that moment another two lads slowly climbed out, acknowledging us with a wave and a grunt. They sat at the water's edge, each one drinking a large carton of orange juice while speaking in German.

"Come on!" I urged. "It's nearly ten fifteen!"

"It will only take a few minutes to get to the Tunnel Bar," Tony replied. "But we'll go now; I'd rather be early and make sure of a parking spot."

We drove along the road adjoining the beach, past the various training schools and 'Alex's' cafe. Tony pretended to shout, but only I could hear him, "Ha! We don't need your help now, you miserable old bastard!"

"He was about the same age as us!" I giggled as we headed for the main road.

We turned down a narrow street and saw an open piece of waste land.

"Don't see any reason why we can't park here," Tony looked at me. "it won't be in anybody's way!" After pulling into the side near an untidy hedge, we both climbed out onto the hot gravel. We walked purposely, we had something to aim for, and we intended to achieve our aim.

We arrived at the Tunnel bar, just around the corner, at five minutes to eleven and in Tony's hand he held the video with the details very neatly printed on a stick-on label, *"Video of wind-surfers at Vassiliki, July 1992, See Tony or Di, at blue and white VW camper"*

To our dismay, we found that the Tunnel Bar was closed. So we walked up some steep stone steps between the buildings that led to a very old church. At least the tall buildings on either side offered some kind of shade. We sat on the steps and took turns to see if there was any sign of movement in the bar.

Tony kept glancing at his watch. "It's turned a quarter-past!" he sighed, grunting his annoyance.

"Look!" I exclaimed. "There's a girl on a bike stopping there." We both got up and walked down to the bar. As we got nearer we realized that it was in fact not a girl, but a slim, young lad with very long blonde hair. He was wearing a brilliant, yellow shirt and around his neck hung amber glass beads.

I saw Tony's look of consternation, which implied, "I don't believe this!" as he eyed the lad's blue and yellow floral pants. Then in an effort to hide his embarrassment he spoke quickly, "I'm looking for Rob or Kev."

The lad made a slight grimace that almost resembled a smile, at least one half of his face moved upwards and his eyebrows raised as he answered, "Yes, well I'm Kev."

He tossed his long hair out of his face adding, "Rob will be along in a few minutes, he's not up yet." He looked from Tony to me and said, "What did you want anyway?"

"The Thompson rep asked me to drop this video off here," Tony explained, holding the cassette out to him.

"What is it?" he said looking slightly alarmed and puzzled.

"It's a film that I made of some sail-boarders yesterday..." Tony began. I could see that he was beginning to falter.

I joined in, coming to his rescue; "Yes, you see we've been selling copies of a film of the island at Agios Nikitas, but we thought that we would come here to Vassiliki to see if anyone would like a film of themselves, or of a group, on their sail-boards..."

I hesitated momentarily when he shook his head saying, "No! I don't think we would be interested."

"But the Thompson rep **asked** me to leave it here!" Tony insisted.

"Oh! Okay then, but we have our own videos, of Hawaii Surfing."

"Yes but we can make a professional video for someone if they want." Tony illustrated his point with his hands, we have all the equipment and they can see the film before they buy it if they like, at our camper, down on the beach..."

"It's a really good idea!" I enthused. "I'm sure when your customers see that film everyone will want one."

He turned to open the door of the bar saying, "Well, we'll have to see won't we?" Then he added with an air of nonchalance, "but Saturday night is definitely a Hawaii Surfing night!"

We were both standing in the open doorway looking into the dark, dingy bar; it smelt strongly of alcohol and cigarette smoke.

Tony called after him, "Of course we aim to cut anyone in on every video that we sell, but we can discuss the details later. I have told the Thompson rep that!"

The lad made a gesture that plainly showed his annoyance. "Look! I really have got to start cleaning this place up!" He sighed affectedly. "It's a frightful mess!" Then flicking his hair back he looked angry. "And Rob doesn't do his fair share; he leaves it all to me!"

"Right then," Tony said as he backed away. "We'll leave it with you and we'll call back in a few days, to see if you have any orders for us."

"Yes, well as I said, leave it if you want to, but I've got enough to do."

We walked back to the van around the corner in complete silence. Neither of us new what to say. I looked at Tony, his face had an expression of total amazement as he voiced his thoughts; "Well that is our main disaster of the day, isn't it?" He shook his head slowly, "I mean it does average at about one enormous disaster a day doesn't it?"

"Yes, it does seem to." I had to smile weakly, before we both started to chuckle as he unlocked the van and we climbed inside.

Suddenly he pointed at the wind-screen. "What's that?"

"I don't know!" I said as I jumped out and took the piece of paper tucked behind the wiper, and handed it to him.

He read it, and then put his head down on to the steering wheel. "Oh! No! This can not be happening!" He gave a moan. "Did I say it averages at one major disaster a day? Sorry correction, this time we've had **two!"**

"What is it?"

"It's a parking ticket," he replied. Then he shouted, **"It's only a bloody parking ticket!** That is about all we need!"

"How much is it for?"

Tony stared again before he read out, "Nine thousand drachmas, that's about twenty-eight quid!"

"Do we have to pay it?" I was mortified. "I mean, it doesn't say that you can't park here does it?"

"Oh! I don't know!" Tony moaned. "I suppose that yellow circle with the red border means something like that, but I thought that we would be alright for a couple of minutes. I didn't think that the bar would be closed, anyway this is just a piece of waste land!" He continued to hang his head in despair; his voice was low when he spoke. "It's so bloody hot!"

"I know!" I answered sadly. "It makes you fed up and you can't think straight, but let's go and find the police station, we'll see if we can talk our way out of it, maybe if we apologies right away, they will be more lenient."

The police station was only a few yards away,

"How convenient for that copper!" Tony remarked. "He must have been on his way on or off duty; he must have thought it was his lucky day!"

"Well he could see that we didn't know that there was a police station that close, he could also see that it was an English number-plate, so we obviously didn't know that we were breaking any laws, or we certainly wouldn't have left it virtually outside the police station!" I was feeling pretty angry by now, especially since my son was a 'bobby,' I was not unduly perturbed by the sight of their uniforms. I had spent too many hours washing and ironing police shirts and moaning at my son to hang his uniform up!

We mounted the iron stairway that led to the police station on the second floor of a ramshackle building. I opened a dark blue door and found a burly looking policeman sitting behind a large desk, in front of him, lying on the desk, was a big revolver.

"Signomie, Milatei Anglika?" (Excuse me do you speak English?) I began.

"Ohi!" He replied curtly.

So there was nothing else for it but to do my Scarlet O'Hara act.

I took a deep breath and said in the best Greek that I could, "Well mister policeman..." I remembered that part from a lesson we had done at night school, I also used some other parts of that same lesson whenever I could.

"It is like this. My husband and I only parked our caravanette for a few minutes so that we could take some photographs of the beautiful church around the corner, and when we came back, we found this." I held the parking ticket in front of him.

He read the ticket and spoke quickly in Greek, "There is nothing that I can do! You should not have been there. There is a notice."

"But we didn't see this notice it was half hidden in the bushes!"

At this, he merely shrugged his shoulders.

Not deterred, I continued, "I ask you, is this any-way to treat a visitor? I am a stranger here in your country, but as you can see I have taken the trouble to learn your difficult language! I have studied hard for hours every day to do your country the honor of speaking to Greeks in their own language."

He acknowledged this remark with a definite nod of his curly black head.

Suitably encouraged I went on, "So, why do you treat a guest in this way?"

I took a step nearer to him and I raised my voice, my hands open in front of him imploringly, "I ask you! Why, Eh?"

I glanced at Tony hovering in the doorway and saw that he was a lather of sweat and visibly trembling, his eyes were staring as he whispered, "Steady on Di!"

My performance was good. I knew that so I carried on. "We didn't want to do anything bad! Only to take some photographs of a beautiful church to show my mother in England."

"Madam, it is only a fine; you can go in front of the chief of police and tell him what you have told me..."

"The chief of police!" I repeated horrified, hanging my head and looking totally distraught. "I don't want to go in front of **him**!" I began to wail at this point. "I am afraid of all this, I am a stranger here! How would **you** like this to happen to your wife, your sister, your mother...If they were in **my** country and a policeman tells them to go in front of the chief of police?" By this time the tears had come and I let them run freely down my face as I looked into his dark, alarmed eyes.

He spoke quietly, reassuringly, "Madam, the chief... he is a very nice man. He will listen to you!" Then he restated, "It is only a fine!"

"Only a fine!" I repeated." It is a very big fine! It is a lot of money... for a few minutes... to take some photographs," I tried to smile bravely through my tears. "Sir, they will indeed be very expensive photographs to show my mother!"

His face had taken on a sympathetic expression, now he was smiling at me.

This was my moment. I spoke solemnly, addressing him directly. "Sir, I sincerely hope that **you are never put in this position by the English police force**, if you are ever a guest in **my** country!"

This final remark must have pricked his conscience sufficiently, because he picked up the parking ticket and tore it in two. Then looking directly in my eyes, he spoke solemnly in English. "No stress… Madam!"

"Efharisto!" I simpered, making a bowed, but hasty, retreat.

"What the hell was all that about?" Tony asked as we were walking back to the van. "I didn't know what on earth you were saying; I could see that bloody big gun! Christ Di, you had me scared to death!"

I looked at his worried face and couldn't help smiling, as I remarked smugly, "Well, it got us off the fine, didn't it?"

♤♧

"From the very day we came here, we've had no luck whatsoever!" I complained, as Tony and I lay, somewhat uncomfortably, on our beach mats. They were held down on the sharp stones with a heavy rock at each end to keep them from blowing away in the strong wind that seemed to constantly blow through the valley making the conditions so congenial for sail-boarding.

"Maybe we'll get some orders from the Tunnel Bar." Tony answered. But his tone was bland. We had just had our usual early morning swim, instead of a shower! At least the temperature of the sea was quite warm, but being shallow it was not easy to swim, also it was painful on our feet, stepping gingerly on the sharp stones to the water's edge. Then we had to walk quite a way, feeling the muddy bottom squelching under our feet, until it was deep enough to be able to submerge ourselves. Although it was relaxing to our aching bodies, after sleeping in the van, we did not feel clean, or very refreshed, as the water left a film of sandy grime all over us.

It was Sunday and the lads had not emerged from their camper, although it was almost ten o'clock. We knew that they were there, as four flashy motorbikes stood outside and their sail-boards were scattered around, along with various other expensive belongings, from wet suits to 'Reebok' trainers, left untidily where they had kicked them off outside the door.

Eugene opened the door of his van and made a sleepy acknowledgement towards us.

I spoke to Tony, "I wonder what he does. You never see him with anybody."

"No, he seems like a bit of a loner."

With that a slim fair haired lady came by and stopped near our van, we had seen her the day before, but then she had stopped further up the beach. She slipped her T-shirt off and underneath she wore a one piece brown swimming costume. She secured her towel and T shirt under a stone and turned towards us, we were surprised to find that she was English when she said, "Will you keep an eye on these please, because there is an Albanian woman who works at the Hotel." We followed the

80

direction to which her glance had gone, to the far end of the bay in the opposite direction to where we were, as she continued. "Keep an eye on her, she walks this way in the morning and she steals things that she can sell."

I looked at Tony. "I think I've seen her, she wears a big white scarf wrapped around her head. She walks along looking all over the beach."

"That's her!" The lady stated positively. Then she crouched down to talk to us better as we were craning our necks and shielding our eyes from the glare of the sun, which was already very strong. "Are you staying here in the van?"

I rather ashamedly replied, "Oh, only for a week or so, we have an apartment at Agios Nikitas"

Then we told her of our intention to make videos for the sail-boarders; "I'm sure you will do very well!" she seemed to genuinely believe that it was a good idea.

"Are you on holiday?" Tony asked, as we got the feeling that somehow she wasn't.

"No, I have lived in Lefkas for a number of years." She told us her name as though she half expected us to know of her. Her expression was enquiring and her eyebrows rose, a smile played at the corners of her mouth, as she added, "I'm a writer!"

"Oh!" We both replied.

"That's wonderful! I would love to be a writer," I said. I was remembering how I loved to have to write a composition at school, for homework. I could hardly wait to get home to begin. I knew that the teacher would read it out to the class the following day, and I always got a grade A for it.

After she had left us for her morning swim, which took her right across the bay, some two miles or so, I said, "I wonder if she is famous."

"Maybe!" Tony answered back thoughtfully.

After she returned and said, "Goodbye" to us, she roared away on her motorbike.

"It seems to me," I began, "that everyone thinks that our idea is good, except these flipping instructors."

"And the other stupid morons like that lad in the office that we have to deal with," Tony added.

"Yes well I've been thinking," I was speaking slowly, with emphasis on my words, "maybe we **don't have** to deal through them!"

"What do you mean?" he looked inquisitively.

"We can put some posters on the van advertising our videos and, we can go up to people and ask them if they would like a video made."

At this point Tony shook his head from side to side, which was the reaction that I had expected.

"Oh! No, I am definitely not going around bothering people!" he stated emphatically. "No way!" Then he crossed his arms in a defiant gesture. "I am sorry Di, but you can count me out of that one!"

"Okay," I agreed smiling now. "But we could try the posters and park the van in a more noticeable place, like half-way along the beach, say near Alex's bar, so that the surfers can see the posters."

"Yes that sounds like a good idea; I'll go along with that!"

We had to write the posters out by hand with a thick, black, felt pen, but although we did them as neatly as we could, when we put them up on the windows of the very dusty van, we couldn't help but notice that they looked a bit amateurish!

We parked at the edge of the beach opposite Alex's cafe, where we sat alongside our van on our little folding chairs, with our large diary and note-book on the folding table between us, and a pen at the ready, to make appointments and take details for filming.

Tony managed to put the sun umbrella up over us, wedging it with a heap of stones, because the ground was so very hard.

We waited for what seemed like hours, feeling very embarrassed when occasionally someone strolled by and stopped to read the posters. Sometimes they just walked on, other times they would turn and look at us as if we had two heads. However, the worst thing was when a group stopped to read the posters out loud and either laugh, or merely smirk and titter amongst each other as they walked away. This reaction really upset us!

"I really don't see what's so bloody funny!" Tony finally declared. He was speaking for the benefit of two lads and a girl who were sniggering at the posters on the other side of the van.

As they came around and into sight one lad with an Australian accent yelled with a mocking drawl, **"Professional video, eh?"**

"Yes, that's right!" Tony replied defiantly.

"It doesn't look a very professional set-up to me!"

"Well you can come and view the videos and judge for yourself."

"No Thanks! I've got better things to do than watch videos!" He grabbed the girls arm and dragged her off sniggering. The other lad sauntered behind them smirking and shaking his head in a bemused fashion.

"This is no bloody good!" Tony grumbled. "We are rapidly becoming the laughing stock of Vassiliki!" he was exaggerating. "I bet everyone is talking about the two English idiots in the old van who are trying to make videos, and they are all having a good laugh at us!" His smile, with a quick spurt of anger, became supercilious, as he continued in an Australian accent. "Hey man lets go and have a laugh at the English, out-of-work, computer manager. He can't even sell videos now!"

"**Stop it**!" I spoke firmly, but touched his hand in an understanding manner. "Don't let these silly young people get you down!" I tried to see the lighter side of things. "They are only showing off to their mates and the girls." I shrugged, smiling at him saying, "It's all bravado!" Then, with a laugh I added, "You just wait; they will all want a video in a couple of days!"

"I wish!" Was Tony's acid reply.

It was getting towards the time when people were leaving the beach to get ready for the evening, our notebook was still empty and our diary still unopened. We had sat there all day, apart from taking an occasional dip to cool off, taking it in turns in case we should miss a customer!

"Well I think this has been our disaster of the day!" Tony grinned as he stood up stretching himself. "I think I have had enough humiliation for one day!"

"Okay!" I agreed. "But we had to try, you never now some people might think about it and approach us during the next couple of days."

He put his arm around me saying, "Oh! I do love you!" And as he cuddled me he added, "You are the eternal optimist! And who knows, maybe you are right!"

That evening we strolled along the beach towards the bright lights of the tavernas on the harbor. There was a lot of noise, chattering people, the intermittent extremely loud shout, with occasionally a stream of equally loud utterances from a Greek. It made no difference if it was a man, woman, or child, they were all apparently oblivious of feeling self-conscious about making themselves heard at all times, their very nature and ego, distinguished them from all others in that respect. There was also the sound of lively music coming from every bar and eating-place. Cars hooted at every whim and headlights flashed, passing dodging people as they pushed their way along and across the cluttered street.

We found a table at a café bar and ordered a couple of beers. It was nice to feel that we were part of the happy crowd, instead of bystanders, which is how we had been feeling of late. We were there, but not to enjoy ourselves like everybody else.

I smiled at Tony and took his hand saying, "Tonight we are going to relax and enjoy ourselves and soak up the atmosphere."

A middle aged couple came and joined us at our table. I began talking to the woman and before long I had told her all about what we were doing.

"You should show your video outside our hotel," she said.

"Yes it would be quite an attraction, I'm sure that you would sell quite a few," her husband said good-humouredly. Then he added, "We've been meaning to get a camcorder for some time."

"But I won't let him until I've lost some weight!" his wife giggled. "But I would love a video of this place!"

"Yes, so would I!" her husband echoed.

When they had left and we were on our own I turned to Tony saying, "What do you think?"

I knew that my eyes were bright, excitement quivered down my spine. "Shall we have a go at showing the video outside the hotel?"

Tony didn't say anything for a while, but thought hard about it. "Oh! I don't know! Sometimes I think people are just being polite!" He sighed, whistling through his teeth. "Anyway we haven't featured this place much!"

"No. But we could use the film of the island and edit it down so that it doesn't feature Agios Nikitas, just show it briefly and so all we would need to do, would be to film this part by night and put it together with some good music!"

"Maybe," Tony replied thoughtfully.

Seizing the opportunity to catch him momentarily off his guard, I joked, "Well we've got nothing else to do!"

"Might as well try, I suppose!"

And so with eagerness now I suggested, "Let's go and get the camera and tripod!"

"What now?" There was a faint tinge of disappointment mixed with surprise in his voice, "I thought we were going to relax tonight!"

"Well if we don't do it now, we will have to wait until it is dark tomorrow, and then we will need to edit it. If we do it now..."

"Yes, all right, we can work on it tomorrow, instead of sitting on that bloody beach like a couple of idiots!"

I giggled as I called the waiter over, so that we could pay for our beers.

Maybe it was the bit of encouragement that we had been given, or maybe it was the couple of beers, that had raised our spirits. But we definitely felt more light-hearted as we made our way back along the busy, curved harbor to collect the camera and tripod. A slight wind had risen, coming off the sea; we enjoyed the feel of it on our faces. I hoped that it might miraculously blow away the heaviness from our hearts and minds and maybe change our luck a little.

We had already taken a long-distance shot of the harbor-front by day, so it would be a dramatic effect to suddenly change the scene from day-time to night-time.

After we had taken this shot we headed back towards the harbor. Drawing nearer we took another mid-shot, from the jetty across the glistening dark sea. Brilliant lights of many colors from all the taverna bars reflected in the still water, and the moon shone above the black mountain, behind the whole bay. It looked magnificent!

We made our precarious way along the quay-side, dodging people, who ambled along.

We managed to take some interesting shots of the busy tavernas, with good humored waiters balancing trays of food and drink, transporting them from the kitchens, across the road to the tables at the harbor-edge. Occasionally we had to suffer the constant pest, who at the sight of a video camera couldn't resist the compulsion to have his tonsils filmed! But these interruptions could always be edited out. And of course, there was the 'hand' syndrome! Someone is always bound to stick his hand in front of the lens!

This irritation can also be omitted, but sometimes we had to take the shot again. Such is life! Nothing is ever straight forward. We had come to realize that, more and more every day.

By midnight we had finished filming and sat down for a beer before we made our weary way back to our little humble bed. We lay there in companionable silence while we looked at the stars in the clear night sky.

₧₨

On Monday morning we couldn't wait to start our new version of the film, featuring Vassiliki.

"Why didn't we do it in the first place?" I asked.

"Well we intended doing videos of the surfers!"

At daybreak we were parked under the shade of a large tree in a small clearing of waste land where a rusty wreck of a car was gradually falling apart, a little way from the beach.

It was dusk when we finished the film, but when we watched the end result I cried out, "It's wonderful, simply wonderful!"

Back at our usual place we noticed a young girl walking towards us.

"Hi!" she said, and then rather shyly she asked, "I wonder if you would do a video of my husband for me?" She blushed and giggled. "I've been trying to pluck up the courage to ask you all day!"

"Of course!" Tony answered. This seemed like an answer to our prayers!

"How much do you charge?"

"Four thousand drachmas," Tony replied.

"Right!" she said, "could you film him now, there is a really good wind today."

"Sure!" Tony answered looking very happy. "I'll just get my camera and tripod and you can point him out to me."

"My name is Elaine and my husband is Simon," she was talking as she led us to the spot at the water's edge, where we could see her husband clearly.

We filmed Simon doing some extraordinary maneuvers on his board and it was quite a job to keep him in shot, as he moved so quickly and turned with such skill, but luckily he kept within our range of distance, so we were very pleased with the footage. I suggested that she should also be on the video.

"No!" she cried. "I am only learning I would be hopeless in the strong wind."

So we arranged for her to stand in shot watching him, before walking towards him as he came out of the water to give him a congratulatory pat on the back. Then we asked them to kiss for us to fade out on, adding a touch of romance to their film.

She was delighted with this suggestion. "Oh, thank you so much! That will be wonderful!"

"Cheers mate!" Simon said shaking Tony's hand.

They agreed to come to the end of the beach to collect their film the following evening. It was quite late before we sat outside our van eating a fry-up that I had hastily prepared.

"Seems like we've cracked it!" Tony remarked winking at me as he gulped on his bottle of 'Amstel' beer.

"Yes, and did you hear what she said, that she had been trying to pluck up the courage to ask us. Maybe people are a bit shy and self conscious about asking us, maybe we should ask them!" Tony was definitely of the same opinion as the last time I had brought that idea up, by the expression passing over his face.

"Alright!" I hastened to add." It was merely a suggestion!"

We began editing their film that night, where we were parked. We were out of earshot of the taverna and it was nice to work in the reasonably cool evening air, instead of the heat of the day. We wanted to make an excellent job of their video, because we were so very pleased that they had asked us; and we hoped that they would tell other people about us.

We worked until very late. Then we put all the equipment away.

"That's it, I'm worn out!" Tony breathed a long sigh as he stretched his arms out.

"So am I!" I agreed. For a long moment I rested my head on his shoulder, content that our task had been successful.

We were soon stretched out on our bed, listening to the chattering people at the taverna and the sound of cars and motorbikes that came and went, at different times of the night. But there was a sense of unbelievable peacefulness on us. Soon we were slumbering, happily dreaming of making more videos, like the one we had just completed.

₰)ℙ

"This is the life!" Tony said with a contented sigh, as we sat gazing across the sea, idly watching the lady writer swimming in smooth, steady, strong movements.

There was no sign of Eugene, or the lads in the big, black camper, but we had come to accept their spasmodic appearances. We were eating boiled eggs at our table and sipping black coffee.

Suddenly a rather plump, middle-aged lady, wearing a pink swimming costume came cycling up to our van. She dismounted and smiled at us, pushing back a loose strand of dark, short hair into a pink headband.

She spoke in an accent that sounded like German, "You make ...the video, Yes?"

"Yes! We do!" we both answered, our duet made us all laugh.

"Well I want very much that you make video, with my family..." She paused to see if we understood.

"Yes!" Tony stressed and to add emphasis he added, "Of course!"

"Ah! Then this is good!" She looked delighted. "It is me, my husband and my two children, boys, one big." She held her hand above her head to show us his size, but since she was as short as I was it really was no indication of his age, not that it mattered a jot! We would have been quite happy to film anyone! She continued as we smiled at her and her dark eyes shone, "This one he is twelve years, name Bernd, the other one..." She held her hand just below her shoulder, "This one Ernst is small, only seven years". She shook her head and winced, "This one he is very, how do you say...bad boy...very, very naughty!" But she spoke with a note of humor, which broke into a laugh, so we both laughed with her.

"Are you German?" Tony asked.

"No. We are Swiss." Then without hesitation she asked, "You can film us today, yes?"

"Yes!" we both answered again in unison, making us all laugh again.

Before turning to leave, she called, "My name is Mathild, my husband is Hanz, he will come to show you where we are to do filming, yes?"

"Yes, that will be fine!" Tony answered. With that she rode off on her bicycle.

Tony shook his head in amazement. "Well, you never know the minute do you?"

"No. They'll soon be queuing up for videos," I replied. "And we'll have to say sorry, we just can't fit you in; we are in such demand, don't you know!"

It wasn't long before we instantly recognized Hanz riding up on his bicycle. He was very slim, with flaxen, cropped hair that was slightly incongruous with his dark suntan. His eyes were brilliant blue and he wore a loose pale blue T-shirt and strange baggy floral print trousers that were narrow at his ankles.

"Hello!" he called pleasantly. "You are ready for the filming, yes?"

"Yes," we both answered. We looked at each other and began to chuckle.

"We really must stop doing this; we're beginning to sound like a double act!" Tony said smiling at me.

We followed Hanz in the van and were surprised to find that he turned away from the beach.

"Where the hell is he going?" Tony exclaimed. Then we noticed that he indicated to us to stop.

"Please to leave van here." He was at the window of the van shouting,

"Sure!" Tony answered before he asked, "Where are you taking us?"

"Mathild, she did not ... say?" He was laughing.

"No!"

He put his head down. "Ah!" his voice dropped. Then there followed a short exchange of varied glances between us before he spoke with some authority.

We understood that he wanted to start the film with them all at their camper in the camp-site, after that they would all get onto their bicycles and ride out of the site. He paused to tell us that he would like us to film them leaving from one way, then

87

they would all stop around the corner to give us time to move our position so that we could film them coming out of the gateway and turning down towards the beach. Again they would pause to give us time to move our position to enable us to film them arriving at their row of sail-boards. Only after all that, did he want us to film them on the sail-boards. First we would film the youngest, because he didn't go far out, so that would give them time to warm up and practice before we filmed them in action.

"Is this... suitable, yes?"

"Oh, yes," Tony answered, but his voice did not betray his feelings.

Satisfied, Hanz got back on his bike and rode on ahead smiling and shouting over his shoulder, **"I go to make ...ready!"**

"Does he think this is a bloody TV production?" Tony exclaimed.

I had a desire to laugh, but I stopped myself. "He's certainly put a lot of thought into it!"

"You're not joking!" Tony replied as he puffed and panted with the camera in one hand and the tripod in the other. "He must be a bloody film director!"

"Come on!" I urged. "It will be alright!"

When we finally arrived at the enormous camper, Tony's face was scarlet. His hair was damp and sticking to his brow and it was apparent that he was exhausted.

Next to the camper Mathild and Hanz were sitting at their table pretending that they were finishing breakfast. Hanz instructed us to begin filming, so Tony did.

Subsequently with one motion of his arm he suddenly hollered, **"Cut!"**

Then he told us to film inside the van where the boys were supposed to be still asleep. The plan was that they should pretend to wake up and come out of the camper smiling.

This was all very well, but the younger one, Fritz did not want to have anything to do with the film! From the moment Tony pointed the camera at him he began to wail loudly. Both Hanz and Mathild coaxed and cajoled him. First Hanz urged him to smile and tried to bribe him with sweets. Then Mathild stroked his head gently and kissed his brow whispering soothing words trying to persuade him to let us film him. This proved to be useless. Finally Hanz ordered, "Film him anyway."

So Tony, who by now, was growing weary, began filming the two boys, the elder one, Bernd was trying to restrain the younger. All of a sudden Fritz broke free and took a flying leap in the air and kicked Tony hard right on his shin.

His parents were concerned and apologized. Tony replied, with a forced laugh. "It's alright, really!"

"He is very bad boy!" Mathild reminded us. "I tell you this!"

We forced a smile.

From then on Fritz seemed to join in with the plans, occasionally pointing to Tony's leg laughing very loudly. His father rubbed his son's fair head, expressing amusement. "He is very funny, yes?"

"Bloody hilarious!" Tony whispered under his breath. However, he answered with a smile, "Yes, he is a very funny boy."

We managed to complete the rest of the film the way that Hanz had planned it and we were surprised to see how well even Fritz had mastered the sail-boarding skills.

Tony whispered to me, "Spoilt little bugger, you should see the bruise on my leg." Then he added, "I wanted to kick him back, the little sod!"

We filmed the rest of the family doing all sorts of jumps and turns on the white water. Hanz was exceptionally good; he waved to us as he went flying by. Bernd was good too, so we held him in shot until he went so far out that you could hardly see him. Then Mathild was near, so we captured her doing some feats until she and Hanz crossed each other, making a lovely shot. We filmed them for about half an hour, ending with them both jumping off their boards and walking up the beach, hand in hand. This was a good point to fade out on. So we asked them to kiss and they delighted in obliging us.

We put the camera and tripod back in the van.

I looked at Tony saying, "I think we deserve a pint!"

"I think we deserve a medal!" He retorted standing worn out by my side, "But I'll settle for a pint!"

We worked all afternoon on the Swiss family's film and we had just completed it by sunset. It wasn't worth putting the equipment away, to enable me to cook, so we settled for some tuna, sliced tomatoes and cucumber, with some bread that had gone rather dry.

"I really won't mind if I never see another tomato or cucumber when we get home!" Tony said looking up from his modest meal.

At 6.30pm Elaine and Simon arrived.

"Have you done our video?" Elaine asked excitedly.

"Yes it's all ready," Tony answered. "would you like to see it?"

"We certainly would!" Simon answered.

They were thrilled with the quality and the effect of the music combined with the sail-boarding techniques.

"It's absolutely **great**!" Simon cried out with glee. "You should do really well making these videos!"

Elaine summed it all up by saying, "I think you've had a wonderful idea, doing this." She turned to Simon saying, "This holiday was in fact our honeymoon." She was blushing as she continued, "It's been like a dream to us, and now that we have this video we can always relive it. We really do appreciate what you have done."

We felt so happy that we had pleased them so much. We stared at the four thousand drachmas that we had earned, as if we had won 'The Lottery!'

That night we planned to go to the Tunnel bar, so we tried to tidy ourselves up. It was no easy task when we had no bathroom, or any decent washing facilities.

With a large plastic container, Tony stealthily made his way to a tap that he had spotted near the 'Cosmos' training school. He was not going to take the chance of asking if he could use it, in case that awful girl refused and made him feel even worse than he already did, at being forced to steal water! Just so that we could have a wash!

We both had a swim first to freshen up a little bit, as we had been sweating all day working. Then Tony poured some water in the washing-up bowl and I washed my hair in it, on the table outside. This was very awkward, but the best we could do. Then I lathered myself with a soapy flannel and finally poured more water from the bowl all over myself. It was the nearest thing to a shower that I had experienced, since leaving our room in Agios Nikitas. Then Tony did the same.

"Now all we need is to see how many orders there are for us at the Tunnel Bar!" Tony said as he put on his last clean T-shirt, tucking it into his cut-down jeans that he had worn since we arrived in Lefkas. I had washed them shortly before we left Agios Nikitas, but now they were definitely looking a bit grimy.

I brushed my short hair back, noticing that the sun had lightened it considerably. I was glad that it was a nice easy style to manage. We both had good sun-tans, in spite of the fact that we had kept mainly in the shade, working! Tony's fair hair was now quite blonde.

I outlined my lips with a pink pencil and stroked a brush of misty grey eye-shadow to enhance my green eyes and tone in with the blue cotton blouse and trousers that I was wearing. It was the first time, in a long while, that we had dressed up smartly! We both eyed one another and decided that we looked quite presentable, considering we were living in a van at the end of a beach!

"You'll do!" Tony said, as he playfully patted my bottom when I jumped out of the van.

We entered the Tunnel bar and directly became aware of eyes peering at us. The place was jam-packed with beautiful people, all sporting outrageously elaborate fashions and fancy hairstyles. Music pounded so loudly that it vibrated and a thick haze of smoke encompassed everywhere. A young guy, wearing many strings of colorful beads on his bear brown chest and a pair of fluorescent pink Bermuda shorts came towards us, "Can I help you, man?"

Tony spoke straining against the noise, "I was hoping to speak to either Kev or Rob."

"Yea! Well they're kind a' busy right now, can I help you?"

We could tell by his amused expression that what he really meant was, "You don't belong here!"

Tony tried to speak against the racket again. "I left a video here, of sail-boarders. The Thompson rep asked me to…"

"What?" he looked confused.

"I said, I left a video here that I made of some sail-boarding." This drew the attention of some lads who were sitting nearby, so they turned and started sniggering.

"Oh! Look, It's Jeremy Beadle!" One of them screeched.

This drew great hoots and hollers of laughter from the rest of the crowd. We recognized some of the lads, as the ones who had been smirking at our posters on the van. We laughed along with them, thinking that this was the best way to deal with the situation. Then the guy said, "Hang on a minute, I'll see if I can find anything out."

He walked to the back of the bar and shouted through a dark doorway.

"Hey Rob, there's a … kinda … old couple … here"

After a short pause he glanced at us and yelled, presumably in reply.

"Well, he's wearing specs and he's got a pot belly and she's kinda … small and … fat."

That was about all we needed! We looked at each other in mutual dismay.

He swaggered back and handed us the cassette saying, "Sorry mate! Rob said to tell you that he was not impressed!"

"Thanks." Tony muttered, as we both walked away.

We felt a sudden complete loss of confidence, now we felt old-fashioned and absurd.

At the harbor-front we sat at the same table where we had met the couple who had given us the encouragement to make us compile a fresh version of our video, sipping our beer. Neither of us felt like talking. A dreadful melancholy consumed us.

We were mindful of the gaiety surrounding us, but we did not feel able to adopt the same attitude of the happy people all around. Their merriment and exuberance made us even more aware of our gloomy predicament.

After a while Tony looked intently at me for a moment, his eyes were sad and his voice was low and dismal. "I've had it here, Di!"

"I know! I feel the same!" we walked back to our van with heavy hearts, we had thought that things were improving, but we had been made to feel so foolish and dejected that we felt compelled to give up.

ഇരുഃ

The next morning we took our last early morning dip in Vassiliki.

Just as we were walking out of the sea, our friend 'the writer,' came along on her scooter and stopped. We told her that we were leaving, since we were not having much luck with our videos.

"You surprise me!" she said. "I thought that you would do very well. I think it's such a good idea!"

"That is what we thought," I said.

Tony pointed out that we had only made two videos for people since we had been there.

"And this is our seventh day!" I broke in. "But at least they were happy with their videos..."

"Well the young couple was!" Tony interrupted. "And I'm sure that the family that we filmed yesterday will also be pleased with theirs, when we give it to them today."

"I'm sure they will!" She replied. All of a sudden she cried, "There's that Albanian woman I was telling you about." She pointed to the hunched over figure that had passed us by. "There are a few Albanians working around here, they don't get much money and they get pretty rotten jobs. They are so desperate you see. There is a lad who works at the taverna over there," she pointed behind the trees. "He is ever such a nice chap; actually he runs the place, for buttons!"

I turned to Tony. "That must have been the lad who was so impressed with our video. After this little final chat we said, "Good-bye" and wondered if we should have known who she was. She had been our only real acquaintance in this place and her regular visit had given us a comforting feeling in our unpredictable environment.

"What do you want to do?" Tony asked.

"Well we can't afford to stay in rooms, since we haven't earned much money, so how about going to Kathisma, at least it's a lovely beach and the sea is so clean, also there's a loo and a shower at Yiorgos' Beach Bar, it's not good! But at least it's better than nothing!"

"That's a fact!" Tony laughed. "Right, let's head for Kathisma and take a few days break!"

Suddenly he remembered that he had forgotten to pick his watch up from a large smooth stone that he had left it on, while we took our dip. "It's gone!" he cried in dismay. "That Albanian woman that passed by when we were talking!" I said, "She must have picked it up."

"Well, that's today's catastrophe!" Tony exclaimed.

৪০ঞ

We ate our boiled eggs hastily, somehow once we had decided on our plans we wanted to be off. We were fed up looking at the beautiful, strutting people, with their slim young bronze bodies, continually carrying sail-boards in and out of the sea.

All packed up we drove away from our corner and headed for the Swiss family's camp-site. We had promised to be there for 10am and we were dead on time, as usual. Tony was very particular about punctuality!

We left the van outside the site and walked to their impressive camper.

Hanz and Mathild were sitting outside and they greeted us warmly. Tony put the video tape on the table.

"Ah! The video!" Hanz cried out smiling at us both inclining his flaxen head towards us. "Maybe we can look, yes?"

"Do you have a video player and television?" Tony asked.

"No! But we can look... er... on your...television...yes?" He looked from Tony to me saying, "Fritz, he want's very much to look! This is no problem?"

"No! No problem at all!" Tony answered. "The van is where we left it before, if you can come there in a little while I will set it up for you."

"Ah! Yes, this is very good! We come...soon."

For a moment I saw a dark look spread over Tony's face. I knew that he was tolerating pain in his arm and shoulder. I didn't want him to put more strain on it, but he assured me, "It will be alright, I can rest it later."

He set up the equipment and started the generator saying, "But I must admit I was hoping that they would just pay us, so we could have been on our way."

"Never mind! It won't take long." I was trying to console him. It was unbearably hot and there was no shade.

The family arrived and the two boys climbed inside the van to watch the film.

We all stood outside, around the doorway in the intense heat and watched the film. There were gasps and delighted cries from the whole family as they watched. Hanz and Mathild were very impressed with the music that we had chosen to accompany their sail-boarding skills. Tony explained that the whole film took almost one and a half hours. So, after about half an hour we were relieved when Hanz decided that they would watch the rest when they got home.

"How much?" Hanz asked.

"Four thousand drachmas," Tony replied.

"No! No!" He cried. "You have made us something very wonderful. We will always have this...to remember our holiday." He pushed six thousand drachmas into Tony's hand saying, "Thank you so much!"

Mathild kissed us on both cheeks saying, "We will always be so happy, when we look at our video. It is indeed...wonderful!"

Chapter Five

The sea at Kathisma looked incredible! We drove down the steep, rough, winding road, and we both felt a strange happiness and relief. We were excited at the thought of camping there, because it was so beautiful and peaceful.

We chose a convenient opening among the small prickly bushes and sharp grasses that fringed the edge of sand where it met the road. We pulled up and felt that we had somehow arrived home! For this was to be our home for the immediate future.

First of all we ran across the burning sand into the welcome embrace of the cooling, crystal, turquoise water. We dived into the silent blue world of tiny silver fish, and then we lay on the top, basking in the warmth of the sun. Letting the sun's rays toast our skin. Our bodies suspended, gently rocking with the rhythmic motion of the sea.

Then, by the side of our van, under the shade of the umbrella we sat gazing across the wide expanse of soft sand, eating Russian salad with crusty bread and tinned tuna.

There were a few campers parked along the edge of the long beach at reasonable distances from each other.

We had planned to show the video again at Agios Nikitas later that evening, but when we approached the street we found that it was quite impossible to park anywhere. So we decided to leave the van at the top of the street, and take a walk down to look at the bay again.

As we passed the little supermarket we heard a deep voice calling, "**Mr. Tony! Mrs. Diana!**"

We turned to see George smiling broadly at us. "**I look for you everywhere!**' His face was flushed and his mouth was open and he took in big gulps of air. '**But I not find you.**"

We explained as best as we could that we had been working in Vassiliki.

He closed his big brown eyes, to collect his thoughts in English. "Er... My mother and my father say...Er... you will come to my sister's birthday tomorrow?"

We must have appeared a bit confused because he went on to explain, "Er... we will have nice time here on the beach, swimming, and later we will have a party, a birthday party." He beamed, showing perfect white teeth." You will come, yes?"

"Yes, of course!" I replied.

His eyes held a strange expression, of distraught young innocence. Then as he excitely ran away he called back, "I tell my family."

"Well that's taken care of tomorrow!" Tony stated flatly.

I looked into his eyes and said, "What else could I say?"

We walked up the steps of the Poseidon and were instantly bombarded with hugs from fat Yani, who continually thumped Tony on his back in a gesture of friendship shouting, as usual, "**Hallo Tonic!**"

Then little Thanai came to us, smiling shyly, and showed her pleasure at seeing us by continually snorting and grunting like a little pig directly in front of us, while she chuckled and chewed the ends of her plaits.

Sylvia greeted us warmly, and asked how we had got on at Vassiliki. She was surprised to hear that the expedition had not been as much of a success as we had hoped.

Kostas came out of his kitchen saying in his odd voice, "Ah! My friends, you come back!" Then he gave a little laugh. "You...miss my mousakas...Eh?"

"Yes, that's right!" Tony laughed back, before ordering two helpings with Greek salad and chips, and two beers.

It was a nice feeling being there again.

Vassilis was still dancing around much to the amusement of all the new visitors. He had developed a new trick which he performed for us. He sat a very bashful Thanai on a plastic table and proceeded to lift it, holding the corner of the table in his teeth. Then he was twirling it around in time with the music. Everyone applauded much to his eminent delight. They were still playing the same tape, and towards the end of the night the two older girls danced with him, joined later by the boys.

When we decided to leave we asked for the bill. We were surprised to find that we had only been charged for the Greek salad and chips.

Kostas popped his head momentarily out of the kitchen to shout, "You not argue... with Kostas!" Then imitating himself on the video he called, "Aye! Aye! Aye!"

As we walked out of the Poseidon fat Yani ran noisily after us calling in his deep voice, **"Bye-Bye Tonic!"** His smile to us was friendly and genuine.

We returned to Kathisma to find that our space was still vacant. It was easily recognized by a large white stone. We parked horizontal to the beach so that the side door of the van could be left open to the gentle breeze from the sea. The clear night sky was full of stars and they looked remarkably near. It was a lovely relaxed feeling lying in our van with the side door wide open, so that we could listen to the hushed sound of the dark sea caressing the glistening shingle. The tension and disappointment of the previous week seemed to ebb away, and we were intuitively aware of an impending happy time ahead. The world was suddenly a beautiful place again.

We slept soundly that night, comforted by the knowledge that we had friends near at hand. We were not alone anymore, in a hostile environment.

I awoke very early and I looked out. Yiorgos, who owned the nearby ram-shackle beach bar hadn't even begun to put his sun-loungers in position. I struggled out of bed and jumped onto the warm sandy roadway.

Tony yawned and spoke sleepily, "What time is it?"

"What does it matter?" I replied. Since he had lost his watch, and the strap on mine had snapped, we only had the clock on the dashboard, and anyway time seemed unimportant somehow now. We ate when we were hungry, and slept when we were tired.

"I think we should try to wash some clothes," I said. Noticing Tony's puzzled expression, I explained further. "We will have to put our shorts and T-shirts on, and swim in the sea." Tony burst out laughing, but I insisted. "It's the only way! Come on let's do it before many people see us."

It was a peculiar sensation walking into the calm morning sea in our clothes, feeling them sticking to our bodies. We swam around and after a while came out of the sea to take the soaking garments off and wring them out. We tried washing our towels and our smalls, and had quite a job to hang onto them, as they tended to fill with air and float away. So we resorted to putting another set of shorts and T-shirts on and began swimming around again. We did not use soap of any kind, but merely removed the dust in the clear salty sea. Then we rigged up a washing line, from the umbrella to the side mirror of the van and in hardly any time at all our clothes were dry. I was amazed to find how clean everything looked, slightly faded, and smelling of the sea, but definitely fresher.

After breakfast we drove into Lefkas town to buy some fruit, vegetables, bread, and some tins of ham and tuna. We could not buy fresh meat or fish unless we were eating it that day, as the van got extremely hot and we found that the cooler was not good enough. We were permitted to put our cooler packs in both Yiorgos' fridge and the Poseidon's' fridge, but we didn't like to request this favor continually. Tony often said, "I **do** wish we had invested in a proper fridge!"

Our food shopping done, we entered one of the numerous toy shops and bought a colorful, plastic ferry-boat for Antigony to play with on the beach, and a 'Barbie' doll to take with us to her party later.

We strolled down the street at Agios Nikitas, acknowledging happy smiles and greetings from many local people and children.

Little Constantino ran out from his father's fish taverna shouting, "Video!"

He pointed up the street where some other children came to join him and waited anxiously for our reply.

I told them, "Maybe if there was room to park, and if they were quiet."

Down at the beach, as we stepped onto the hot sand we heard excited cries, **"Mrs. Diana! Mr. Tony!"** George and Fotis, wearing brilliant swimming shorts that showed the depth of their sun-tanned bodies, were running to meet us, followed by little Antigony in a fluorescent-pink bathing-costume, looking extremely proud of herself. She poked a stubby little brown finger into her podgy tummy, and with her other hand she waved four little fingers in the air.

"She is telling you that she has closed four years now!" George explained with a grin.

"Auraia!" I exclaimed.

Tony patted her head of curls saying, "That's lovely! Happy Birthday!"

"Kronia Pola!" I translated.

"Efharisto!" she reciprocated very loudly.

The afternoon was spent pleasantly, but rather noisily by our standards. Tony and I felt embarrassed by the degree of deafening shouts and exclamations emanating from our friendly Greek family.

As we anticipated, George asked, "Mr. Tony, my father... he ask you want to swim with him?"

"Yes, I'd love to!" Tony responded looking worried.

"Please don't go too far out!" I called to ease the situation.

To which Tony laughed saying to George, "Tell your father that Mrs. Diana worries if I go far!" Then he turned to me saying, "You worry too much!" But there was a grateful look in his eyes just the same.

We had taken a video camera with us and captured the day for them. We knew that they did not have a video player themselves, but that Demetrius' brother had one, so they would be able to see the film at his house, and eventually they would probably buy a player themselves.

They were all delighted with the idea of being on video, and this added to the riotous, excited behavior.

George and Fotis dived and splashed, hollering and bellowing in the sea, while Antigony ran around in little circles squealing with joy. She wasn't sure why, but the boys were definitely excited about something, so she also joined in. Mata laughed self-consciously, and tried to hide her ample proportions behind a big red towel, while Demetrius, as composed as ever smiled nonchalantly.

Antigony loved the toy boat and insisted that I played with it at the water's edge with her. I put different sized pebbles into the boat, calling them by all our names, and pushed it to float on the water, until it sank and I cried in a high pitched voice, "Voithia!"(Help!)

This game was enchanting to her and it never lost its appeal. Every time the boat sank it was every bit as funny!

We left at around 4.30pm to enable us to shower at 'Yiorgos' free shower, back at our base. Then we could change in the van for the evening party at the Tsetikas' beach-side apartment.

There was a ludicrous queue outside the shower, everyone standing with a towel and shampoo, intensely aware of feeling rather degraded. It was rather humiliating to wait in line for someone to step out from behind the torn plastic sheet that was the entrance to the corrugated makeshift shower. It was actually, merely a hose pipe running across the scorching earth from a huge metal tank that had been heated by the sun to a pleasant degree. The head of the shower had a habit of falling off, so that you were suddenly drenched by a solid blast of water. The base in which you stood was made of rough concrete, so that should you happen to drop the soap it became quickly embedded with small pieces of gravel, making it comparable to sandpaper! Everyone kept their swim-wear on and came out to dry themselves while they walked back to their various tents or campers. It was also disconcerting to know that directly adjoining the shower was the toilet. This too, consisted of three sides of corrugated aluminum sheeting and a shoddy wooden door with an unreliable catch, which was in fact a small piece of wood nailed on the door that swiveled on a bent nail in the frame!

The whole procedure was quite amusing, but nevertheless it was disconcerting to know that while you were in the shower, someone was in the toilet alongside, and there were little holes in the aluminum adding further to the embarrassing situation!

However once we had overcome this calamity we dressed up in our best clothes.

I wore a green dress with tiny white daisies on it, and Tony wore some casual navy slacks and a short sleeve blue shirt, these clothes had been retrieved for the occasion from the case on the roof of the van. Thankfully they were made from polyester, and crease resistant. I was glad that I had thought of that when packing.

As we past the Poseidon we heard a long drawn-out whistle, and looked up to see fat Yani and his Aunt Sylvia smiling down at us.

"Very smart!" Sylvia shouted.

And fat Yani bellowed, "**Auraia!**"

We were greeted at the door by George. Then again at the top of the stairs by Mata, who introduced us to a rather attractive woman in her early thirties, who was Demetrius' sister called Voula, and then to a pleasant stout mature lady who wore her white hair in a bun. Although she was wearing a simple black and white print dress there was something regal about her appearance. She beamed at us and hugged us affectionately. She was Demetrius' mother, also called Antigony.

On the balcony overlooking the bay was young Antigony and her three little friends, one of them a boy also called Yiorgos, which of course was George's name. They were all staying in adjoining apartments.

Demetrius sat quietly watching the children in his imperturbable manner. As we walked out onto the balcony, he stood up and welcomed us formerly, shaking our hands, and offered us some wine.

We gave Antigony her parcel and Tony filmed her opening it, much to everyone's delight. Thankfully she was thrilled to find the doll, and played very happily with it.

After a little while Mata brought a big creamy gateau with four candles lit on the top. Everyone clapped and there were cries of, "Auraia!" from everyone. Then the children gathered round Antigony who had suddenly become very shy and demure. Everyone sang a little song that was equivalent to our 'Happy Birthday!'

At the end of which Antigony blew out the candles. Tony caught the happy expressions with the video and we felt sure that we could give them something that they would treasure for ever.

After the children had finished eating they went off to play in the main room and Tony I were left to chat with Mata and Demetrius, with the ever-willing assistance of George.

Mata carried out to us, two big plates full of tasty bits of food. We were not sure what some of them were, but they were thoroughly delectable. I was simply delighted to have the opportunity of speaking Greek again. I relayed the story about our parking ticket to them and they were amazed and amused. Mata explained that

Demetrius had brought his mother and sister with him that day to spend Antigony's birthday with them and also to meet us.

It turned out to be a lovely evening, and despite the language barrier between Demetrius and Tony, they seemed to share a kind of tranquil empathy.

As we left, George asked, "We will see you again tomorrow?"

"Not tomorrow," I answered. "But we will see you again soon.

We were walking up the street when we heard George running after us. "Please to stop!" He said panting. "My father and my mother say they... want for you to come on Sunday... and they take you to very, very nice place... for to eat!" He was looking from Tony to me, as he went on. "Er... we will meet here at seven ..." He took a deep breath, and pleaded, "Please! Yes?"

"Well that would be very nice," I replied.

"Yes," Tony responded hesitantly.

"I go now to tell them, yes!" He beamed running back to the apartment shouting very loudly, to Fotis who was standing waiting at the doorway. "**Ne!**"(**Yes!**).

We had to smile at their apparent joy at our acceptance.

Tony laughed. "The man from Delmonte, he say ... **yes!**"

When we arrived at our place on the beach we were surprised to see that there were a few more campers parked along the road. There were also two quite large tents erected on the sand itself and a big camp-fire crackled and glowed in the darkness. We could see the black silhouettes of many children seated around the fire. Soon the delightful sound of children singing filled the night.

We both sat outside the van on our chairs watching and listening in wonderment. It was 11pm but there were still some Greeks swimming in the calm dark sea. Their voices carrying clearly on the water, in the still night air.

We eventually climbed into the van and drifted to sleep to the sound of the happy singing.

In the morning we were up early, since Tony had anticipated a queue outside the free toilet, and this was something that we both really dreaded.

As it happened there was no-one around, much to our relief! (To use a pun!) So we were able to enjoy a day on the beach. We swam; lay in the sun, then swam again, all day, just as though we were holiday-makers. It was nice to have a quiet day on our own after the riotous previous day. Although, it wasn't exactly quiet, because the children who were camping quite close-by were all in the sea making a lot of noise. Every time a wave came crashing over them they would all scream in unison! This appeared to be the favorite game of Greek children, screaming in the sea! Or screaming anywhere for that matter. But after a while we became used to it.

We wondered if it was worth trying for a parking place in the street again, and decided not to bother. It was Friday night; Agios Nikitas would be packed, so we opted for a relaxing night on 'our' beach.

Towards the evening the large group of children gradually left the sea, and began a game of volley-ball using two large pampas grass canes from the side of the road, a long piece of string, and a Coca-cola tin. They had a fantastic time, and made a tremendous amount of noise as they became more and more excited. When somebody scored a point there was an enormous cry of applause, which made us laugh. It was very entertaining to watch their play, and to learn their names and idiosyncrasies.

Later they lit their bonfire after gathering driftwood and bits and pieces, and roasted chicken and sang cheerful Greek songs again, long into the night.

We were awakened early on Saturday.

"Auraia thalassa!" (Beautiful sea!) The cries were right outside our van. I peeped out to find that to the right of us a dilapidated car was parked. In front of it, at the side of the road, were three camp beds on which lay three sleeping adults.

A little further down the sand were four sleeping bags, and four excited children, two boys aged about twelve and five, and two girls of about ten and eight. It was the girls' high voices that were particularly noticeable. Especially the older one who had run up to the camp beds and was trying desperately to waken her father.

"Papa! Papa! Auraia thalassa!"

We climbed out of the van just as the parents were awakening.

I called to them. "Kali mera!"(Good morning)

"Kali mera sas!" They returned the greeting to us.

It was a little later when the third person emerged from under the pink blanket, and we discovered that it was in fact a very elderly lady. The youngest boy ran up to her with a bucket of sea-water carried painfully across the hot sand. Into which she put her twisted hands and splashed her wrinkled face. As she did so she let out a gasp, which made the attentive children laugh and the eldest boy mutter, "Po! Po! Yia- Yia!"(Oh! Grandma!)

They soon assembled in a circle on the sand, and began to eat bread and cheese from a large plastic cooler bag. Then they began to peel oranges, and eat them very noisily.

Our avid attention was drawn away by the sudden arrival of another old battered car which parked on the other side of us. The doors flew open and we were amazed to see how many people scrambled out. There were five adults and five children, and a baby.

The children immediately headed for the sea shouting, **"Auraia thalassa!"** The adults smiled at us and followed, carrying sun-umbrellas, towels, bags of food, and an assortment of beach toys.

Soon another car arrived and drew up with a screech of brakes alongside the previous car. Greek music from the radio blasted out and a young couple stepped happily out. The woman was carrying a young baby and the father opened the back door for two pretty little girls to climb out.

As soon as their bare feet touched the sand they were off running towards the sea whooping, "Auraia thalassa!" in squeaky little voices.

Tony turned to me shaking his head saying, "You'd think these kids never saw the sea! The way they keep going on about how beautiful it is!"

"I know! And they really do mean it!"

The father smiled at us and nodded towards our GB sticker saying, "From England?"

"Yes!" We answered, and Tony began to explain that we had traveled by road.

He put his hand up to show that he did not understand. "Only leetle beet English!" he explained holding his thumb and fore-finger close together for emphasis. So I did my best to explain in Greek.

"Auraia!" They both exclaimed, and praised, unreservedly, my achievement of conquering such a difficult language. The woman told me that my grammar was exceptionally good. I was thrilled! I wished that my teacher at night school could have heard her. I noticed that the father was carrying a long fresh loaf, and since we needed some bread I enquired where he had bought it, as most of the shops were closed on Sunday. Immediately he broke the loaf in half and handed me the warm crusty portion with a smile. "For you!"

I smiled gratefully. "Efharisto poly!"(Thank you very much))

Later that day Tony and I were swimming in the rather more-crowded sea than usual, and I sat down near a young woman with a baby. She was one of the five adults who had arrived in the first car.

Feeling confident with my ability to manage the Greek language now, I remarked, "Ti auraia pethi" (What a charming child!"

"Efharisto!" she replied, smiling.

After a moment I asked, "Poso meenes einai?" (How many months is it?) Children are neutral gender in Greek.

"Theka meenas," (Ten months) she replied proudly.

"Kalla!" (That's nice) Suitably encouraged I asked, "Einai koritsi ee angoory? (Is it a girl or a boy?)

"Tee?" (What?) she asked with a bewildered expression.

I repeated, "Einai koritsi ee angoory?" (Is it a girl or a boy?)

At this, she picked the child up and quickly moved away throwing me a very displeased look.

Sitting down next to Tony I commented, "I only asked if the baby was a girl or a boy! I mean how can you tell when they are wearing little pants?"

After we had eaten our lunch in the narrow shade of the van we returned to the beach again and headed for the sea.

I noticed the other young mother who had complimented me on my Greek language and we smiled. We spoke in Greek to each other for some minutes. I was saying how lovely the sea was here and what a beautiful island Lefkas was.

After some time of chattering like this, I ventured to talk about the baby.

"Einai omourfi pedi!" (It's a beautiful child!)

"Efharisto!" she replied, with a lovely smile.

"Tee einai?"(What is it?) I asked. "Einai koritsie e angoory?" (Is it a girl or a boy?)

"Tee?"(What?) she stared at me with a somewhat severe frown.

I repeated the question and got a similar confused response. Then she hastily took the child out of the sea and walked quickly up the beach to talk to the child's father, who looked equally annoyed with me.

Towards the end of the day a red rusty truck slowly drove along the road. It was carrying all kinds of fruit and vegetables. I wanted tomatoes and a cucumber, so I walked up to the fat little owner and spoke in Greek. "Tesera tomates, kai ena Agori"

The man placed 4 tomatoes in a bag and spoke in English. "Why you ask me for one boy?" Agori means boy!" He explained.

I pointed to the cucumbers, whereupon he let out a loud cackle saying, "Angoori!" as he handed me a cucumber.

"So that is why I was getting such funny looks!" I turned to Tony. "I have been asking people if their child is a girl or a **cucumber!**"

Tony went into fits of hysterics until he recovered enough to say, "Don't you think you should go and explain to the people?"

I approached the woman whose husband had shared their loaf with us first, and did my best to explain my mistake.

To my relief they both burst out laughing, and the mother hugged me affectionately. Then she said, "Einai **Agori!**" (It's a **boy**!)

The father speaking in English now said, "NO a cucumber!" And we all giggled again.

I then made my way to the other young woman who apparently had already heard my explanation to the previous woman, and she and her husband were already expressing amusement as I drew near.

The father cried, "**Angoori!**"(Cucumber!) He hollered with laughter while pointing at the baby, who was now quite noticeably a boy, since he was without his pants. Soon everyone within earshot was enjoying the joke!

I turned to Tony. "What a good job that truck came or I would have been insulting people for the rest of our stay!"

As evening neared, our new 'friends' with their two little girls and baby packed their belongings into their car and came to us to say, "Adio!" They were still amused at the idea of their baby being called a cucumber! They were waving happily to us as they departed, with a loud tooting of the horn, and a roaring of the engine, as the car made its boisterous way up the winding steep road.

Similarly, a few minutes later, the five adults and five children and baby boy also took their leave of us with dramatic waving of arms through the open window of the old jam-packed car.

Everyone who was left settled-down to enjoy the renowned, beautiful sunset at Kathisma. All around us outcries of, "Auraia!" could be heard. As dusk descended we could see fires being lit at different locations.

Tony opened a litre of wine, and we sat on our chairs near the van sipping the cheap white wine as though it was 'Mouton Cadet'!

Half way through the bottle Tony lifted his glass to the moonlight saying, "This is a particularly pleasant little wine!"

"Yes! Very good!" I chuckled, enjoying the mood of the evening.

The family on our right began to make a 'fire-place' using stones collected from the beach. Then the father, a tall slim man with thick curly black hair and a bushy moustache, filled the centre with coals which he set light to, much to the mounting excitement of the four children. When the fire was glowing white he placed pieces of chicken on two long skewers, and rested them across the fire where they immediately began to crackle and the fire started to spit and dance.

We watched and wished that we could light a barbecue, but we had no room to keep coal as well as everything else in our van. But the smell of roasting chicken was making us very envious; it had been a long time since we had tasted fresh meat.

As though sensing our desire, the father looked towards us, and with a warm smile he beckoned to us.

It was such a friendly gesture that I would have got up straight away and gone over if it hadn't been for Tony saying, "No! We can't intrude on their evening!"

I hesitated. But the father spoke to his wife and his mother, and they both looked towards us gesturing, "Ella! Ella!"

I turned to Tony saying, "I think we should go they really want us to!"

"Okay!" Tony's replied reluctantly.

The elderly lady waved her hands and indicated for us to sit.

Tony was self-conscious but smiled at them all and sat cross-legged next to me. We were between the two older children. He had brought the half full bottle of wine with him and he handed it to the father, who emitted a long whistle expressing amusement, as he began pouring it into plastic beakers for himself and his wife.

The elderly lady shook her silvery head saying, "Ohi! Ohi!" She showed us what she was drinking. "Cola!" She said with a cackling laugh.

Soon the father lifted the luscious smelling chicken from the skewers carefully, and handed us a plastic plate each, onto which he dropped a succulent portion. Then he did the same for his mother and his wife, and finally the excited children who were calling, "Patera emena!"(Father me!) while holding their plates in front of each other. The father laughed and pretended not to give them any, which increased their enthusiasm in the squabbling game.

We devoured the sizzling chicken with great relish, the hot fat running down our chins. There was a general mood of light-heartedness and gaiety as everyone chatted around the hissing flames.

They told us that they made the trip from Athens quite often at weekends during the summer, to enjoy the fresh clean air, and the beautiful sea.

The elderly lady held her nose between her thumb and forefinger saying, "Atheena, Phew!" This made everyone laugh, and the younger children imitated her with amusement.

Our hot faces were illuminated in the heat of the brilliant fire-light, and the wine had made us yet further relaxed. Even Tony who preferred to keep a low profile delighted in the atmosphere, and in the knowledge that these little chats gave me such great pleasure because of my genuine liking of people and my interest in them. I told them of our journey to Lefkas, and about our video. They were eminently intrigued, and listened engrossed. The children had fallen silent, their thoughts and imagination completely spellbound.

As the embers were dying the elderly lady noticed that the two younger children had fallen asleep, where they had lain, quietly listening. The father picked the boy up first and while his wife opened the sleeping bag some distance from the fire the father kissed his brow and laid him down placing a cover over him. Similarly they did the same with the slightly older girl, and then he put the remains of the fire out by kicking sand over it. Eventually we all retreated to our simple beds. As we climbed into the van we called out, "Kali nickta sas!"

"Kali nickta sas!" They all murmured from their beds beneath the stars!

The air was still and warm; only the slightest pleasant breeze from the sea prevailed.

Within a few minutes we could hear the sound of loud snoring from the father, which was soon combined by the whistling exhaling of the old woman as she breathed steadily. We giggled quietly lest we wake our new acquaintances.

"You couldn't sleep like this, without any fear whatsoever, in many places!" Tony remarked.

"No! "I agreed," I wouldn't like to try it where we live at home!"

⅚⅛

When we awoke on Sunday morning our neighbors were already in the sea, all

except the granny who was folding up the sleeping bags and putting them in the open boot of the car.

"Kali mera!" she cried on seeing us emerge from our hot van.

"Kali mera sas!" we called back before we raced directly into the refreshing cool sea. Plunging headlong into the hushed depths, because we needed to clear our heads after the quantity of wine that we had drank the night before.

We surfaced; shaking the water from our hair and eyes, and our new friends greeted us.

Tony held his head in his hands and used the Greek exclamation, "Po! Po! Po!" This really tickled them all.

Some waves arose, first quite small, but in a short space of time they became bigger. This was the cue for the screaming game! All the children screeched at the top of their voices. **"Patera!" (Father!)** Shrieking as loudly as they were able every time a wave smashed into them, knocking them over with a powerful blow.

We decided to shower and change a little early as we were meeting the Tsetikas family at seven. To our mutual joy, we were able to use the shower without queuing! So we were both ready in good time.

We said "Good-bye" to our friendly family because we knew that they would have gone by the time we returned.

Tony retrieved his last clean white shirt from the case on the roof of the van and I wore a cotton trouser suit of subtle shades and obscure patterns. We felt respectable again after our few scruffy days!

ഇരുൽ

It was almost seven when we met the Tsetikas family who all looked very smart! It was evident at once that they were all pleased to see us again.

George looked very proud of his new spectacles which made him look considerably older, as he and Fotis ran to meet us smiling. There was a gleam of excitement in their brown eyes.

Antigony also ran to us wearing a little white skirt with a matching top. She threw her arms around us both in turn. Mata embraced us both and Demetrius had a gleam in his eyes that definitely belied his outwardly detached demeanor. He shook our hands and bowed his cropped, silver haired head, in a gesture of respect.

Voula was with them, and George explained that she had come back with his father from Agrinion that day so that she could spend the day on the beach and come out with us.

I spoke first. "You look very intellectual in your glasses George."

"Yes quite the smart young man." Tony added.

"Thank you," George touched the frame and seemed to grow a few inches stretching his head high with pride.

"Did your father go there and back to-day?" Tony asked.

"No. He went back on Thursday night ... to open the shop the next day." George replied. "But he ... er... left early this morning ... because the shop is closed ... and my Aunt Voula does not have work to-day." Then he explained further. "My father will be leaving with his sister straight from our meal to-night, because. he has to open the shop in the morning, and Voula has to go to work in an office."

Mata looked anxiously at us, and George asked Tony, "It will be alright... for you to bring us?" He indicated to his mother, Fotis, Antigony and himself, "Er...in your van ... back here! Yes?"

"Yes, of course!" Tony answered.

So we set off, up the street, to where we had left the van. Demetrius had left his brown 'Mazda' saloon about 200 yards further on, so George suggested that he, his mother and Antigony came with us.

"So that I can say... the way to Mr. Tony!" he justified, as he climbed into my usual seat in the front. Voula and Fotis went with Demetrius.

George obviously enjoyed being in the front with Tony, while Mata and Antigony sat in the back with me. They both seemed enamored with the VW and examined all our little amenities with great interest and there was considerable hilarity when they discovered the porta-potti!

Antigony squealed, "Auraia!" This made Tony roar with glee. This confirmed his belief that this expression seemed to be used for just about everything!

We followed Demetrius' car, with Fotis leaning right out of the window flapping and waving his arms in the air with frenzy.

George spoke English to Tony, while Mata spoke Greek continually all the way; I was quite surprised that I was able to understand almost everything that she was saying.

We arrived in Lefkas town and everywhere was bustle and excitement. We pulled up next to Demetrius' car and we all got out. It was nearing eight o' clock, so the streets were lit up and crowded. Greeks were strolling around in their best clothes, and little girls were paraded in elaborate dresses, while little boys wore fancy outfits. It was all very interesting to see.

George spoke with excitement in his voice. "First we take a walk...er...then we go to a very, very nice restaurant. It is not known by many people on holiday, it is very, very good place to eat!" He smiled to see if we understood before continuing. "Many, many Greek people go to this place...er ...because it is very... very beautiful place! Er... It is big, big... garden!"

"It sounds wonderful!" I answered.

"Auraia!" Tony exclaimed, much to everyone's delight.

We walked in a kind of procession, which seemed rather comical to me. Especially as Tony was walking alongside Demetrius, almost in step, and neither of them could say a word to each other!

Mata and I walked with Voula, and Antigony who had slipped her little hand into mine and was happily skipping along.

George and Fotis followed behind stopping to look and blurt out sudden exclamations loudly whenever they saw something that took their fancy. After some little time George went into a shop to buy something and we all stood and waited.

He came out grinning and waving big black flippers in the air shouting, "**Frogs Foots!**"

A little further along the street Fotis disappeared in a colorful shop and came out wearing a white captain's hat with a black peak. This emphasized his beautiful features and made him look quite stunning! Antigony then decided that she too wanted a hat, so after searching among an abundance of various assortments, she eventually picked out a straw hat with a red ribbon round the brim which made her look very cute.

We heard the sound of a brass band, and soon a boys brigade marched joyfully by.

It was such a pleasant sight and sound, that we continued our stroll roused by a nice happy feeling!

Tony took a photo of us all.

Then Demetrius asked if we would like to eat? And we agreed that we would. He led us away from the tourist area and turned down a narrow side street that we would never have noticed.

The restaurant which he led us to was hardly splendid, but we thought that like all Greek tavernas it would be friendly. We entered through the door and walked inside.

I was surprised to find that we appeared to be standing in an enclosed garden. The roof was made up of the tree tops that met so densely that it was almost impossible to see the sky and stars through the branches and fragrant leaves, and all around were the trunks of trees which formed irregular walls. Bordering the edges of the restaurant flowers of many vibrant colors grew. Canaries and other tiny birds of unusual tinted feathers fluttered freely, singing sweetly in the boughs above, and even descended onto the tables to pick up some crumbs. The whole place was altogether extraordinary and bewitching.

We showed our delight at being in such a wonderful place, and the family was ecstatic! A waiter welcomed us and called to another waiter so that they could put two tables together for us all. Demetrius then organized who was sitting where, so that George was on one corner, next to Tony to enable him to act as interpreter between the two men at either end of the table. Antigony insisted on sitting next to me, which pleased me a lot. And Mata sat opposite me with Voula by her side. That left Fotis to sit on the other side of me. There were no written menus. Instead a waiter came to the table and recited very quickly what there was to eat, before he suggested various dishes.

Tony and I chose pork chops, not wanting to take any risks! The family had a variation of food from beefsteaks to fish and Antigony had a sort of hamburger. Demetrius ordered wine, which came in a large pottery jug, and an assortment of soft drinks for the children, with two bottles of iced water, and two beers presumably for the men.

The starters arrived first, there were two big hot cheese pies, cut into sections, three big Greek salads with juicy black olives, three plates of feta cheese, two plates of tsatsiki, and three baskets of hot, crusty bread!

Tony looked at me and there was a brief look of panic in his eyes. His indication was obvious without him saying a word. "How much is all this going to cost?"

Our pork chops were quite delicious! Grilled on charcoal with herbs and served with half a lemon that was to be squeezed on to the sizzling meat which almost melted in our mouths.

The wine flowed and it was very gratifying to sit in this way and chat to a Greek family in such lovely surroundings. I told them the story about how I had mistaken the word for 'boy' (agory) for the word for 'cucumber,' (angoory) and they found it very amusing indeed. Even Demetrius forgot his self-control, and chuckled heartily. Mata and Voula had to dry their eyes on their napkins. George erupted into loud heehaws, while Fotis and Antigony giggled shyly. Then George, still laughing jokingly asked for a plate of agory. Fotis followed suit and asked for half an agory! - Everyone laughed again.

Suddenly Antigony stood up and startled us by shouting, "**Stamata**!"(Stop!)

She whispered into George's ear, and he repeated in English. "She say, er... not to laugh at Mrs. Diana!"

"Efharisto!" I said to her as I bent to kiss her warm little brow.

Demetrius whispered, "Yiorgo..." and then spoke rapidly to him in Greek.

George made a sigh to him before saying, "Er... my father wants for me to... speak some English."

So Tony and I obliged, we chatted about school and hobbies while the adults listened in proud amazement. Tony was pleased to be able to speak freely for a change.

At around 11pm Demetrius called the waiter over and asked for the bill.

Tony got his wallet out to contribute, but was instantly halted by a solitary signal of Demetrius' hand and one word spoken in English, "No!"

He then spoke quietly to George who translated. "My father say that you are our... guests in our country, and... we are always too... your friends!"

I stressed how very appreciative we were of their friendship and hospitality.

Mata smiled saying, "Filoxinia!" interpreting the word for hospitality.

Demetrius suddenly and dramatically stood up saying, "Prepi na figo!"

George justified his action saying, "My father say... he has to leave!"

So Demetrius walked first towards Tony and took his hand, shaking it firmly. Voula took her leave of us with much kissing and shaking of hands.

ℰᗡᑕᎡ

Then Demetrious took my hand in a strong grip as I said, "Efharisto." I told him that we would both always remember his kindness. He made a slight inclination with his head to signify that it was nothing, simply saying, "Parakalo."

I had a feeling that we had somehow achieved a mutual respect. He paused at the entrance to turn briefly to say, "Adio" then he was gone.

A few minutes later the rest of us walked out of the restaurant together.

George and Fotis shared the front seat next to Tony and sang a jolly little Greek song about Kirios Antonis, (Mr. Antony) They were laughing as they sang, *"Oh Mr. Antonis, how we love you! As the stars jump and we count the fires until the rain comes."*

I looked towards Mata puzzled and she tried to explain that it was a very old song that didn't really make sense even in Greek. She told me that Nana Mouskouri sang it.

However they sang it all the way back to Agios Nikitas. Mata and I spoke quietly in the back so as not to waken the currently slumbering little girl.

When we approached the village Antigony stirred and her little face rosy from sleep, creased in a drowsy smile, when she looked out of the window to find that we had arrived and said, "**Auraia!**" which made us all smile.

We dropped them all off outside Iro's rooms, where we could pull into the garden to turn and they stood waving as we drove back up the street and on towards to our beach.

"**See you again soon!**" George shouted.

ℰᗡᑕᎡ

We found that the beach was curiously deserted as we pulled up in 'our' spot. All the happy weekend visitors had left, and the silence was to some extent strange. We had got accustomed to having company, now we were alone again.

110

We lay in our bed listening to the hushed sound of the sea, thinking about the evening.

"Wasn't it lovely?" I sighed.

Tony lifted his head slowly from the pillow to glance once more out of the window as the headlights from a car winding it's way up the hill momentarily lighted up the inside of the van. His eyes were shining. "Yes, it was one of those nights that you know you will always remember."

Chapter Six

When I awoke on Monday morning there was a bright streak of yellow light across my pillow, the sun was already up and getting hot. I stretched my legs downwards until my toes stuck out from underneath the sheet, with my arms upwards. I looked at Tony sleeping peacefully and felt strangely happy inside. I lay for a while breathing deeply and gazing at the deep blue sky. It was a beautiful day! Like every day, and we had nothing 'scheduled,' nothing that we 'ought' to do! We could do anything we wanted to. Well so long as it didn't cost money. We could relax and soak up the sun and indulge in our favorite pastime, observing people and everything else.

I glanced at Tony and he was smiling. "What plot are you hatching now?"

I swung my legs out of the bed and answered, "I was just thinking, that we should just enjoy the day here, taking it easy on this beautiful beach."

"Sounds like a good idea!" he replied and followed me out of the van. "Race you to the sea!" The sand was hot under our feet. I sat in the sparkling white foam that was just like a bubble bath.

The beach was strangely empty of the people who had inhabited, albeit for a short period of time, various places along the shore. Now all that was left to verify the fact that they had been there, were depressions and hollows, and many footprints in the sand. Even their bags of rubbish had been collected by the van that called every morning.

So we enjoyed the peace and tranquility, and each others company.

"Shall we try to show the film in the street to-night?" I asked.

"Suppose we should!" He answered as he gulped cold water from a misted plastic bottle that he had just bought from 'Yorgos.' Caravan shop. "We could do with earning some money!" he said. "We'd better keep the price at 4,000 drachmas though."

ဆာ

That night we drove to the wide opening at the top of the street and it was readily apparent that there was no room to park.

"Well that's that!" Tony stated looking at me with disappointment. Again our hopes and plans had been thwarted.

"Never mind!" I sighed, "We could try showing the film here!"

But he was not easily cajoled. "Nobody would see it here!"

"They might!" I retorted. "And anyway what else can we do? So stop moaning!"

We parked opposite the opening to the street, and Tony set up the equipment and started the generator again. It looked ridiculous somehow. Our van parked by a heap of rubble, and us sitting there playing the video in a completely desolate black space.

"What the hell are we doing here?" Tony wailed after about an hour, and we hadn't seen a single soul! "We are just wasting our time sitting in this God-forsaken hole!"

"But we really need to earn some money!" I insisted. At that moment we became aware of footsteps approaching, and I squeezed Tony's arm in an effort to stop him from speaking. We heard the sound of voices speaking German and when I peeped out of the corner of the mesh-covered window of the van I saw that a middle-aged couple and two teenage girls were standing looking at the television screen. We sat silently for some time hoping that they would become interested in the video, and when we heard outcries that distinctly proved that they were stirred, we made a few slight movements before I drew back the curtain and said, "Do you like the video?"

"Yes!" They replied altogether. The woman added, "It is very good!" She turned to her husband and spoke to him. Then she said to me, "We will buy one please."

This was like an answer to a prayer!

When they had gone we looked at the 4,000 drachmas she had given us, and felt immensely happy.

"See!" I said, "I **told** you somebody might pass!"

"That will do for me!" Tony answered as he gently planted a kiss on my forehead before he began to put the equipment away.

We walked down to the 'Captains Corner' and sat at Zak's bar enjoying a glass of nice draught beer, when he came and sat between us and enquired how our business was coming along.

"Etsi ketsi!" (So so!) I replied. To which he laughed loudly.

Then he surprised us by asking us to make a video for him at his bar. "Tomorrow. Yes! Yes!" He insisted!

When we awoke on Tuesday morning we decided to go into town to buy some provisions and to get some petrol for the van and for the generator. This done, we strolled through the ever busy streets after finding a parking place down a dusty side street covered in rubble. We walked quickly in the narrow shadow of nearby buildings, trying to avoid the searing heat of the July sun.

At the market place I bought some fruit and vegetables, picking them from wooden boxes stacked on the cluttered narrow pavements. It was amazing how cheaply we could live not buying meat. Then we made our way to the supermarket.

"Let's have a beer first!" Tony suggested, looking longingly at the little bar that we frequented when in town.

"You go!" I answered. "I'd really rather finish shopping so that we can get back and make a start on Zak's film."

Tony didn't need any persuading! I went into the welcome shade of the dark supermarket that was quite familiar to me by that time. I felt that I knew where everything was kept, and I was able to ask for exactly what I wanted along with all the Greek women at the delicatessen counter. I bought some cooked ham and some cheese that the somber faced man wrapped in patterned blue paper lined with a plastic film that helped to keep it moist.

When I crossed the busy noisy street I found Tony looking completely at home in his usual seat watching the world go by, along with several Greek men of varying ages.

"You look like a local!" I laughed, as he helped to carry the bags to the van.

It was afternoon when we stepped around the corner of Zak's bar and we became immediately conscious of a change in the impression of the place. Zak was wearing a brilliant white T-shirt with 'Captain's Corner' printed on the front, and so was his wife, who had normally always worn black. His plump teenage daughter appeared, trying to stifle her giggling, in exactly the same top. And so did his 12-year old son who swaggered proudly like his father, between the tables. The place which was normally reasonably tidy was in fact strikingly clean. There wasn't an empty glass or stain on any of the tables.

Tony asked if they were ready to be filmed, and after a lot of laughing from them all, they consented.

Zak behaved as though we were not there at all! He wandered about moving chairs and looking out to sea, and conducted himself like a true professional actor!

His wife appeared to be less confident, and couldn't stop smiling and occasionally burst out laughing. Their daughter was quite overcome with embarrassment and took a fit of giggles and this made the otherwise cool-headed boy laugh as well. Then Zak asked us to film the arrival of his friend who was also wearing an identical T-shirt. He was the local Jack-the-lad!

It took us several 'takes' before we got it right! He wanted to make a 'cool' entrance, but since everyone was giggling he couldn't stop himself from laughing. Eventually, he was satisfied with his performance. Then he asked us to film him getting into Zak's little boat that he ferried people to 'Milos' beach in. This was a new attribute! A few weeks ago when we were staying at Agios Nikitas there was no other way of getting to that beach except to scramble over the headland. Now Zak was charging 300 drachmas a trip. A profitable venture we thought. Again, it took us a few attempts to film the fellow who was definitely a first class 'poser'! He strutted down to the white boat wearing gold rimmed, sun-glasses, and ever so casually started sailing away! If he felt that some minor hitch, like someone on the beach walking in front of him, might have spoilt his performance, he insisted on doing it all again! We wouldn't normally have minded but the heat was so very intense!

Everyone on the beach found his repeated performances, and affected behavior, tremendously comical.

When we finished filming we were brought two large beers by Zak.

"I feel that I bloody well deserve this!" Tony said with a sigh.

Zak asked when he could have the film and we told him Thursday night. We told him where we would be parked and he assured us that he would be there some time after nine to see the video and to pay us. This arranged we headed back.

We were glad to get back to Kathisma and compose and refresh ourselves in the cool sea again. Then as the sun began it's decent, we enjoyed some ham and salad in the shadow of the van, before taking a bizarre shower together in our swim-wear.

It was 9pm when we parked in the same place that we had used the previous night, feeling slightly more optimistic. "Maybe word has got around about us!" I said hopefully.

"Yes, maybe!" Tony agreed.

After about half an hour a young couple came by and stopped to look at the screen.

I made myself visible and they both said, "Hello!" They told us that they were Swiss. Then the girl explained that some people, who were staying in the same apartments as they were, told them that they had bought a video from us last night, so they had come to see if we were here tonight. "We will buy one please," she said.

It wasn't long before another couple, who were English, came past after spending the evening at the Poseidon. It was lucky that the film was at the part featuring the Poseidon.

"Look, there's Vassilis!" The girl whispered and they were both enraptured by the rest of the dancing and merriment.

"I'll take one please!" The young man said smiling. "I'm really glad that we came this way for a change tonight or we wouldn't have seen you."

Then the girl said, "You should be in a much more prominent position, you'd do a 'bomb'!"

"It's very difficult to get a parking spot!" Tony explained.

"Well we will certainly tell people about you!" The young man enthused. "I think this is a brilliant idea!"

"Yes you've caught the atmosphere of this holiday for us! And I'm sure there will be a lot of people like us, who will love to have this quaint little place on video!" The girl added,

"8,000 drachmas, that's nearly twenty-five quid!" Tony said with a nod of his head. "Let's go for a drink at the Poseidon and see the crowd"

We were welcomed with friendly greetings as soon as we turned inside the doorway. Fat Yani waved his arms frantically and bellowed in his now familiar way, **"Hallo! Tonic!"** We ordered two bottles of beer and settled to watch the dancing.

Sylvia came and sat with us, to take a break after a busy night. "I would like to buy two videos from you please?" she said. "One is for my parents in Switzerland

and the other I will keep until one day we will have a video player." She continued with a smile, "It will be nice to keep it for the children when they are grown up."

We promised to bring her two videos the following night.

This request threw us into a bit of a quandary as we did not like to charge them since they had been so kind to us! Yet we desperately needed the money.

ഇൽ

On Wednesday we were determined to edit Zak's film for him. Despite the scorching heat we sat in the sweltering van on Kathisma beach when everyone else was under the shade, or in the water, and we worked almost solidly for most of the day. Only stopping to throw ourselves into the sea to cool down, then to find that by the time we had walked back to the baking van over the burning sand we were every bit as hot as we were before!

We finally finished Zak's film and were very pleased with the results. We sincerely hoped that he would be too! We labored so hard on it because we wanted to please him, and surprise him. Satisfied with the result we then started to edit the film that we had taken of the Tsetikas family on the beach, and at Antigony's birthday party. We added this on the end of a video of the island.

When we had showered and dressed, we parked the van in our new parking location and walked down the street and along the little bay to the Tsetikas' apartment. George and Fotis ran down the stairway to greet us excitedly. We handed the video to George, and told them that we were not sure when we would see them again.

George explained, "My mother and us children will be staying for another three weeks, but…my father …he will only be coming on Wednesdays, and at weekends."

Mata and Demetrious waved to us from the balcony, and beckoned to us to come up, but we declined, I explained that we had to go to work, and they understood.

George waved the cassette in the air excitedly and shouted, in his usual boisterous manner "**Video!**" The delight in his voice was very pleasing to us. His parents also thanked us profusely.

So, then we began our nightly vigil. It was only eight o'clock, but we didn't want to miss Zak. He usually passed that way on his motorbike, on his way to join his wife after she had opened the bar.

We waited and watched, but there was no sign of anybody!

Around 10pm we became restless and fed up! "**Where the bloody hell is he?**" Tony cried in dismay, "We've worked our butts off doing this blasted video and he doesn't even bother to come!"

"Let's take it to him then!" I suggested.

"I'm not running after that little pipsqueak!" Tony argued. "Anyway, I wanted him to see how good it is!"

"So did I" I wailed, "But the main thing is that we get the money! After all he will see it when he takes it home." After some deliberation I suggested, "I'll take a walk down to the bar and just see what's going on."

When I got near I was almost deafened by the blaring jazz music from Zak's bar. That wasn't the type of music that he usually played.

When I entered the bar there was a lot of high spirits and gaiety. A large group of Germans were singing and dancing, most of them were quite obviously drunk. Zak grinned at me in a half-witted fashion and came towards me with open arms saying, "My friend!"

The place vibrated with the intensity of the music and the crush of people gathered inside and out, were shouting and singing drunkenly. Zak's wife looked at me and put her hands to her head looking annoyed.

It was impossible to speak against the clamor, so I yelled to Zak. "**Video!**" I pointed to my watch to indicate that the time was almost 11.15! He grinned stupidly back at me and shrugged his shoulders. Then he turned away and was swallowed up in the crowd. This was the final straw! I fought my way through the bar and out into the fresh air.

Outside, I paused to collect my thoughts and then I marched vigorously up the street.

I was angry to think that we had worked so hard to please Zak and I felt that he had let us down! As I neared the top I found that I had to slow down, my legs were aching and I was out of breath. I could just distinguish the van in the darkness, and the light from the portable television looked quite absurd in the wasteland. I felt so sorry for Tony sitting there! I couldn't help feeling that the situation had become nonsensical.

"Any luck?" I asked.

"Not a bloody sole!" He replied. "What about Zak! Did you see him?"

"Oh! I saw him alright!" I replied. "He's as drunk as a skunk!"

Tony looked disgruntled. "What now?" He looked defeated. "I feel silly sitting here night after night in the vague hope that someone passes."

"Yes," I agreed. "But first let's take this tape to Zak, his wife will pay us anyway." Tony switched the video off and started to put the equipment away saying, "We'd better take these films to Sylvia as well." Then his face became troubled as he added, "We can't charge them can we?"

"No!" I agreed.

We entered Zak's bar. "**I see what you mean!**" Tony shouted above the noise.

Zak was at that time slumped in one of the chairs half asleep among the din.

Tony walked over to him and handed him the video.

"Ah! My friends!" Zak slurred the words; his eyes were glazed and hypnotic.

"**The video you asked for!**" Tony's voice showed his annoyance.

"Dhen pirazi!" Zak shrugged his shoulders.

"It doesn't matter?" Tony had some knowledge of Greek language. "It might not matter to **you**. But it bloody matters to **me**!"

"How much?" Zak's lethargic reply came with a yawn.

"Four thousand!" He was holding four fingers right in front of his face.

Zak beckoned to his wife who took the money out of the till and handed it to Tony saying, "I am sorry!"

We had seen Zak in an entirely different way and we had not liked it.

"Isn't anything reliable around here?" Tony was whispering as we walked into the Poseidon.

"Hallo Tonic!" Fat Yani called with a big grin from behind a crumbling wall.

"There's your reply!" I answered.

"Oh! I forgot about him!" Tony laughed.

Sylvia came over to us smiling, and we handed her the two cassettes. She thanked us and within a few minutes she was back with twelve thousand drachmas.

"Oh! No!" We both cried.

"Yes! You must!" she insisted. "It is your **business**!"

"But you have been so kind to us we want to pay you back!" Tony explained.

"No! No! You made video of the Poseidon, and many people see it, and they come here!"

"Well anyway we are only charging 4,000 drachmas now for a video!" I laughed.

"Then I have had a bargain!" she chuckled as she pushed eight thousand drachmas into Tony's pocket, before she walked away. As she did so she called over her shoulder, "And I only take them if you let us give you Kostas' mousaka!"

We looked at each other in wonderment.

"Some things stay the same!" I said as we sat down at an empty table and were immediately brought two beers by Vassilis, one was balanced on his head.

After we had eaten, Sylvia joined us at our table and spoke, thoughtfully. "I think you should go to Nidri!" She nodded her head positively. "There are many people there and I think you would sell many videos!"

"You think so?" I asked.

"Yes! Yes!" She replied emphatically. Then she added, "But we will miss you!" She held her forefinger up in a reprimanding fashion. "You must come back to see us often!"

As we walked out of the Poseidon Tony confirmed my feelings. "She might be right! It's worth a go!" We waved to our friends and felt a bit sad at the thought of moving away from them again. They had always cheered us up, when we were feeling down-hearted, with their constant show of affection and joviality.

"I'd better change some more money while we're here." Tony said. And we walked into the Car Hire office.

Liana looked up and smiled saying, "You have come back!"

"No! We have decided to go to Nidri," I answered.

Tony added, "There is no-where to park around here."

"Yes, I know!" She agreed. "It is very... big problem!" Then she said with sympathy, "Maybe... you leave some videos here with me and I show one in my hotel to people having dinner, Er...and... breakfast..." She held her hands palm outwards in a questioning manner, "Maybe I can sell some for you! Er...I don't know!"

"That would be **great!**" Tony cried enthusiastically.

"We would be very grateful!" I added.

Then he remembered to add, "Of course we would give you something for every one you sell."

"**No! No!** "She put her hands out defiantly, "I do not want anything....only to help you!"

We arrived back at Kathisma and felt a little tinge of sadness, knowing that this was to be our last night. Tony opened a bottle of cheap wine and we put our chairs and table in front of the open doorway, and sat facing the midnight sea. We looked up at the sky, studded with sparkling stars, and felt very insignificant.

"It's funny to think that we can't go home!" Tony said. "I mean we've got no house to go to!"

"Not for a while yet anyway!" As I was speaking we saw the bright lights heading down the hill towards the beach. Our eyes followed the direction they were heading and we were surprised to see, as the vehicle got nearer, that it was another old VW like ours. The only difference was that it was cream colored.

"It's got a German registration." Tony observed.

The van pulled up along side of us and a young man leaned out of the window calling, "It is alright...for to stop here?"

"Yes!" We both answered. Our voices seemed to be obtrusive in the stillness of the night.

We were half way through our bottle of wine when the tall, fair haired man walked up to us. "It is very beautiful here!"

"Yes!" We answered again.

Hesitantly he asked, "You mind if my wife and I come and sit with you?"

"No!" We replied.

He called to his wife, "Freda! Come!" Then went to his van and brought two folding chairs like ours, under his arm and a bottle of wine in his hand.

"I am Karl, how do you do?"

We sat talking and drinking wine, as he seemed to have an endless supply! And it was not the cheap wine that we usually bought. I brought out some cheese and tomatoes that we ate with some crackers, and felt glad that we had something to offer them.

Karl enquired if we had actually driven from England! And we went on to tell them about our venture and the reasons for our doing it.

It was a strange sensation to be talking of personal things, and sharing food, with complete strangers, whom we would certainly never meet again, well into the early hours of the morning. But we were becoming used to these peculiar incidents, and furthermore we quite enjoyed them.

Dawn was breaking when we wished each other luck and happiness in our lives, and climbed into our humble beds for a few hours sleep.

In the morning the sound of children's voices awoke us, and when we looked out with bleary eyes we found that our German friends had gone, but there were quite a lot of people already on the beach. Yiorgos was strolling around collecting the money for his sun-loungers. "He's having a good day!" Tony remarked. "They must all be tourists!" We had noticed that, like us, the Greeks, usually sat on beach mats. "I need to do an oil change." Tony suddenly stated gloomily. "I think I should do it here before we move on."

It was already scorching hot so we took our morning dip first, and then he started the messy job. I helped by holding the sun umbrella over him as he lay on a beach mat under the van doing whatever he had to do. Soon all the dirty oil was drained into a red plastic bowl, the filter cleaned and replaced, and the engine filled with fresh oil. Then there was the dirty job of filling the four litre container with the dirty oil which we would deposit at the garage. This had been a major achievement in such heat, and something that Tony had been meaning to do since we had arrived at Kathisma, but had left it until the last minute, as one usually does!

We both took our last erratic shower at 'Yiorgos' and said 'Good-bye' to his wife.

As we climbed into the van to leave we noticed Yiorgos on his usual sun-bed under a huge umbrella, a straw Stetson placed precariously on his head so providing even more shade for his sleepy dark eyes. He saw us leaving and raised his thin arm to touch the rim of his hat and made a movement with his hand that signified that he had acknowledged our departure. Tony responded with a 'toot' on the horn and we headed up the winding road.

Sadly I said, "Goodbye beautiful Kathisma."

After depositing the dirty oil at our usual garage we headed for the mountain road that eventually led to Nidri.

"I'm taking you a different way!" Tony said, as the van trundled along the hot dusty road. We passed some ramshackle homesteads where a scraggy mule or donkey stood sleepily under the inadequate shade of a tree. Scrawny hens ran about squawking noisily. Occasionally an old man sitting on a rickety chair in the shade of his shoddy home would raise his slumberous head to look at the van, his attention drawn to the GB sticker. We passed white crumbling walls covered with brilliant flowering shrubs and half-hidden gardens. Then turning further inland we headed up a long steep road lined with sweet smelling wild herbs and shrubs.

Behind us we could still see the beautiful blue sea at Kathisma.

In the distant shimmer on the road we saw an odd black shape which appeared to be floating above the haze.

"Whatever is it?" I asked.

"Blowed if I know!" he replied, "Looks bloody queer though doesn't it?"

We strained our eyes to try to make out the external outline of the thing. As we got nearer the configuration became clearer, and we saw to our relief that it was an extremely old looking woman dressed entirely in black sitting on an equally old looking donkey which was tethered to another donkey, so loaded with branches of greenery that it resembled a walking bush.

As we passed slowly by, she waved her hand at us and her wrinkled face, enfolded so completely in shawls that it was almost obscure, broke into a smile. It was a curious sight and we both waved back.

The aspect of the countryside changed as we headed even further into the mountains and on either side, beyond the yellow daisies and monstrous thistles lining the track, were vast plains of grape vines. In the distance women of varying ages were gathering potatoes. Some old women wore unusual pointed wide-brimmed hats and long black dresses that swept the red dusty earth beneath their feet. I remarked to Tony, "I don't know how they can do that! It's so very hot and they have no shade whatsoever!"

"No, it must be dreadful!" Tony replied.

We made our twisting way still higher noticing that the old van was struggling slightly, when we turned a sharp corner to find a small herd of sheep nibbling on the sparse grass at the side of the rough road, while a shabby herdsman in a threadbare jumper idly coaxed the scurrying procession with clicking hooves over the countryside, by prodding them with a twisted stick.

Now we were passing cropped fields of gold where the yellow corn had been harvested, and fire-red poppies stood proudly among the tall white grasses fringing the fields.

Ahead, we spotted some crumbling ruins, and a little further on we saw an ancient chapel, perched absurd on the mountain peaks. Even in its broken-down state it still held a peaceful beauty of bygone days.

Something stirred within my heart and I touched Tony's arm. "Let's stop here for a minute!" I pleaded. "I'd love to take a look at this place."

"Okay," he replied, as he pulled up at the side of the road and turned the engine off.

It felt eerie and silent, apart from the sound of crickets and our footsteps, as we made our way gingerly through some brambles and gorse. I longed to pick the tiny pink flowers like pom-poms, and delicate baby bells of powder blue and lilac hues. Miniature, blue butterflies danced among the blooms, and brilliant yellow larger ones fluttered around me, occasionally settling momentarily to tremble on a flower and hover with enchanting characteristic movements of their powdery wings.

Tony smiled as he watched me make a posy but after a few minutes he said, "Come on! We will have plenty of time later on for your flower arranging, but first we have to find somewhere to sleep tonight!" His words startled me; I was so completely lost in my thoughts.

"I feel as though I have done this here before!" I said.

"Well you've probably done it in some other similar place."

"No!" I answered spontaneously. "I'm sure that it was **here!**"

"But you have never been here before!" he insisted.

I saw a huge patch of bright yellow daisies and quickly changed into a dress with daisies on it, that was in the back of the van. I pleaded for Tony to take my photograph.

I was aware of something forcing its way into my mind, something that I couldn't quite remember. Like a vivid dream that is forgotten the instant that you awake, but still lingers haunting in some minute shuttered window in your mind. I walked dream-like towards the fractured doorway of the little church and paused to whisper, "Inside on the wall there is an icon of the virgin and child."

"Well, there usually is!" Tony replied cocking an eyebrow at me. "I mean, that's a pretty safe bet!" But nevertheless his features took on a slightly puzzled expression when we came upon the icon, and I felt a leaping unexplainable delight. Tony spoke gently, "You've probably been somewhere very similar on one of our holidays."

"Maybe!" But I was not completely convinced.

Back in the van, the spell was broken by the engine jumping back to life.

We seemed to be driving through some ruined grounds where flourishing trees of oranges and lemons grew together filling the air with a delicate smell of citrus.

I saw some stone steps leading to an old white house.

"**Stop!**" I cried. "I really have been here before!"

"Don't be daft!" He jerked the van into second gear and threw me an impatient glance as we headed further up the twisting, rough road. There was nothing distinguishable ahead, only the brow of the hill and the cloudless blue sky.

"If you would just listen for a minute..."

"I am listening!" he droned, and there was a somewhat impatient note in his voice.

"Right!" I replied, and pointed in the direction that we were heading. "Just over the hill we will see a beautiful view of the sea." His expression made me carry on, "Then on the left there is a path." I closed my eyes to enable me to concentrate. "It's covered with trees and bushes... and there are a few houses at the bottom... sort of farm-type places, with goats.. and hens... Oh! And a pig!" I opened my eyes to look at Tony, who was smiling broadly now.

"Listen!" I enthused. "The path leads to a stream, with a little metal bridge and some stones... big stones...that you can walk across the stream on. Then the stream gets wider and opens into a river, and goes along the side of a field, and further on, it goes under a big stone bridge, which supports the road!"

"Honestly Di!" He was laughing. "Your imagination runs away with you sometimes!" He shook his head good-humouredly.

"Right! Well a bit further on to the right of the road there is a church... a big one...with a reddish dome and a lot of steps with a graveyard all around...and it all looks down on the sea!" I sat back exhausted and waited for a reaction from him. I didn't have to wait long! We ascended to the top of the hill and the sight that met our eyes, made our hearts race! He whistled out through his teeth in amazement. There was a fantastic view of the sea, and he looked at me rather oddly.

"See! I told you!" I remarked excited now by the weird feeling that was filling my being. It was no more than a minute before we both saw the path on the left.

We had passed it because it was almost hidden by trees.

"There it is!" I was excited and Tony stopped the van in a small clearing at the side of the road. We jumped out onto the hot road and were instantly aware of the loud noise of crickets as we entered the welcome shade of the overhanging trees. My steps grew faster and my excitement mounted with every sight that met my eyes.

"There's the little farm house!" I cried triumphantly. There were chickens running about and a rooster strutted proudly across our path. Then with a startling, flapping of wings, it flew onto a nearby gate adjusting its wings and stretching its scrawny neck. It shrieked its cheeky familiar cry of 'cock-a-doodle do!' This made us laugh as we walked on by.

"There are the goats!" I cried, pointing at a small enclosure where four black and white goats lay dreamily chewing on dried-up leaves.

"But there isn't a pig!" Tony retaliated in mock reproach. Then around a corner we saw a row of small dilapidated houses, where threadbare mats hung over rusty iron banisters, above some old worn steps. Washing hung between intermittent painted gourds. There was a water pump and a concrete trough, along side which a mangy black dog was lying asleep in the shade.

"I told you there were some houses here!" I insisted quietly, so as not to disturb the unhappy looking creature. The whole place seemed empty of people; there wasn't a single person around.

We crept passed the dog and heard the sound of lapping water, and as we turned the bend we saw the little rusty metal bridge that provided a crossing over the rushing stream. There were large stones among the many smaller stones and Tony looked at me in astonishment saying, "This is really uncanny!"

"Look!" I shouted. "There, follow the river through that field of sheep, look there's the big bridge!"

Tony screwed his eyes to see and his brow furrowed. "I don't understand this at all!"

We walked back up the lane in complete bewilderment and climbed back into the van in silence. Tony started the engine as I said, "I still think it's got to be a coincidence!"

It was a few moments later when we saw the red dome appear on the horizon on the right of the road. I grabbed Tony's arm and we both gasped when the rest of the church came into view. It was painted cream and it was indeed big, and there were many steps leading up to the massive dark wooden doors. All around the church were crosses and shrines of various elaborate designs, and behind it all was the perpetual sea.

Tony stopped the van without saying a single word, and we both got out, and walked timidly into the cemetery. We had only walked a few hesitant yards when we both stopped abruptly. On a grave nearby was a photograph of a little girl aged eight.

"Mariana Panayiotis" I whispered the name on the gray headstone beneath the picture, in a gold colored frame.

"Good God, that's just like the photo that your mum's got of **you** on her sideboard!"

"Yes," I replied. "And look at the date!" I pointed to the inscription saying, "She died on the nineteenth of October nineteen forty one! That's the day that I was born!"

I looked at the smiling young face on the faded photograph and felt an instant emotional reaction, and an overwhelming sensation of peace.

Tony put his hand to his brow saying, "This is all very weird!" Then he took a photograph.

I was still holding the flowers that I had picked, so I knelt down and lay them upon the white pebbles on the grave.

ഇൽ

We arrived at Nidri around 5pm to find the usual bustle of honking cars and revving scooters, and sun-burnt people heading from the beach, carrying all sorts of beach accessories, or walking back into the town dressed-up to enjoy a meal at one of the many colorful restaurants.

They resembled a procession of ants all making their treacherous way in one direction carrying things, while another row headed, with similar determination, in the opposite direction.

We were forced to drive very slowly since we found that foreigners on holiday in Nidri appeared to feel completely indestructible! Once they were rigged in shorts and flip-flops, they acquired a certain mode of walking, and main roads seemed to mean nothing to them any more!

We had passed a camp-site about 10 kilometers before Nidri called 'Episkepos,' but we were hoping to find another one either at Nidri, or nearby.

The rugged coastal road from Episkepos was exceptionally hazardous, since there were many pot-holes, and no lights. To add to this, the headlights on the van were not very good. So Tony was not keen to make that journey every night!

We headed further south, passing some fantastic scenery.

The gulf of Vlychou lay behind us, magnificent and peaceful in delicate shades of blues shimmering in the afternoon sun.

"Well we haven't found a camp site Tony."

"Looks like we'll have to go back!" he sighed, as he turned the van around.

128

"First let's find somewhere where we can have a picnic!" I suggested. "We passed a lovely little wooded area a little way back, and I'm starving!"

"Good idea!" He agreed.

We pulled in beneath the shadows of the leafy trees and found that the grass was unusually green at that particular place.

"Isn't it nice here?" I felt happy sitting under the screen of leaves that almost shielded us from the sun. The light filtered through in places creating parallel shafts and beams that lit up patches of grass so that they glimmered in the flickering rays. The whole place was enchanting, and we sat dreamlike, enjoying the peace and rest that it offered, with only the pleasing company of sweetly singing birds, and the ever-present sound of unseen crickets. We were tempted to linger, mesmerized as the sun began to set, and the spot took on a completely different appearance of subtle hues of emerald, and depths of darkest green. Our thoughts were so fully occupied with the strange events of the day.

Tony spoke, startling me momentarily from my confused reflections, "Come on! Lets head back to Episkepos, and get settled-in for the night."

හඟ

We entered the huge metal gates under a big sign that read, 'Episkepos Camping'. Tony jumped out of the van and made some enquiries about the terms at a shabby reception building.

"Not bad!" he said, as he got back in and started the engine. "1,700 drachms a night, that's about a fiver." He smiled at me and added, "We can park anywhere we like!"

There were a few campers about and a few more tents scattered around. Everyone's main priority was to find some essential shade. We found an unclaimed large tree, and were instantly filled with delight! We parked the van at an appropriate angle to give us some privacy, and then proceeded to make our claim on the rest of the shade. We opened-out our table and chairs, and hung a washing-line between 'our' tree and another nearby tree.

Next to us was a typically Greek-style family tent. It was one of the old army-brown ridge tents that we had become accustomed to seeing at Kathisma.

Nearby there was a concrete washing area with stone sinks and along-side was an old-fashioned communal fridge. It was the sort of fridge that one saw in the shops, used mainly to keep bottles cold. It had sliding glass doors, that were cracked, and it emanated a rather unpleasant odor! But we were grateful to be able to keep things cool. Next to this was a concrete block of toilets and showers.

This indeed was a real luxury!

There was a building in the middle of the site that combined as a shop that sold necessities, and a humble snack bar. A few rickety tables and uncomfortable wicker-seated chairs stood outside, under a few straggly trees. Alongside our parking spot was a wire-netting fence, and beyond was a clearing with two large trees. Under the first tree a white goat was tied. And under the second there were two little white lambs. We settled down in our new home under the tree and listened to our radio while we drank a bottle of cheap wine to celebrate. We were not sure what! But it seemed fitting to celebrate something!

Our new neighbors arrived back from a day at the beach and welcomed us to the site, which seemed a friendly thing to do. Like most of the people that we met, they were amazed to learn that we had driven from England!

I walked into the concrete building that housed the toilets and showers, with my towel and bag of toiletries. It seemed unusually civilized and almost refined compared with the facilities at Kathisma. But I was surprised to find that this place seemed a hive of activity. There were women and girls of all ages and sizes standing around, some still in bathing suits, while others were either dressed up to go out for the night, putting the finishing touches to their glamorous dark features, or they were in nightdresses. They were all talking loudly, no matter what they were doing! There were conversations going on between some, in knickers and vests, who were vigorously brushing their teeth, and others who were steaming in the shower cubicles, and someone else who was in a toilet.

I showered quietly and brushed my teeth, standing amongst them, but although they smiled at me, I felt curiously alien to them all!

I was soon back again in the van and I scrambled under the covers.

Tony arrived back smelling fresh from his favorite soap saying, "Gosh that place is like a bloody party! I've never heard such a racket! Why can't these people do **anything** quietly! They never pause for breath!"

"I know!" I laughed back." It was the same in the ladies block!"

"I heard!" Tony said with a laugh," The two blocks are back to back. There is only a narrow gap, at the top, between them."

"Still it's better than Yiorgo's loo and shower."

"Only just!" Tony's retorted with a snort.

We lay in our bed under the tree and listened to the crickets.

"It's been a funny sort of day!" I sighed.

"Not half!" he agreed with a laugh. "Wonder how we'll get on at Nidri!"

"Aye! I wonder!" I replied sleepily. "Surely we should sell some videos there!"

"Well, we will have to see." Tony concluded, as he turned over and promptly fell asleep.

ဆဝ

We were awakened by the squawking of a cockerel and the clucking of hens in a nearby shoddy enclosure. Then we heard the pitiful sound of the lambs bleating. I climbed out of the van to see a few people strolling either towards the toilet block, or away from it, in their night attire. I slipped on my flip-flops and grabbed a towel and soap and followed their example.

Thankfully I found everyone was a little more subdued, and simply said, "Kalimera!"

"Kalimera!" I answered.

We ate our breakfast of fresh bread, delivered to the site, and strawberry jam with a mug of steaming black coffee. I had left it too late to cook, as the van was already baking hot by 9.30am. The lambs were still bleating and I was relieved to see an old woman dressed in a long black dress and shawl walk towards them. She dropped some pieces of red water melon near them and they excitedly jumped about to eat them, but some had fallen a little out of their reach and they struggled wildly, trying to reach the succulent morsels. But they were tethered very close to the tree, so that they could hardly move at all!

"Why doesn't she give them some more rope, she can see that they can't reach the food!" I moaned to Tony.

"Don't go getting upset!" he said patting my arm. "These people don't regard animals the same way that we do!" He was looking at me a little sadly. "To them, they are just a source of food."

I was pleased, however, when I saw the old woman bring the goat some leaves, which it devoured with great relish, while she began to milk it. Then she placed a bottle into the bucket of milk, and when it was full she put a teat on the end, and began to feed in turn, the hungry squabbling lambs.

131

"Are you happier now?" Tony laughed.

"A bit;" I replied." But I still don't like to see them tied so close to the tree!"

After we had eaten I decided to do my washing. I stood at one of the stone sinks with my load of washing on the concrete floor beside me. It was a peculiar feeling to be amongst so many Greek women, all doing their washing and talking incessantly! I thought to myself, If only my friends could see me now! I was scrubbing the sheets against the rough stone side.

Later, we drove to Nidri and parked on the busy harbor front where there were a lot of vehicles already parked. It was quite a distance from the popular places that we wanted to film. So we had to carry the camera, tripod, and batteries in the blazing mid-day sun.

By the time we arrived at the stretch of beach, we were puffing and panting, and the sweat was pouring off us! But in due course we managed to take some interesting shots of the micro-light taking-off, soaring above, and eventually coming down again.

Then we decided to change our location, so we walked the curve of beach along the waters edge, avoiding splashing children and beach balls. At the other end we were able to take a pan of the beach from a different angle first, to establish the position. Then we filmed the colorful Para-glider gracefully lifting into the air from a nearby wooden platform. We filmed the banana-ride being towed swiftly over the gentle waves, full of laughing children, who were intermittently thrown into the blue sea. This was particularly amusing and Tony got some really good close-up shots of the surprised expressions on the children's faces.

It was around 2pm when Tony said, "It's Amstel time! Let's take a break! I'm parched!" We sat in the shade and enjoyed a cold beer, before continuing our filming session.

Slowly, we walked to the high-street and took several shots at different positions. This proved to be quite difficult since the road was always very busy so we were glad when we had enough footage, to add to the original film of the island.

Hot and weary from our efforts we made our way back to the van. We decided to stop at a lovely little bay called Nikiana for a dip to cool off. There was only one other couple with a boy, who took a photo of us, on the stony beach.

Nikiana was so very small that it was hardly a resort at all, but merely a street with a few tavernas, and this pretty pebbly bay. But the sea was clear because of the lack of any sand, and it shelved quite steeply so that once you had suffered the uncomfortable maneuvers of the sharp, white stones you could allow yourself to be supported by the buoyant water.

"This is more like it!" Tony laughed as he swam towards me and dived under my legs, to lift me onto his shoulders and throw me back in the sea again with a splash.

We stayed in the sea as it was too hot to sit out in the sun, but as soon as we spotted a vacant tree on the shore we scrambled, none to elegantly, towards it and spread ourselves under it. When the sun became less intense, we decided to make a move back to the camp, where I could prepare some food.

When we arrived back, I was delighted to find that my sheets, towels, and clothes on hangers, were lovely and dry. I had never experienced the same joy when I had used my £400 washing machine at home!

I made a tasty fry-up of tinned ham, onions and potatoes, which we washed down with a bottle of cold beer.

At seven o'clock we headed back to Nidri, and took some more interesting shots of the same places at night.

It was 10pm when we finally arrived back at the camp and made a start on our new version of the film.

As there was no-one around, we were able to work until two in the morning. We had placed the generator beside the wire fence so that it would not disturb anyone.

We didn't even hear the Greek family arrive back, they must have been very late, and gone straight to bed.

Tony opened the cupboard in the van and took out a bottle of Metaxa and poured us both a nightcap. We were standing outside in the darkness clicking our glasses.

"Here's to us! Let's hope we have some good luck at Nidri." Tony said with a wink. Shortly afterwards we fell into our nice clean bed, worn out, but content, and were soon fast asleep.

₧₨

The crowing of the nearby cockerel awoke us very early, and we were glad because we wanted to make copies. Since the film was 25 minutes long, each copy took the same length of time to make. So we ate a cheese and tomato sandwich while the film was being copied.

We worked solidly from 8am until 7pm, when Tony said, "That will have to do! We've got twenty copies now."

We took our showers, amid the customary rumpus, tingling with excitement at the prospect of showing the film at Nidri.

"We need to sell two a night! One will pay for the site and our petrol and another will cover our daily food." Tony speculated.

"What about our beer?" I laughed.

"Ah! Yes, well we need to sell three really then!" He added with a smile. "Of course **that's** in a perfect world!"

We had learnt to live very economically. A tin of tuna or ham was our only extravagance, and sometimes we even went without that. But a bottle of beer or cheap wine was a necessity. We had to keep our priorities right!

"Let's go!" Tony was turning the van around, and I ran along side helping to direct him between tent pegs and hanging branches of the trees. He stopped for me to jump in and we were off.

Our hearts were racing when we arrived at the beginning of the bustling roadway and again we had to drive extremely slowly.

We were disappointed to find that the first street that led to the harbor front was blocked off by a shabby concrete-based road sign stuck in the middle of the narrow street. We ultimately found another similar street much further along the main road and turned down it, but found that the area where we had intended to park was also blocked off. There were a vast number of cars and vans and trucks all parked 'Greek style', bumper to bumper, without a thought how any of the owners would be able to get out. But of course in Greece this is not a problem; the owner merely holds his hand on the horn of his car until somebody comes. If the offending car is alarmed, as it usually is, since Greeks love anything noisy, then so much the better! The alarm would be set off to attract a hasty response. These noisy occurrences happened quite frequently we were to learn. But it did not make our task of selling videos to the public any easier!

"There is absolutely **nowhere** that I can park!" Tony looked distraught.

"Can't we go past that silly bollard?" I asked. "It really is the only place that we can show the film!"

"No! We can't!" Tony replied emphatically. "I'm not going through another experience like the one in Vassiliki!"

"But there are loads of cars down there!"

"Yes, well maybe they have a permit or something." He had found a vacant spot among the mass of vehicles in a large parking area. "This will have to do."

He switched the engine off, and as the headlights went out we found ourselves sitting in almost total darkness.

"This is no good!" I moaned." Nobody is going to see the video here!"

"Well it's the best that I can do." Tony declared flatly.

After sitting there for some time feeling fed up and defeated, I ventured," Come on then, let's have a go! Maybe someone will see us and come down here."

Tony started the generator and he put the video on. But we were so surrounded by cars and trucks, that the whole situation was ridiculous. After about an hour and nobody had paid us the slightest attention, I went to buy some provisions from the many shops on the high street.

I passed along the side of the busy tavernas, where everyone was having a good time, and the food smelt delicious! On a table near me some people had left more food than we ate in a week! There were bowls of spaghetti, pork chops that had only been picked at, and half-eaten chicken portions. How I longed to taste chicken again! I was tempted to try to sneak one of the pieces into my bag, knowing that the food would only be thrown away. This is how it must feel to be a tramp! I thought secretly, while smiling at the waiter who came to clear the table.

I was walking back with my bag full of the cheapest food that I could buy, and a bottle of water, when I found it hard to remember where the van was parked. It was then that I could just make out the small light from the television screen at the side of the van.

I was walking behind a couple when they suddenly stopped in front of me, and I heard the woman say, "Look! What's that light down there?" pointing in the direction of our van.

"It's a television!" the man replied. "Silly buggers! Somebody's watching television... in the middle of a car park!" And they both burst out laughing.

Suddenly we were deafened by the sound of another horn blaring. Greeks were running around shouting to each other wildly, until someone came and amid a stream of erratic dialogue, cars and trucks were started, and the trapped car moved off accompanied by a lot of cheering and much loud laughter.

Tony was terrified incase someone blocked **us** in! As there was **no way** that **he** was going to create **that** sort of noise!

"Right! **That's it!**" Tony said in disgust as he switched the TV off and began to put the equipment away." Let's go! I've had it with this place!"

I knew that he was right, the situation was quite impossible. At that moment I spotted a policeman strolling along the harbor.

"Hang on a minute!" I called as I ran towards him shouting, "Signomi!"(**Excuse me!**), "**No! Diane, don't!**" Tony shouted after me looking alarmed. But I knew that it was our only chance.

The policeman armed with a big gun stopped abruptly and stared at me. His face was stern and I felt my heart racing as I spoke. "Milatei Anglika?" (Do you speak English?)

"Ohi!" (No) he retorted.

So I had to try to explain as best as I could in Greek.

I told him about our videos, expressing how very grateful we would be if he would allow us to park down at the other end where the tourists walked by. It would bring more tourists from all over the world to Lefkas when people see our lovely video.

His stern face broke into a wide smile as he answered me in stilted English.

"No problem... madam!"

"**Really?**"

Suddenly he leaned forward and surprised me even more by hugging me. Then he laughed very loudly saying, **"Of course!"**

"But the bollard!" I said, not knowing the Greek word. He looked confused, so I pointed to the post in the middle of the street.

His face now broke into a huge smile. "No problem!" He made a movement with his arms to indicate that we simply move it. I suppose we should have known: What else would you do? I wanted to make sure that it would be alright so I asked if he would please tell this to my husband who was very reluctant to break any laws. He promptly walked with me and as we approached the van Tony's face was a picture! I heard him give a small incredulous gasp. I tried to reassure him immediately by saying, "It's okay, we can park down there tomorrow. We just move the sign."

I looked at the policeman for reassurance and he said cheerfully, "Yes! Of course! my friend! Why not?"

"So we won't get a ticket?" Tony enquired.

The policeman looked at me, "Tee?"(What?)

I translated Tony's question in Greek. "Then echamai isitirio?"

The policeman smiled, softening the grimness of his face. "Ohi! Ohi!" Then taking a deep breath he said," I... Yiorgos ...say...Er...permission...okay?"

"Efharisto!" we both replied.

We drove through the crowded road now full of inebriated noisy teenagers and masses of cars, all parked along the side of the pavements making the road a nightmare to drive through.

Tony shifted in his seat, "No wonder there is so much utter chaos, and nobody takes **any** notice of the traffic laws!"

"But isn't it good that we can park at the other end?" I enthused quite proud of myself for organizing this accomplishment.

"I hope we can! But if we get a ticket I don't fancy saying, but Yiorgos said we could!" We both laughed when he added; "Almost all the blokes in Lefkas are called Yiorgos!"

"Well we must give it a go!" I insisted.

"Too right;" He was laughing while he patted my knee. "You did very well!"

The rest of the journey needed all of his concentration as it was particularly dark, and traffic sped past at an alarming rate. It took us all our time to try to avoid the huge pot-holes and maneuver round the hairpin bends that had no rail between the uneven road and the sheer drop below.

We were always pleased when another vehicle came behind us and lit up the road a little until it overtook us, and disappeared out of sight.

"I should have got these lights fixed," Tony complained. "They are hopeless!" But with our roads at home being mainly lit up, plus the fact that we hadn't driven much at night in the van, we hadn't realized how bad they were. Another car with flashing headlights sped past, honking irritably at us.

"Where the hell are they all rushing to?" Tony sighed, glancing at the clock on the dashboard. "It's 11 o' clock for goodness sake!"

"They're probably only going to a taverna, where they will sit for an hour over a coffee!" I replied with a smile.

Greeks seemed to take on a completely different attitude once they got behind the wheel of a car! Their otherwise slow mode of life became wild and perilously rapid.

We were glad to reach the camp-site in one piece.

Tony parked the van in its place saying, "This calls for a drink! I need one after tonight!" Then he added," There is no way that I will be drinking alcohol before we get back here tomorrow night."

We were sitting in the still night air, at our table under the tree, with only the nearby sleeping lambs and the goat for company, enjoying our wine with some bread and cheese.

I giggled as I said, "You looked terrified when you saw me coming with that policeman!"

"Too right;" He laughed back." I thought he was going to ask about our equipment. And if we had declared it at the customs!" He took a sip of wine and continued, "I thought to myself, what the hell, has she done now?"

I almost choked on my wine." Oh! I had forgotten about that."

"Yes, well I hadn't!".

I raised my glass, and looking into his weary eyes said, "Well here's to better luck tomorrow!"

"Yes indeed, to better luck!" He added. "We weren't exactly a roaring success to-night."

"No," I agreed with a chuckle, the wine was beginning to go to my head.

I looked around the camp-site, silent except for the heavy snoring coming from the nearby tent, and out into the countryside beyond the wire fence. It looked dark and strangely hostile, but I reminded myself that this was only a small corner of this interesting island. I remembered the magnificent views and wonderful sea all around.

With an ardent sigh, my feelings were so intensified I said, "Isn't it beautiful here?"

"What?" Tony gulped on his wine and stared at me. "Beautiful? Here?" he laughed. "It's not a five-star hotel you know."

"No! I mean here in Lefkas!" I was opening my arms to illustrate my point. "I feel as though we have escaped into another world somehow. A world that only a few people know about, and that makes it sort of special, don't you think?"

"Yes, I know what you mean!" He was smiling now. "But not many people would envy us living like this!" He filled both our glasses again saying, "Just think what most of our friends would say if they saw us here!"

"I was thinking just that when I was doing the washing over there." I swept a glance towards the now deserted stone sinks that had been such a hive of activity.

"What would Maureen say?" I laughed, knowing how particular my long-standing friend was. "She would be horrified!" Then mimicking her I said, "Good God Di, what are you doing here! Don't be silly! Go home!"

Tony added quickly, now caught in the mood, "And what about Kathisma! What would she make of Yiorgos' free loo and shower?"

"Don't even think about that!"

"And then, stuck at the end that of that beach in Vassiliki; with **no** toilet or shower! **That** would have been the last straw!"

As we reflected we both began to laugh. We felt light-hearted and stupidly giggly.

"I expect she and Cliff will have been to one of their 'Cheshire Set' cocktail parties or something." I was speaking while staring into my half empty glass.

"Well they won't have had as much fun as we're having." He paused for a moment. "But, I wouldn't mind having a holiday in that luxurious company villa though in Val de Lobo, Portugal it would be heaven after this camp-site."

"Yes Tony, so would I but it's no good thinking about the things we can't have, lets think about tomorrow, how nice it will be to swim in that beautiful sea again and who knows what tomorrow will bring. That is what is so great about what we are doing. How many people our age could do this? Opt out of the rat race for three whole months!"

"I suppose so; we've made such huge adjustments to our life."

I looked out of the open doorway at the moon, and began thinking about the days when I would meet Maureen in Chester city to go shopping with our gold credit cards and stop in a swish café to have a nice lunch. And the other nice meals we had, had at classy restaurants with Maureen and Cliff, who was a director in a big soft furnishing company called, Montgomery's of Chester.

Maybe it was the wine, but after a while I said, "Oh! It's so funny the things we think about!"

"It certainly is!" Tony replied with a sleepy smile.

⁜⁝

Over 1,500 miles away Maureen looked out of her bedroom window at the moon, while Cliff lay by her side. They were in their huge bed in their large country house surrounded by four acres of gardens.

They had tried to sleep and failed. Pictures danced disjointedly behind Cliffs closed eyelids. He had so much work to do. The company was expanding at such a rate it was hard to keep up with the demand on soft furnishing. One of the other directors was retiring, that would mean another load of work for him to deal with.

"Can't you tell me what's on your mind? Maureen asked quietly. "I'm worried about you Cliff, you haven't looked well for ages now, I think you are heading for a heart attack or a breakdown."

"I'm so very tired Mo, yet I can't sleep for thinking about things that have to be done and I just don't have the time."

"You'll have to take someone on," she was speaking earnestly now.

"The fact is we need an IT manager..."

He hesitated for just enough time for her to ask, "Tony?"

"Yes," he sat up in bed. "But where the hell is he? And how can I get in touch with him?"

"Oh, Cliff if would be **so** good if Tony could work at your place."

"I know, and I also know that he is just the right man for the job! It's so frustrating!"

"Maybe they will be home soon."

She was beginning to tremble with excitement. She had missed her friend and had longed to be of help to her and Tony in their distressing situation.

Then she turned over and prayed silently, "Please let them come home soon."

Chapter Seven

I didn't bother to dry my hair, or use a towel at all, when I came out of the sea, because the heat was so intense it was unnecessary. I licked the salt off my lips and scrambled under the low branches that offered some dappled shade. Sitting down next to Tony, I noticed that he had fallen asleep while I was swimming.

I shook him gently saying, "Wake up! You're burning!" Go and cool off in the sea. It's lovely!"

He groaned and turned his face towards me. The imprint of the towel and pebbles underneath was visible in red blotches on his skin.

He sat up lethargic in the afternoon heat. "Christ! It's scorching!" he was rubbing his face with his hands.

The little beach at Nikiana was at that time of day quite empty of people, most of the Greeks were having their siesta. But we had nowhere to go for a comfortable rest during the heat of the day. The sweltering van was quite unendurable! So the sea was our only refuge!

He struggled to his feet saying, "I suppose I'll have to brave the stones once again!"

"It's okay once you're in though!" I answered cheerfully.

The sea was motionless and undisturbed as he stepped falteringly and clumsily on the sharp stones. But soon he was sighing, and exhaling audibly with long deep breaths of relief murmuring across the calm water to me.

"Oh! This is ecstasy!" The smooth rhythmic movements of his swimming left a v-shaped trail on the glimmering sea.

I sat, looking out into the distant blue horizon and thought, if only we had got the money from Tony's redundancy, our lives wouldn't be so bad. However, I had noticed that the warmth of the sun had helped to reduce the pain in his arm.

I saw him wave and smile at me and I waved back momentarily interrupted from my thoughts. Then I continued thinking again: I remembered how hard he had worked to achieve our standard of living and I frowned at the unfairness of the way that he had been treated. I wished with all my heart that I could do something to help to remedy the situation. However I had thought of this idea, and so far we were enjoying ourselves in a rather odd, if inconsistent way. At least Tony was not suffering despondency; his attitude was becoming far more light-hearted. This casual way of life had altered him a lot. Before, he had always been meticulous about everything! He had shown such attentiveness to all aspects both at his job, and at home, with scrupulous care! His demeanor had been quiet, reserved, and basically shy. Now he was beginning to be more self-assertive and to even lose his temper on occasions. I found this new dimension of his personality both intriguing and amusing.

I was gazing dreamily through the liquid shimmer of heat on the beach when I became aware of him struggling over the stones towards me, making quick short gasps of pain, until he dropped beside me under the silvery tree. His legs, still wet, stretched out before him.

He was smiling with pleasure, but I felt that I had to say, "I suppose we must think about going back early today. We've got to prepare for tonight."

Stretching and yawning, he let the words out with a contented sigh, "Oh! In a while! There's no rush."

ℰℭ

It was still scorching hot at the deserted camp-site, people were either out for the day, or asleep in their tents. We sat under our precious tree while I wrote out some posters with my felt-tip pen and paper. I took great care and made them look as professional as possible.

Tony glanced across at them and said with some surprise, "That's not bad at all, considering the conditions available here! They really do look quite artistic!"

"Thanks!" I answered feeling quite happy, as I wiped my hands and face on a towel. It was impossible to perform the most minimal act without becoming soaked with perspiration.

I threw some pieces of red melon to the lambs, which were still in my opinion suffering needlessly, by the side of the big tree. They seemed to spend the whole of their paltry existence laboriously seeking some relief from their tortuous plight, struggling around the tree seeking what little shade that was available.

"It's disgusting!" I moaned to Tony who was just as appalled as I was by the conditions that many animals suffered abroad. "They haven't even got any water!"

"Well you won't find any 'animal rights' organizations here I'm afraid!" He shook his head sympathetically. "I know it's sad! But you can't do anything about it, so try not to look at them." He was gently steering me away from the wire netting. I knew that I was beginning to care for the poor little things too much. Probably because they were always there, so near to us. They had in a way become our distant companions.

141

We set off for Nidri feeling a bit more confident than we had done the previous evening. The fear of the unknown was gone. We knew what to expect and we had the permission of the policeman to park where everything was going on.

"We should do alright tonight." Tony was swerving the van around one of the hairy bends with vigor and confidence.

"Here we go again!" he sighed as we entered the resort.

I laughed as he had to swerve to avoid hitting some foolish youths sluggishly strolling along carrying a ghetto-blaster that was blaring rap music. As we passed closely by, one of them hit the van with his hand and bellowed some obscenity.

Tony leaned out of the window and yelled back, "**Thickhead!**" Then he turned to me. "Honestly, they are definitely lacking in intelligence! The way people treat this main road."

"Yes! Yes! I know!" I answered becoming bored with this nightly bothersome encounter. But I didn't have to undertake the responsibility of avoiding hitting them.

When we reached the first street Tony stopped the van and I jumped out. I picked up the heavy metal post with a round red no entry sign at the top and heavy concrete base, and dragged it to one side to enable Tony to drive past. Then I replaced it and climbed back into the van.

We entered the lively harbor front where music pounded from bright and crowded tavernas. People were strolling along in both directions. We found a good position opposite the illuminated boats offering trips by day to otherwise inaccessible beaches, a few advertised night time cruises with Greek dancing and free wine. On the other side of us were many welcoming tavernas where sprightly, bright-eyed waiters danced about between the tables greeting people with cheerful willingness.

Tony switched the engine off and smiled at me saying, "This is looking very good!"

"It's great!" I was rubbing my hands together with glee.

We both leapt out and immediately started setting up for our first showing. We decided to forget the previous night.

I placed the posters on the inside of the windows, and one beneath the television on a white folding top that proved ideal for the job. Already people were showing interest in the activities around our van. Tony lifted the equipment from under the seat, and placed it in its usual place on our revolving table, in front of the seat that we both unobtrusively sat on.

A waiter from a nearby bar came over to investigate what all the commotion was about, and when he realized that we were going to show a video, he began shouting excitedly at the top of his voice, a quality that Greeks of all ages seem to have.

"**Ella! Tho! (Come! Here!)** We were instantly surrounded by numerous interested waiters and old Greek men from the nearby boats and even some Greeks who were having a meal nearby. The video started and as the music began, a hush fell on the noisy throng, so that when the picture of the drawbridge at Lefkas town appeared on the screen, a tumultuous applause rang out. "**Auraia!**"

Tony and I looked at each other in amusement. But we were very pleased with the reception that we were getting. After a few minutes a young waiter, who was also keeping a watchful eye on his taverna, asked me, "Nidri Yes?"

"Yes," I answered. "in a minute!"

But he was impatient and repeated, "Nidri?"

"Yes!" I answered. "Se theo lepta!" (In two minutes!)

This satisfied him so he yelled to everyone around him, "**Nidri se theo lepta!**" Everyone then began to get very excited. When the establishing shots of the main street appeared on the screen there was a tremendous cheer accompanied by a lot of jubilant laughter and exclamations as people recognized various shops or lads on scooters, or simply individuals walking about. Then as the harbor came on the screen, and the different tavernas came into view, there was uncontrollable hilarity, and shrieks and yells rang out as they identified the numerous places.

The microlite accompanied by a good rock beat, caused quite a sensation, as did the Para-glider, with a nice romantic tune! There were sighs again of, "Auraia!"

When the banana-ride threw all the happy children into the sea, everyone clapped and laughed with unrestrained delight.

Suddenly on the screen, the harbor was transformed from daytime to nighttime; this effect on the crowd was amazing. They gaped open-mouthed in total awe. Tony and I had to smile when we saw them looking from one to the other repeating, "Auraia! Eh?"

We had filmed the Greek ship called, 'The Odyssia' that took people for the Greek dancing, evening trip. This looked particularly impressive, floating along so brightly lit up, against the blackness of the night. The illuminated masts and ropes were reflecting on ink-colored sea. We had managed to film some close-ups of the dancing young man, and added our own bazooka music, but since the movements of the dancer were completely in time, no one would guess that it was not the music that was actually playing at the time. Again the crowd, now so large that it was becoming difficult for people to pass on the roadway, roared with appreciation.

When the film finally came to an end the applause that rang out was almost deafening. There was a sudden rush of bodies towards the van and numerous hands pushed crumpled drachma notes at us. Tony handed me the cassettes; I handed him the money and everyone was laughing so much that the atmosphere was quite unbelievable. Tony's' gratification was apparent; "This is more like it!"

He put the tape on again and the whole procedure started again; only this time with a different audience. The attention of some holiday-makers at nearby tavernas had been alerted and they came over to see what was going on. Most of them were English and seemed very interested in the whole idea. One couple, around our age, asked how long we would be stopping as they had run out of money and wanted a video.

"We will be here for a few weeks," I assured them.

"What a brilliant idea!" The man exclaimed. "I bet you've made a fortune!"

"Not exactly," I replied. "But things are beginning to look up now."

"We've been in the wrong places. This is our first night here!" Tony explained.

"Well I think you'll do very well!"

We sold ten copies to the Greeks at the first showing, and another six to British tourists with a few more intending to buy one the following night.

Tony worked out our takings; he was beaming with joy. "76,000 drachmas, that's about 250 quid!"

Then we were suddenly surrounded by children, and young lads on bikes, who either dropped their bicycles against the van or left them so that no-one could stand near the screen. Some began climbing on the bumpers and rocking us, Tony became anxious about the generator so we decided to close for the night and head back to our camp. He was grinning as he lifted the generator back into the van saying, "Anyway, we've only got three copies left!"

"We've done very well!" I said. "I think this calls for a decent bottle of wine!"

"But first we'll go and eat." He seemed to have grown younger in the last few minutes. "I'm fed up watching everybody eating lovely food and were existing on cucumbers and tomatoes!"

"I do make a good fry-up though!"

He kissed the tip of my nose saying, "You've done remarkably well!" Then he looked straight into my eyes saying, "I don't know what I would do without you!"

"Don't be daft!" I replied suppressing a lump in my throat.

We walked into the taverna that I had passed the night before, and we ordered chicken and chips for two, with a bottle of wine, feeling like royalty.

෨෬

The next day was spent making more copies, from dawn till sunset, an extremely uncomfortable task in the muggy van. We were still parked under our tree with raffia mats draped over all the windows, and with the curtains closed, to try to keep it as cool as possible. But it was still stifling! We kept taking turns to run to the cold shower, for a few minutes to cool ourselves. By 7pm we had made and checked 20 copies.

"That will have to do!" Tony said, hurriedly putting the equipment away. "I can make some more as I'm showing the film." Then with a hasty glance at the dashboard clock he asked, "Ready then?"

"Ready!" I answered. It had been a pretty horrendous day, but we were eager to get back to our spot on the front and earn some more money. I quickly threw the remains of our melon to the lambs, which seemed to have got used to us being around all day. As I climbed into the van one of them bleated.

"Bye-bye little fellow;" I called. And as if in answer he bleated back.

We arrived at the same place to find that there was a motorbike parked diagonally across our spot.

Tony looked furious. "Just look at that! Some mindless yob has taken up two places!"

No sooner had he had uttered the words, when one of the young waiters came running over shouting, "**Hallo!**" He put his hand out in front of our windscreen saying, "One... moment!" Then he moved his bike out of the way and came towards us grinning happily saying, "I keep ...er...for you this place!"

"Thanks a lot mate!" Tony replied feeling sincere gratitude.

"**Okay! Mate**!" He shrugged as he ran back to the bar.

The evening began quite similarly to the night before and we had sold seven copies by the end of the first showing. Then the couple that we were half expecting came and bought their copy and another one, for some friends of theirs, who were staying at their hotel.

"We've told everyone about you!" the lady said, peeping into the van to speak to me. "My name is Ann and my husband is Tommy we are from Warrington, England."

"We're almost neighbors!" I cried. "We are from West Kirby, near Chester, England."

We went on to tell them why we had decided to try this idea and they were very interested. It turned out that Ann knew someone who worked at the same company that Tony had worked at, and that she was vaguely related to somebody who lived in our road!

"Isn't it a small world?" She laughed.

Some other people then wanted a copy so they left saying that they would help us if they could, by telling their 'rep.' about our idea the following day.

"That would be great!" I replied and Tony agreed.

We sold another copy to a German couple, who seemed thrilled with the idea. It was particularly amusing because the man had a very expensive video camera. Tony made a reference to it and the man laughed. "Yia! But I not... do good like this!"

"With the music... it is very beautiful!" his wife added.

Tony was smiling. "Well I think that just about wraps it up for tonight: Ten copies that's 40,000 drachmas, that's just over 130 quid."

"Not bad for a nights work." Then I yawned, "I'm worn out."

"Yes it's been a long day!" He started the engine and suddenly the smiling face of the waiter appeared at the side window shouting, "**Here! For you... tomorrow**!"

He pointed to the parking spot and patting the side of the van. "**Bye -bye**! **Mate**!"

We were back at our camp site by 11pm.

We sat on our chairs feeling a need to unwind slightly, after the treacherous journey home. Tony opened a bottle of 'Boutari' red wine and we sat down to enjoy our drink and celebrate our changing luck. "Here's to us! And more good times ahead!"

"I'll drink to that!" I answered, clicking my glass to his, and we smiled contentedly as we drank the rest of the bottle.

"It seems like you've got yourself a 'mate!' And a regular parking place!"

"Yes," Tony laughed. "You can't help liking these funny people," he sipped his wine, before continuing, "they may be noisy and over-confident and sometimes rather arrogant, but their hearts are in the right place!" He nodded as he reflected, "That waiter chap is quite likeable!"

"I think he is rather sweet!" I answered with a provocative smile.

"Oh! Yes?" Tony laughed quizzically chasing me into the van.

We lay in the van in the moonlight looking out at the stars through the gaps in the branches, and listening to the ever existent sound of crickets, until we fell into a deep uninterrupted sleep.

₧₧

The crowing cockerel woke us with his habitual early cry.

Tearing ourselves out of our bed I said, "Let's make an early start on our copies. If we start at seven we'll have twenty done by five o' clock."

Tony yawned before replying, "Then maybe we could have a quick dip at Nikiana, I've really missed having a swim."

"Anyone would think you were here on holiday!" I teased.

The day passed in the same laborious way as the one before, but we both agreed that it was more important to get as many copies done as possible.

"After all," I remarked trying to be sensible. "It would be awful not to have enough!" Then I added, "We can always take time off when we have an adequate supply."

Having worked an extra two hours we now had thirty-four copies in total.

₧₧

That night when we pulled up in front of the motorbike our friendly waiter ran out shouting, **"Okay, Mate!"** Then having moved the bike he stood grinning, waiting for us to open the doors and step out. He held out his hand to Tony saying, "My name...Yiorgos."

Tony smiled and whispered to me, "Tell me something new!" Shaking his hand he said, "My name is Tony."

Then Yiorgos turned to me with a smile that was quite dazzling, while he took my hand and slowly raised it to his lips. "And Madam?"

"My name is Diane," I answered.

He peeped up from under his thick black curls that had fallen across his forehead, and with my hand still raised near his lips he sighed, "Ah! Lady Di!" Then with an impudent, but agreeable, wink he touched the side of my face with his hand, adding, "No! Elizabeth Taylor!"

"It's a long time since anyone has said that I look like Elizabeth Taylor," I said smiling at Tony. "I think I'm in love!"

"Come on! Let's get the show on the road!" His eyes twinkled as he laughed.

We had only just got the video going when Ann and Tommy appeared.

"We told our 'rep' about you!" Tommy cried excitedly. "She wants us to buy her a video so that she can show it on the coach from the airport to Nidri." He paused to observe our delighted reactions before continuing. "She rang the Thompson company and they have given her the permission, and have agreed to pay for the video; so if you can give us a receipt for her to claim the money back."

"We'll **give** her a video!" Tony was clearly excited. "We are only too pleased that she will show it!"

"No! No! It's all arranged." Tommy insisted. "Just write out a receipt on this." He had even brought a note pad and pen with him.

Tony handed him a video and Tommy said, "Our 'rep' thinks that this is a wonderful idea, she said that if you would like to write out some notices she will put them up at the various Thompson apartments and hotels so that more people will know about you!"

"This is fantastic news!" Tony was overjoyed. "It's ever so kind of you to do this for us."

Ann replied, "We really wanted to help you!" Then she looked inquisitively inside the van and asked tentatively, "Do you live in here?"

"Yes!" I answered.

Her face took on a sympathetic expression as she merely replied, "Oh!"

We arranged to meet them the following night and I promised to have some posters for them.

Tony smiled happily at me. "Well, you've got your work cut out for tomorrow!" Then he added, "And I'd better make some more copies!"

഼ഽ

When we awoke the next day we were slightly confused as to what to do. We had only sold seven copies the night before.

Tony was sipping his coffee. "It's not bad though really, we made 85 quid." Then he added, "I might as well make some more copies while you write out the posters."

He glanced inside the van at the clock on the dashboard. "If I make a start now, I'll have ten done by 2 o'clock, and then we can go to Nikiana and have a swim and a bit of relaxation." He finished his coffee. "Surely forty copies should be enough! Then we can just make a few each time we show the film"

By 2 o'clock we had our posters written out, and our copies complete and checked. He was still meticulous about giving everyone a faultless copy.

147

Half an hour later we hurled ourselves bodily into the sea at Nikiana. It seemed to soothe our aching bodies and appease our anxiety.

"This is bliss!" I murmured with closed my eyes.

"I could stay here forever!" Tony replied letting out a long sigh of immense pleasure.

Later sitting on our towels on the stones he sliced a honey-dew melon in half, and we ate it hungrily beneath the low branches of one of the silver-leafed trees. Then we lazily watched the small black and white birds ducking and diving above the tranquil water, and flutter chirping in the branches above our heads.

Tony wiped the perspiration from his brow. "There isn't a breath of wind today! Not even from the sea!" We had expected the weather to be hot but this sort of heat was unbelievable! It was Sunday the 9th August, and we had been in Nidri for one week.

Suddenly and unexpectedly a Greek woman sat down heavily right beside us, causing Tony to whisper, "What a cheek!" Then he added, "This is our tree!"

"That is not the way of the Greeks!" I laughed. "When in Rome!"

"Yes, well we're not in bloody Rome!"

We were suddenly surrounded by four screaming children and an extremely old man who didn't look too clean. The woman told the children to go for a swim, while she indicated to the old man to sit down. He looked at us both and his face broke into a toothless grin, before he squeezed himself beside us.

Tony looked horrified. "This is ridiculous!" he moaned a bit too loudly for my liking, making me feel rather embarrassed.

"Be quiet!" I whispered.

"Well! Why did they have to sit here! There are plenty of other trees!"

"I don't know! Maybe they like this tree!" I had long given up on understanding some of the Greek manners.

The woman fanned her face with one of the children's straw hats smiling at me saying, "Whew! Zesti!" (Hot!)

I smiled back and replied, "Ne, zesti!"

The old man began rummaging in his trouser pockets before bringing out some sticky sweets in a crumpled grubby paper bag, and then he held them out to us both saying, "Ella!"

"Ohi! Efharisto." We both cried shaking our heads.

"He must be joking!" Tony whispered in my ear.

The old man was dressed in a tattered brown suit, underneath it he wore an old faded blue jumper, and under that he had a thick check shirt, it seemed the customary shirt that apparently all the old men wore.

"I bet he's even got a vest on under all that!" Tony chuckled.

He kept his flat black cap on but began to take his shoes off.

"Oh, no!" Tony exclaimed, as the man started to peel off his socks. "That's done it!" while he quickly got to his feet. "We're moving!" Then gathering all our things and putting them into our bag, he moved away.

"I don't think we should have done that," I said reluctantly following him. "It seemed a bit rude!"

"Rude! You must be kidding! These people don't know the meaning of the word. They plonk themselves all around us, when there is plenty of room." He nodded his head at the almost deserted beach.

"Yes, well they were probably just being friendly."

I was watching the old man struggling across the stony beach to go for a paddle.

I began to ponder so I said what was in my mind.

"I think that we should go back to Agios Nikitas to see if Liana has sold our videos, and see if she wants any more."

Tony nodded his head thoughtfully, "Yes, we've been so busy, I had forgotten about that."

"Pity we couldn't have gone today," I replied gloomily, "we could have seen the Tsetikas family. They are bound to be there on a Sunday. "

"We will definitely go next week," Tony promised.

The old man was enjoying his paddle immensely, cackling loudly, with a cigarette still in his mouth, all the children were squealing with delight pretended to splash him. There was so much joyful activity that we also couldn't help laughing.

"This is probably his yearly paddle!" Tony said.

It was then that the woman shouted something to me and exploded into unrestrained laughter as she wiped her face on a grubby towel.

I smiled back acknowledging her remark with a nod of my head saying, "Ne!"(Yes!)

Suddenly one of the boys aged about seven ran over to us and picked up Tony's flip-flops, and still laughing ran down the beach shouting to us over his shoulder, "**Efharisto**!"

"Hey! What the hell's going on?" Tony was worried.

"I think I must have said that he could borrow your shoes."

"Well thanks a lot!" Now he was disgusted. "I thought you understood this blinking language!"

"Yes, well she spoke so fast! And she was laughing!" I replied. "I thought she said, "He should have brought his sandals!"

The old man found that walking in flip-flops was as amusing as his paddle. And the whole performance was extremely comical. Even Tony couldn't help laughing at his antics. When he had managed to seat himself again, the boy ran back with Tony's beach shoes. The old man raised his cap to us and the whole family waved to us smiling and shouting, "Efharisto!"

"Okay! No problem." Tony replied smiling politely.

"You hypocrite!"

"Well! What can you do! You've got to laugh haven't you? At least he had washed his feet in the sea."

After a while the family decided to leave, there was an excessive amount of fussing and shouting as they gathered their belongings together.

Tony was just about to doze off, so he was startled. "What a commotion!" Still he noted the family's departure with some relief saying, "Thank God for that!"

A few minutes later, on the road near us, we saw the same boy leading a scrawny mule wearing a straw hat with holes for its ears, pulling a cart. Inside the cart was the rest of the family, amid bunches of brilliant artificial flowers. They all waved to us.

"They must be Gypsies!" Tony said.

"Well they're a bit like us then!" I said with a chuckle.

The procession stopped abruptly and the woman handed the boy a bunch of silk roses. He ran over to us and smiling shyly, placed them at our feet.

"Well, what about that?" I said. "That's so nice!" I turned and waved to the family as they moved along the road. I could tell that Tony was also moved, by the expression on his face.

∽∞∾

That night at Nidri we met Ann and Tommy and we gave them our neatly-written posters. To our delight they bought two more videos for people at their hotel.

"I'm going on the microlite tomorrow; do you think that you could film me and add it on the end of my video?" Tommy said with a big smile.

"Certainly;" Tony answered.

"I'll pay you of course," Tommy insisted.

Then Ann said, "The other friend of ours, who we got a video for, is going on after Tommy, could you film him as well?"

"Sure!" Tony answered. "I'll add it on the end of his film as well."

"Now this is business!" Tommy said seriously. "Lets fix a price!"

"Okay I'll do it for a thousand drachmas each." Tony stated with a smile.

"But that's a lot of work for about three quid!"

"No! Tommy you have been so good to us"

We agreed to meet them the next morning at half past ten, since his 'flight' was scheduled for eleven o'clock, if the weather permitted.

After they left us we noticed that there was no interest shown in our video at all.

"What the hell has happened?" Tony cried, looking out of the van. "There isn't a soul in sight!"

After what seemed like an age, I got out of the van and looked around.

Just as we were beginning to feel pretty dismal, a long-haired street artist and a young boy assistant came along. They set up an easel along side of us and opened two folding chairs and a table onto which the boy placed a lantern. He had no sooner lit it, when someone came to have a portrait sketched. A pretty young girl sat smiling self-consciously as a young man, perhaps it was her husband, stood watching proudly, while the artist with his sketching pad and charcoal worked with rapid strokes, outlining the girl's features with exaggerated affectation.

Soon there was quite a large crowd around but this did not deter him; he delighted in the attention he was receiving. Occasionally someone absent-mindedly glanced in our direction, but the sighs of admiration at the accomplishments of the artist soon distracted their attention from our video. Eventually the artist showed the finished portrait to the girl, who smiled approvingly. Her male companion handed the artist two thousand drachma notes.

He made a polite inclination of his head, and then he rolled up the sketch and fastened it with an elastic band before handing it to the young girl. The transaction was complete.

No sooner had the seat been vacated, when another young couple stopped and the whole procedure began again.

There were the usual make-shift barbecues along the side of the road, where very senior citizens sat on folded seats roasting corn-on-the-cob. People were stopping to buy some and wandered past our van holding the hot corn wrapped in paper but nobody stopped to look at our video.

People were actually leaning on our van at this point.

This final insult irritated Tony so much that he switched-off the television, and vaulted out of the van saying, "This is just **not on**!"

A few people gave him a passing glance but continued to stare at the artist's performance.

"Well he's got to make a living too, I suppose."

"Yes, and we know what it's like! Come on! We're wasting our time here tonight.""

Tony lifted the generator into the van saying, "I'm not putting up with this."

We did not know then, that we would, in fact stoop to things a good deal lower, in a very short while.

ෑᘓ

Later that night, we sat under the tree in the moonlight drinking our wine and recalling the events of the night.

Tony was shaking his head with disbelief. "It's really strange the way things change. One minute they can't take their eyes off our screen, and the next they don't want to know!" He swallowed a mouthful of wine. "I mean," he added emphasis, by tapping the table with his hand, "we slog our guts out making all these bloody copies and now no bugger wants them!"

"Maybe it will be different tomorrow."

"Well, I bloody hope so!"

151

After a while we both saw the funny side of the situation, and exploded into unrestrained laughter. Touching his glass to mine he said, "Here's to us!"

"Yamas!" I agreed.

⊱⊰

The following morning I was up and showered before Tony awoke. He had drunk most of the wine himself the night before, and as I entered the van he groaned, "Did I have a nightmare, or did last night really happen?"

"Cheer up. We've got to meet Ann and Tommy and their friends today, so go and get a shower you'll soon feel better."

We met up with them at the last snack-bar on the front as arranged, and Tommy was rather apprehensive about taking his flight. But the weather was perfect for it, so it was to go ahead as planned.

"Poor Tommy! He's really scared!" Ann laughed.

"Too right; I'm bloody petrified!" Tommy gave us a nervous grin.

We were in our position at the end of a small jetty and I held a beach-mat over Tony to try to shield him from the exceptionally hot sun.

The filming of the microlite proved to be quite difficult to do, since it soared by very fast and went high into the sky. But Tony did manage to succeed in capturing the stunts and tricks and some very good close ups of the whole performance.

When Tommy was back on land he finished the film with Ann giving Tommy a kiss and a congratulatory pat on his back as Tommy spoke into the camera, "That was great!"

Then it was time to do it all over again for their friend; Tony was already worn out! The sweat was pouring off him and all the muscles in his arms and shoulders ached from holding the camera aimed at the sky for so long. It was impossible to use the tripod for these shots, so he leaned on me to keep him steady. When we had completed the next session Tommy insisted on buying us a drink, and we didn't argue.

"Was it difficult to film Tony?"

"No! Not at all Tommy;" But fatigue was written all over his face.

⊱⊰

Back at the camp it took us the rest of the day to edit the films and add the music.

Tony leapt out of the van saying, "All that work for six quid!"

"But look how they have helped us," I reminded him.

"I know," he answered. "But it has been a hell of a day! I only hope that we sell some videos tonight! "

"Well we can only try!"

We sat in our usual place that night and again nobody paid us any attention.

Ann and Tommy came for their videos and told us that they were going home in three days.

"Let us buy you a meal before we go!" Tommy said.

"Thanks but we have to keep showing the film, but you can buy us a drink tomorrow night if you like, before we start showing." Tony answered looking pleased.

"That's a deal." Tommy said as he paid us the two thousand drachmas and also gave us a tip of six hundred drachmas, before they left.

"That was nice of them," I said, as I settled down in the van.

"Yes," Tony remarked. "they're a smashing couple."

We sat watching the film that we knew every detail of for the rest of the night, which was a very monotonous thing to have to do. It was like some form of torture. Made worse by the fact that not one person bought a copy. At one point I even got out of the van and stood outside looking at the screen with avid interest, making gasps, and sighs of wonder, in the hope that other people might join me. But although my ploy worked for a few moments, as soon as people became suspicious that I was in some way associated with the van, they moved away giving me some very peculiar looks.

Then at another time, when we were both inside the van out of sight, the wire mesh obscuring us in the darkness, I looked at the ground outside and saw a pair of feet. They were men's feet in open sandals standing in front of the screen.

"Don't move! Some one is watching!" I whispered to Tony.

After a while the man put his face up against the window and peered inside. When he saw us both sitting there, he jumped back with alarm, and hastily walked away.

ॐ

The next morning we walked into the café at our site and bought a fresh loaf. The owner smiled saying, "Hello, my name...Yiorgos."

"Hello," Tony answered, giving me a knowing smile.

"Video...er... very good business...eh?"

"Oh! Yes Brilliant!" Tony answered sarcastically. "It couldn't be better!" But the joke was wasted on Yiorgos.

We were eating our bread and apricot jam, when I noticed that the lambs and the goat were getting agitated. I looked with interest at a man and a little boy walking with the old woman in black, towards the lambs.

"Look!" I cried, pointing to them. "There's something going on out there."

The man was very good-looking and wore a short sleeved, blue shirt and a pair of brief, black shorts. His features were very dark and his hair was black and wavy.

"What a handsome bloke!" I was looking at him when he surprised me with a charming smile. I smiled back calling, "**Kalimera!**"

"**Kalimera**! he replied with a bow of his head.

The old woman, shrouded in black, was untying one of the lambs from the tree and she started coaxing it towards the man and the boy.

"Oh! Look!" I said. "He must be going to buy it. Maybe it's for the boy, isn't that nice? Maybe it will have a better life now."

Then I saw the glimmer of the knife his hand.

The lamb was bleating pitifully as the old woman dragged it by its outstretched front leg, the rope tied around its little hoof. I couldn't believe my eyes.

"**Do Something**! I screamed. "He's going to kill it!"

Tony just stared in disbelief, every bit as appalled as I was.

The lamb was struggling violently against its impending fate. It was indisputable that the lamb's frightened cries were for help. But no help came!

There was a look of sheer panic in its black eyes as they rolled upwards showing the whites in absolute dread. I was sure that it knew what the man intended, and I felt a revulsion well-up inside me.

It was as though the poor little defenseless creature, that is the epitome of all innocence, was screaming, *"No! Please! I'm too young to die!"*

Tony grabbed me by my shoulders and whisked me away. He too was trembling with horror.

"Don't look, Di!" We buried our faces in each other, as Tony repeated, "Please don't look!" Then he let out a gasp. "Jesus Christ!"

After a few seconds the bleating stopped and Tony steered me inside the van.

His voice was gentle. "It's all over now! It was very quick!"

Then he looked into my face speaking despondently. "I couldn't do that to save my life! That must be a very hard man!" His face had turned ashen as he said, "Don't move from here! I have to go to the bathroom: I think I'm going to be sick!"

When he came back we both sat dumbfounded with our backs to the wire fence, until we had got over the shock. There was a long silence.

Eventually Tony broke it. "Come on!" he said. Let's go to Nikiana and try to forget it. There is nothing we can do to alter the way they do things in this country. But after that episode I don't like certain Greek practices at all!"

I took a moment to digest this. I could feel a slight color heightening my face.

"Neither do I!" I agreed. "I can't believe that happened. It was surreal," I glanced briefly at the remaining lamb. "I don't think I like the Greeks any-more!" my voice was low and sad. "I think that they are a lot of barbarians!"

There was only a pool of blood on the ground beneath the tree where the man had tied the lamb upside down, while he had skinned it.

"No! It was probably just his job!" Tony replied. "And to give him his due, he did it well!" Then with a brave grin he added, "It's just not the sort of thing you want to watch while you're having your breakfast, especially with sound effects!"

Chapter Eight

That evening we arrived at Nidri earlier than we normally did so that we could meet Ann and Tommy for a drink. We felt distanced from the happy people all around us. The gruesome event of the morning was still haunting our thoughts, and the vivid mental image was still active in our minds.

"Try not to think about it!" Tony said patting my hand affectionately.

I simply pulled a sad face, since there was nothing really to say.

Yiorgos, the waiter, called over to us as we walked into his bar, "**Ah! Yes! Hallo mate**." Then with an exaggerated bow he added, "**And Lady Di!**" We all laughed and sat at a table near the roadway.

Ann and Tommy arrived.

"Did you give the video and our posters to your rep?" Tony was rubbing his hands together and smiling.

"Yes we did!" Tommy replied cheerfully.

Ann sounded just as happy. "She is going to show the film tomorrow when the next lot of tourists arrive." She giggled, excited at the prospect. "You should do really well once everyone knows about you."

"You know, you should think about asking that bloke with the microlite if you could work with him, filming the people that he takes up!" Tommy was looking at both our faces for our response before continuing. "I'm really made up with my video, and especially the part with me on that microlite is going to take pride of place in my video collection." He was rubbing his hands together with delight. "I can't wait to show my mates back at home!" Then he went on to say, "The other chap is just as pleased as I am with his film, so I'm sure there would be a lot of people who would feel the same and would love to have themselves doing something like that added on to the end of their film."

Ann broke in, "Yes and there are so many things here for you to film." She looked around. "Aren't there?"

"Yes," I replied. "actually that was our first intention, to film personal moments, like kids on the beach, and people at their favorite bar, that sort of thing."

I looked at Tony and he continued, "But it's not so easy, people are reluctant to be filmed, and it's so bloody hot!" He was smiling. "We didn't think it was going to be anything like as hot as this!" Then he responded, "But I suppose we could give it a go, I'll have a word with that microlite fellow."

Ann turned to me. "Our rep thinks you're idea is super! She's a smashing girl, her name is Annie, and she's Scottish. She's based at Vassiliki really but she calls at Nidri a few times a week." She paused to take a sip of her beer. "She said that she wished that you were in Vassiliki, because she would ask you to film the sail-boarders, and said that they would love to see themselves doing their stunts and tricks on their boards."

"Tony, did you hear that?" I reacted instantly.

"Yes, Annie must be the girl that we were told about, we wanted to have a word with her, but somehow we didn't manage to." He looked slightly disgruntled. "Looks like we slipped-up there, we should have tried harder to see Annie."

Tommy nodded in agreement. "Well, it's too late now; she's leaving in two weeks."

"But she will be passing the video on to the girl who takes her place," Ann quickly reassured us.

"She has asked us to get her a video for herself to take away with her, so that it will be a reminder of her time here," Tommy added with a smile.

The street was beginning to get busy; people were strolling along looking at the black slate menus, standing outside the various tavernas, and glimpsing the food already on some of the tables, as they decided where they were going to eat that night.

"Well, I suppose we had better open up shop!" Tony concluded slowly.

"We'll see you later to get that video for Annie," Tommy said as they were leaving

We sat in the van with the video playing, and a Dutch couple came and stood looking with avid interest, and then after a few minutes the woman reached into her bag and took out her purse.

I nudged Tony excitedly and he beamed back at me. "She is going to buy one!" I whispered happily. Then I saw her put her purse back and they walked away. And my heart plummeted.

Then two little blonde boys with striking blue eyes ran up to look at the video. They were between the ages of nine and twelve. When the shots of the banana-ride appeared on the screen they became very excited and the younger one pulled at my arm and pointed to the screen and then to himself.

"Oh! It's you!" I said, recognizing him as one of the laughing children.

"Yar!" He answered, pulling his brother and pointed to the screen again.

"Oh, yes, and him too!" I said with a smile.

It wasn't long before a young man came up to join the boys, he surprised us by speaking in a cockney accent, "Give us one of them videos darlin'" He winked as he handed me the money saying, "I think this is a terrific idea!" As he walked away he shouted to us, "Good Luck!"

"Well that was very sudden!" I remarked.

"Maybe he had seen it on one of the other nights," he said as he put the 4,000 drachma notes in his wallet. "Well at least we've sold one!"

Then Ann and Tommy came and bought the video for their rep.

Ann spoke hesitantly, "Would you be offended if I gave you something?"

"No." I was looking at her with some puzzlement.

She reached into her bag and handed me a block of pink toilet soap. "It's new!" she said. "Seems a pity to throw it away!"

I wasn't quite sure what to think, but I thanked her anyway.

ⅎ℞

Back at our camp that night we sat by our table sharing a bottle of 'Boutari', and angrily swatted some persistent flies.

Tony looked sullen. "I'm sure these flies have come because of the blood from the poor lamb."

"Hush!" I said. "Don't remind me about it."

I had secretly checked on the remaining lamb as soon as we had got back, and was beginning to feel that I was getting a bit paranoid about it. I took a big gulp of wine hoping that it would help dull my senses and help me to sleep. Then I spoke with a giggle, "I've never drunk so much wine or beer in my life before!"

"I know! We'll probably be alcoholics by the time we get home!" Tony laughed. Then on a more serious note he added, "But what are we going to do about selling these videos?" He looked despondently towards me. "We are not having much luck now are we?"

"No," I answered sadly. "But maybe it will pick up again after the rep shows the video on the coach tomorrow."

We were both sitting pondering about our predicament.

"Maybe we should have a go at doing some personalized videos," I suggested after a while.

Tony did not appear very enthusiastic, but he was prepared to give the idea some consideration. I grew more forceful as I drank more wine, and I tried to convince him with my schemes.

"Honestly, I think it would be different here!" His face looked doubtful, so I added quickly, "There is so much going on, I think we should give it a go!"

Tony swallowed the rest of his wine. "But how will we ask people if they want to be filmed?"

"Oh! Don't worry about that! Leave it to me!" The wine was giving me false confidence. I knew how he hated speaking directly to strangers. "We'll wait until we see someone going on the microlite and we'll ask." I noticed Tony's expression of instant panic. "Sorry," I corrected. "**I** will ask them if they would like a video of themselves added to the end of a video of the island all put to music." I sat back on my chair, confidently happy. "That's all there is to it!"

"And what exactly will **I** be doing while you are asking people these questions?"

"Oh, you will be standing nearby, looking very professional with your camera on the tripod, or better still..." I ardently added, "You could be sitting under a tree or under the umbrella."

My imagination was growing wild as I conjured up some mental images.

"Yes! We could take the table and these chairs with us and set ourselves up...you know...properly. We'd look like real professionals and we could have a sign so that people could read it and come to **us** to ask us to film them doing whatever!" I ended, on a note of triumph.

"That all sounds very well, but I'm still not sure if it will work."

I finished my wine saying, "Well we will never know if we don't try!"

"Okay," he agreed with some trepidation." I suppose there's no harm in trying."

ℰ⁖℥

We arrived at Nidri 10am and the only place where we could park was at the far end of the roadway, in a big parking area, some considerable distance from the beach. It was a particularly difficult task to carry the folding table, and two chairs, as well as the tripod, camera, and bag of accessories. But we struggled along, and I was determined that nothing was going to deter me from my plans.

"Are you sure you can manage?" Tony sounded concerned.

"Yes, I'm fine!" I answered without hesitation, barley able to walk upright under the strain. The heat from the constant sun was almost overpowering, and people were looking at us with idle curiosity and some amusement.

We finally reached the end of the little jetty where the microlite was situated and we paused to get our breath. After a while we positioned ourselves quite nearby on the sand. Tony opened the table and I opened out the chairs and we both sat down for a rest. The sweat was pouring off us. People all around were beginning to stare; so I pulled out the sign that I had laboriously made that morning out of a discarded empty 'OMO' soap packet, that I had found in a bin. I had cut it and turned it so that the inside was facing out with my carefully written notice plainly visible. I placed it on the table, while Tony set up the tripod and the camera. All around us people were sunbathing, and they raised themselves lazily to see what was going on.

I smiled at them saying, "Video!" I hoped that this was some sort of explanation as I was not sure what nationality I was addressing.

"Oh!" Some of them merely answered, before resuming their prostrate positions.

After a few minutes I walked over to the man who was reclining on a sun-lounger near the microlite.

"Excuse me!" I began. "Do you speak English?"

He tilted the black cap from over his sleepy eyes. "Only... leetle beet!"

So I decided to explain our plans and hopes to him in the best Greek that I could manage. After my opening sentence, he looked quite interested, so I carried-on. "My husband, over there," I gestured towards Tony who waved pleasantly at that point. He must have realized that I must be explaining what he was going to do.

The man acknowledged with a slight nod of his head.

"He would like to take a video of the microlite when you take somebody up and..."

"Yes, er... of course!" I was interrupted by him answering me in English,

"No, you don't understand!" I continued, now also in English. "We sell the videos to the people and we will give you some money for every one that we sell. Is that Okay?"

"Yes…Why not?" He was looking at me through half-closed eyes.

"Thank you... Efharisto!"

With that, I walked back to Tony.

"Well that seems to be alright!" I announced as I sat down again. "Now all we have to do is wait until someone makes an attempt to go up, then I'll go and ask them if he would like us to make a video for them."

We sat under the umbrella for what seemed like a very long time, people were walking past us and reading our notice with some amusement.

Tony was beginning to look embarrassed, he spoke quietly to me. "I feel a bloody fool sitting here! Everybody is laughing at us!"

"No they're not!" I answered. "Anyway, they will soon realize what we are doing when they see us taking a video."

"Yes, but when?" Tony was looking around in despair. All eyes seemed to be on us, and then we heard a burst of laughter.

I knew that he felt unnerved. His voice was insistent when he whispered, "Why don't you go and ask that bloke what time his first flight is arranged for, maybe it isn't for another hour."

"Okay!"

With only a moment of hesitation, I squared my shoulders and walked across the hot sand and along the water-line. The rippling waves curled around my ankles and I glanced at my watch as I approached the man again.

"Excuse me!" I said with a pleasant smile. "When are you taking somebody up?" I was motioning with my arm to help him to understand.

His tanned face turned slowly towards me and his eyes squinted against the sun.

"Today? ... No! I not go!" He made a gesture with his hands shrugging his shoulders. "Today the weather ees... not right! There ees... too much wind."

"Oh! No!" I sighed. This wonderful idea was turning into a nightmare. I looked at Tony and saw that he was looking extremely embarrassed.

"I don't believe this is happening!" He groaned as I walked back to him.

Wildly I wondered if it was only in my imagination, or was there really mockery all around us.

We folded the table and chairs, our cheeks flaming.

But despite our humiliation I felt a surge of renewed determination, a spark of challenge surged once more through my veins.

"Well after going to all this trouble, carting this stuff all the way up here, I am not going back without having a proper try!"

"So what do you want to do now?" Tony looked exasperated. "How about this couple here!" he was pointing to a young couple who were kissing passionately, their bodies entwined on the sand in front of us. "What about asking them if they would like a video, a blue movie maybe?"

"Don't be silly!" I was trying to keep my composure. "I want to try the other end of the beach where the Para-glider is."

"Right!" Tony swallowed hard his eyes burning bright as fire behind his tinted glasses. The veins in his temples pressed out against his perspiring skin, and a twitch was clearly visible in his jaw. "Right! Anything you say, but let's get to hell away from here!"

We struggled along the curve of the beach, walking at the waters edge because it was slightly easier than stepping over people lying on the crowded beach.

"It's useless, useless, I tell you." Tony kept muttering under his breath as we stumbled along.

We arrived at the other end of the beach totally exhausted. He threw the table and chairs on to the sand and dropped to his knees near them.

"Don't draw attention!" I said quietly.

"Oh! I like that!" He burst out laughing. "That has got to be the understatement of the year!" He repeated sniggering. "Don't draw attention! I'm walking all over the beach with a table and chairs, a bloody umbrella, a tripod and camera, and on top of all that, a soddin' OMO packet! And **you** say, don't draw attention!"

"You know what I mean!" I was slightly peeved, but also amused. "Oh! Come on Tony, you promised that we would give it a go!"

"Okay! I won't say another word." He was frowning. "Except that I don't think you should do it!" He put his hand up to stop me from answering. "But this is your 'baby' so do what you want. I will just sit here and wait for the orders to come pouring in." With that, he assembled the table and chairs again.

When the camera was firmly in position on the tripod he sat down on one of the chairs underneath the flowery sun umbrella, the notice in front of him on the table.

160

I had to stifle a giggle because he did look a bit ridiculous. However I didn't want to admit that I was wrong, so I made my mind up to put everything I had into my plan. All I had was a ray of hope that someone would want to be filmed.

I looked at the platform where the Para-glider took off from. It was not far away, but there was a rough stretch of reasonably shallow water between it and where we were positioned. There were a few people standing on the wooden platform waiting for their turn. A young woman dressed in a bikini top and a pair of tight blue denim shorts was strutting around showing just how confident she was about her own ability, and sexuality.

Suddenly I felt old, frumpy, rather silly, and very tired. However, I tried to convince myself that I could do it. I wanted so much to prove to Tony that my idea would work. And we needed the money!

My heart was beating wildly as though a small bird was fluttering in my chest. Finally, I took my first step towards the platform and I hoped that I would not fall on the slippery stones. I held my shorts as high as I could and waded further, feeling my feet slipping and the water splashing on my legs.

People were mildly curious, but it seemed that everybody stared when I suddenly shouted loudly, "**Excuse me!**"

The strutting woman looked down at me with a questioning expression. "Yes? … What…you want?"

"Er...I was wondering if anyone would like a..."

"**What?**" She repeated, putting her hand to her ear.

I felt my lips quiver I had to summon all my courage to shout even louder.

"**I was wondering if anyone would like a video. Of the flight! It looks very good when we put music to the film...that is my husband over there.**" I pointed in the direction where Tony was sitting. "**He takes very good videos!**"

"**What?**" She said again. Shaking her head from side to side, she turned to some of the people standing on the platform by her side saying irritably, "What does she want?"

Some of them mumbled, some shrugged, but I heard one man say, "Something about a video!" he gave a stifled laugh.

I closed my eyes, and wished with all my heart that I was not there. I felt my body begin to shake and my legs were trembling so much that I was frightened to move.

A woman standing next to the man shouted to me, "**What did you say?**"

"**I said... would anyone like a video taking!**" I yelled back, summoning every once of strength in my body, while everyone around looked at me.

The woman on the platform gave a laud laugh. "A video! ... Goodness! No thank you!"

Now there were shrieks of laughter from all around. I felt like crying. I bent my head and wished that my hair was longer so that it would fall and hide my face. I looked from one to another. My heart was so full I cold not speak.

I turned and stumbled back to Tony, who was looking even more ridiculous than I felt. He resembled a sketch from 'Monty Python'!

"These people are silly, they don't understand anything!" I said, trying to stop myself from crying.

I saw a look of pity in his eyes and at that moment, I was instantly recharged with energy. I looked towards the banana-ride staring with fierce concentration. I saw that there was quite a queue. I wondered if Tony sensed that beneath my attempt at a poised exterior; beat a heart as agitated as if it belonged to a frightened rabbit.

In my desperation I thought. Surely people with children would act differently.

I headed towards them, taking a sly backward glance at Tony who was shaking his head in a bewildered and disbelieving way.

I spoke with as much assurance as I could muster. "My husband can take a video for anyone if you'd like him to. Come on! Surely someone would like a video of the kids on the banana-ride! It will look great with music... We can add it on to the end of the video of the island." I paused for some reaction, but nobody spoke, so I continued trying to sound enthusiastic. "You can come to our blue and white camper van and see it! We park down there by the bar." I was pointing to the promenade.

After what seemed like a very long time a woman gave me a reluctant smile. "No Thanks." She said. "We'll take a rain check!" But she had the look of someone who had hardly bothered to listen to what I was saying.

I stumbled up to Tony, now feeling utterly miserable, and totally defeated, and I noticed that he had packed everything up.

He handed me the umbrella, camera and bag and simply said, "Let's go!"

We staggered back to the van, struggling with all our belongings that kept sliding about. It was almost impossible to keep a firm grip because our hands were sweating and our clothes also stuck to us.

Tony was grinning now.

"We will look really professional!" He mimicked. "We looked more like professional prats!"

"Shut up!" I giggled. "Don't make me laugh or I'll drop something! I just thought that we had to try a gimmick!" I was feeling more cheerful, now that we were out of sight of the beach.

"It's not bloody funny..! That was a bloody nightmare!

I had to agree that the whole affair had been pretty dreadful.

I looked at Tony's dejected expression and said, "Sorry!"

His face broke into an ironic smile.

"What **did** we look like?" He gave a snort: "A couple of right idiots."

"Stop it!" I was beginning to laugh. "You looked so funny sitting there! I should have...." I couldn't speak for laughing.

"What?" Tony was now laughing with me. "What?"

"I should have taken a video of you!" I was now in hysterics and we both doubled up with hilarity. Finally we threw our things into the van, climbed in, and collapsed into our seats.

"What a bloody fiasco of a day, Di!"

We were still laughing as we drove back along the busy road out of Nidri.

When we reached Nikiana, Tony threw back his head and exploded into hollers of laughter again.

"Do you fancy having a go here? Maybe that old man would have liked a video of himself, taking his socks off and having a paddle! I think **that** was quite an important event!"

"Alright! That's enough!"

But I knew that it would be a long time before we forgot the ridiculous happenings of the day. And I also knew that neither of us would ever really want to.

೮೦೧೪

The following day there had only been time for a quick swim at Nikiana, but the water had been wonderful and exhilarating. Large waves rose and fell against our hips and we laughed out loud as the sea splashed us. Already we both felt better. The sky was a metallic blue and we lay back, with our eyes closed against the glare of the sun and let our bodies dip and soar, weightless on the rhythmic swell, until we felt lulled, and totally relaxed. It had been sufficient to refresh and revive us before we set off again for another night's work.

We had come to realize that we had now joined the other various stalls selling unusual toys like yo-yo's, that lit up and sparkled in the dark, and other such amusements. There were also numerous artistic looking young people, who sold hand-made bracelets, necklaces and earrings or gold-leaf paintings.

That particular evening we sat at the bar opposite the parked van in its usual place. We watched, with some amusement, the reactions of passing tourists as they stopped to read the posters that I had placed on all the windows.

"It's funny to think that Ann and Tommy will be at home now."

"Yes." I answered. "And they were sitting right here with us last night."

We observed a lot of noticeably white-skinned people.

"They look lost and bewildered. I wonder if any of them have seen our video on the coach!" I was beginning to feel excited.

"Yes! And I wonder how many of them will want to buy one!"

We set up the equipment, and began showing the film.

"Don't look now! But there are a lot of people gathering outside looking." I said quietly. Tony peeped out over my shoulder to glance through the wire mesh that screened us from our prospective customers. We could see out very well, but nobody

163

could see in, unless they came very near. So we mainly stayed out of obvious sight, inside the van, and only made ourselves noticeable when we felt it was right to do so.

There were quite a lot of sighs, and exclamations of pleasant surprise, emitting from the crowd, and we became quite excited.

"It's really good isn't it, do you want one?" I heard one man say. I looked out eagerly.

"No! I don't think so. We've got enough videos at home!" The woman replied.

After a few more minutes she popped her head inside the van. "Do you have any videos of other islands?"

"No!" I replied.

"Oh! Only we've seen this one now and you don't want to see the same film again! Do you?"

"Well most people like to have one as a souvenir, to remember their holiday, and to show to their family and friends." I explained.

"Oh! Yes," she replied. "What a good idea!" With that they both walked away.

Tony looked perplexed. "Sometimes you wonder don't you? Are **they** daft, or are **we**?"

It was some time later that I spotted two blonde heads in the crowd, "They are the boys who were on the banana-ride!" I cried. "They have brought their mother."

Soon the video was at the point where the banana-ride was featured, and they both became very excited, and worked their way to the front. They laughed loudly when the banana threw them into the sea, and the rest of the crowd recognized them as the stars of that shot, and their happy mood was infectious.

Their mother came up to the doorway. "Yes please. I take a video. It is very good!"

With this action, other people decided that they would also like a copy, and within a few minutes we had sold six more.

"Ironic isn't it? It only takes one to buy a copy, and everybody else wants one!" Tony was shaking his head.

Since it had been quite late when we started selling the videos we decided to show the film again for the fourth time, although it was almost midnight.

"The camp gates will be closed in a few minutes." Tony was looking worried. "At least that's what it says on the board, so I am not driving all that way for nothing."

"Where will we stay then, tonight?" I was feeling a bit perturbed.

"There is a deserted spot that I've noticed, just up the road a mile or so. It's a wooded area, quite a bit back from the road. We'll be alright there for one night."

I was not sure whether I liked the idea, but there didn't seem to be much choice. Then a couple from Athens bought a video, so our prolonged session was quite worthwhile.

164

At around 1.30am we drove into the darkness of the wood, and it felt strange and ghostly. There were some broken-down tables and benches so it must have been a picnic area.

"It probably looks quite nice during the day." I was looking around with some uneasiness.

Since we had been cooped-up all night in the van, we decided to sit out at one of the tables near where we were parked.

"Lets have a bottle of wine! I'm sure we deserve it."

"And we'll have some bread and cheese!" I added. "I've got a box of Camembert, we'll have that."

Once our eyes had become accustomed to the dark, we felt better.

We had a torch that we left switched on, placed on the table, so that we could see what we were doing a bit better.

Our mood became bright, and Tony imitating the woman said, "Have you any videos of other island?" Then with a laugh, he said, "What a silly cow!"

We were both laughing again.

"What the hell did she expect?" he went on. "Oh! Yes madam, which one would you like? We've filmed a thousand islands!"

We were rolling around in our usual hysterics, having just finished the wine and our snack, when suddenly we were illuminated in a brilliant white light that startled us so that we both jumped.

Tony sat up straight and stared intently behind me. The light went out as I turned around and a cold shiver of fear ran through me.

I shuddered as I heard Tony's faint cry of terror, "Christ Almighty! What is it?"

We both stared in total panic as the enormous black shape came steadily and smoothly towards us.

As it came nearer we saw that it was a motorbike with a very large man sitting on it. He had switched the engine off and was pushing the bike along by making strong, steady movements with his black, leather boots on the soft, pine-covered ground.

Then he parked the motorbike behind our van and momentarily disappeared from our view. Tony threw me a quick glance that suggested that we make a run for the van, but before we could move an inch, the figure had emerged again, walking slowly and directly towards us. He was towering above us like a formidable statue, huge and gleaming black in the moonlight. Then he was standing still, a gigantic, dark bulk, with a black helmet and visor against the night sky. Tony's eyes flickered then I saw him walk to the door of the van and pick up something.

"Don't worry I've got a hammer here!" he whispered. It was concealed in his hand, by his side, ready, waiting for him to make a move towards us.

I heard Tony's sharp gasp for breath, and I could feel my own heart racing and the back of my neck tingling. The tension was intense; it was a feeling of frantic despair.

Suddenly he removed his black helmet saying, "What the hell are you doing here?" His voice was pleasant and soft. "I spotted your English number-plate from the road. So I came to see. Hope I didn't startle you!" He paused momentarily: "Sorry if I did!"

Tony let out a long sigh of relief. "No! Not a bit!" He gave me a fleeting look of surprise as he laid the hammer down discreetly on the ground under the table.

"Do you mind if I camp here near you tonight? I've got a one-man tent."

"Sure!" Tony replied. "Be glad of the company."

"Great!" He began to remove his heavy leathers. Somehow he looked completely different in his cotton shorts and T-shirt that he wore underneath. Also being bare-footed, he appeared rather vulnerable.

He joined us at our table to drink a carton of milk that he had brought with him.

"This is both my supper, and my breakfast!" He gave a little laugh. Then he began to tell us how he had come to be there, and it was a long story. He had come on holiday with some friends, all on motorbikes, but he had met a girl in Kefalonia, a neighboring island, and had fallen in love with her, so he had stayed, while the rest of his friends had gone on touring, without him.

"So now I have to head home!" He said. "And I feel really broken-hearted about leaving my girl friend, Maria." He hung his head sadly, and sighed adding quietly, "We spent our last night together last night! And we both cried!" He looked up into my face and smiled self consciously. "Honestly, I really cried! I can't believe the way I am feeling."

"Oh! That's really sweet!" I said. "I do hope that you will keep in touch with her and who knows, maybe one day you will get married."

"I hope so! But I don't know how I am going to explain all this to my family."

"I'm sure they will understand." I was trying to reassure him.

He moved his motorbike to face us, switching on his headlight to give us more light, so that he could erect his igloo-style tent, while Tony and I tried to help him.

"How did you spot our number-plate from the road?" Tony said, while we were struggling with the tent.

"Ah! Well the headlight just caught the van as I swerved around that corner." He was pointing behind him. "I was keeping an eye out for somewhere to put the tent up for the night, and I was surprised when I saw the GB sticker and then the number-plate!" he laughed. "I thought to myself, gosh they are a long way from home!" Then with an amused facial expression, and a knowing wink he said, "And I am trained to notice things: I'm a traffic policeman!"

"Oh! My son is a traffic policeman in the Metropolitan Police, in London!" I was feeling immediate warmth towards him.

After a little while he made his way inside his tent saying, "I will be leaving early in the morning so I will say goodbye now, and good luck!"

"It's been nice meeting you," I said. "I do hope you have a happy life."

"All the best mate! And good luck to you too," Tony added.

When we were inside the van now and Tony reached into a cupboard and brought out our bottle of Metaxa.

"I'm having a brandy! I have never been so frightened in my whole life!"

"No! It did look awfully scary didn't it, when he came so slowly towards us?" I was readily accepting the glass of brandy that he was handing me.

"Well it certainly sobered me up!" Tony laughed. "I was feeling nice and mellow before!" he took a large swig. "But I was glad that I'd kept that hammer ready by my seat!"

"Oh! Yes, I didn't know you had that!"

"Well I am always prepared: Just in case!"

We drank another glass of brandy and I began to feel a bit dreamy.

"Wasn't it nice the way he told us about how he had fallen in love?"

"That is when I should have hit him with the hammer!"

"You horrible thing!" I cried as I pushed him over.

We both fell on the bed laughing. Tony raised his head to glance out of the window and laughed. "I wonder if they spent the last night in that little tent!" He spluttered, "There is hardly room for him! Let alone the two of them. They certainly couldn't get up to much in there!"

We both tried to suppress our outbursts of laughter. Relief and the effect of the brandy was exploding like fireworks inside us.

∞∞

In the morning I awoke very slowly. A bright shaft of light was shining through a gap in the curtains, and I looked out to see if the tent was there.

Tony stopped snoring and spoke sleepily. "Is he there?"

"No!" I exclaimed a little sadly. "He's gone!"

I climbed out of the van and looked about me. I could hear the melodious hum of bees. Through the pines nearby were about six or seven brightly painted bee-hives.

I looked out on a scene of powerful beauty, which the night before had seemed menacing. A high cliff rose sheer on both sides of the wood and far in the distance was the dark blue sea. A small church, white and gleaming stood against the blue sky. A slight wind was getting up feeling nice and cool against my skin.

I glanced at the wooden table beside me, and saw that the round empty Camembert box was still on it. I picked it up and noticed that something had been written on the bottom.

"Just to say, that nothing happened between me and Maria! A kiss maybe, but nothing 'more', as they say!"

I showed it to Tony. "He must have heard us! Whatever must he have thought? And he was so nice!"

Chapter Nine

We spent another lazy day at Nikiana, mainly swimming, and sitting under a tree. I was enjoying speaking Greek to a few people, and playing at the waters edge with some attractive young children. I felt completely captivated by their innocence, and childish games. Three little boys were having a wonderful time playing with some empty orange juice cartons. They had stuck a twig, with a few leaves, to act as a mast into the cartons, and they were sailing them with great enthusiasm and excitement. Their fiery loud outbursts, while they pushed and shoved each other in friendly, juvenile combat, were so typical of Greek behavior; and were amusing to observe.

There was an Italian family, who appeared to be quite wealthy, nearby on the beach and they had a boy of a similar age, around five or six. He had an assortment of expensive toys scattered around him, but he seemed to be bored and unhappy. His fashionable parents pampered and petted him, but nothing seemed to please him. His father gave him some sweets, but he threw them on the ground in a temper tantrum.

After a while the boy strolled indecisively to where the little Greek boys were playing, standing silently watching their play, and the fun that they were having.

One of the make-believe boats sailed near him so he hesitantly pushed it back to the other boys. Then one of them asked him in Greek if he wanted to play with them. The fact that he couldn't understand their language posed no problem; he knew they were including him. Then one little Greek boy ran up to a rubbish bin and came back grinning holding another empty orange juice carton. The little Italian boy ran to a nearby tree and broke off a twig and taking the carton from his new-found friend he stuck it firmly inside and pushed his own make believe boat into the assortment of cartons floating on the sea.

They all played happily for the rest of the day together, and I couldn't help thinking that there was a lesson to be learnt somewhere in that example.

It was soon time for us to head back to our camp so that we could have a meal and a shower before heading back to Nidri to work.

Tony spoke on a sigh. "I wonder what is in store for us tonight."

"I wonder! No two days seem to be the same!

…

At the harbor-front at Nidri people passed our van and some seemed very interested, some were mildly curious, and others were quite indifferent. The latter groups mainly consisted of the very young couples who meandered along with arms around each other, stopping to kiss at every opportunity, and were oblivious of everyone else apart from each other. One such couple stopped momentarily, to gaze at the screen, and I heard the girl read our notice out loud.

"Video of Lefkas!" Then turning to the chap she said. "Lefkas? Where's that?"

"It's **here!** You fool!"

He swung her around to smack her bottom, which was almost visible; her skirt being so short, and made her scream, as he dragged her off.

"Oh! Is it?" She giggled.

Tony turned to me. "They have probably just booked a last minute holiday in the sun, and they don't really care where it is!"

"No, they will probably never bother to even see any of the island, but spend the whole holiday on this beach and at these tavernas, and when they go home, when people ask them where they have been they will say, *to some Greek island.*"

It was the family-orientated group that tended to buy a video, couples over thirty who genuinely liked the place, and wanted to remember it. But there were noticeably less of them around now, and very many youngsters, who were more eager to get back to their room after they had eaten, or go to a disco club, than stand and look at a video of the island.

However a French couple stopped to buy one, then immediately an English couple also bought one and seemed to be very pleased to have it.

The man smiled saying," I'm so glad that we came here today. We're staying at Vassiliki, but we hired a car for a couple of days and we were just leaving, when I spotted the van." Then as he put the cassette into a carrier bag, he added. "It's a great idea!"

His wife agreed. "I can't wait to see the rest of it and show our kids when we get home."

"If only more people were like that!" Tony commented, after they had left.

A bicycle drew up suddenly beside the open doorway and a man spoke in a pronounced German accent.

"Hello, I see the film the other night, it is very good!"

"Thank you!" We both replied.

"I have a very small company, only four yachts, and I want...if you... can maybe make a video ...to promote my yacht chartering holidays...maybe we can arrange something ?" He looked at us questioningly.

We looked at each other in total perplexity. Then Tony stepped out of the van and took him to one side so that they could talk away from the intermittent distractions that our video was causing, because some families with excited children had also arrived.

I could hear the man now. "Can we agree on a price? I think that you will need to spend one week on my yacht and film the places that we call at." He paused to glean some acknowledgment from Tony, before he asked; "Do you think that...Er...you can do this?" He laughed self consciously and added, "But it depends on how much you will charge!"

"I have to be honest with you, I really have no idea!" Tony shook his head from side to side, "You have taken me by complete surprise, but the idea certainly sounds interesting, and it is obviously something that I would thoroughly enjoy doing!"

The man carried on. "Think about it and I will come back in a few days time, and then maybe we can talk!" He got back onto his bicycle. "I live up in the mountains, you can come to my house and we will have some wine and some food and make some arrangements!" Then as he began to ride away he shouted. "That is, if the price is right!"

"Well! What do you make of that?" Tony was dumbfounded, "There's never a dull moment!"

We sold one more copy to an old Greek man who was ecstatic because he had seen himself on the video, standing along side his boat that took people for short trips.

"Well, I think we'll call it a night!" Tony stated, as the film finished. "I think we should head back a bit earlier tonight so that we can talk about this German's offer." He stretched and yawned, "I don't know about you, but I'm worn out!"

I was also feeling very tired and was quite happy to pack up and go back to our camp, although it was only 10pm.

When we got back there was a brown Army tent standing near our spot.

"Oh! Look we've got company. They must be Greeks!" Tony exclaimed.

We sat deliberating over the prospects of making the promotional video, while we drank our usual bottle of Boutari, bought from the snack bar on the site. Yiorgos had it ready in his hand when Tony walked in and he laughed.

"Po! Po! Po!" and wagged an accusative finger at us both.

We didn't understand why, but we laughed anyway.

The idea of being on a yacht certainly filled us with excitement, but it was tinged with apprehension because we were not altogether sure about our abilities to film in those sorts of circumstances. We had managed to put together a very impressive video, but we had done it in our own time, and without anyone supervising us. We did not really like the idea of being stuck with people that we didn't know for a week and even then; what if the video wasn't good enough? What would we do then? It was all very bewildering and worrying. I knew that Tony felt anxious and ill at ease at the prospect of spending a lot of time and effort on something that might prove to have an unsatisfactory outcome.

We finished the wine as I said," Well how about charging him 500 pounds! He can take it or leave it!"

This more or less settled the issue, except that we wondered if the German would be prepared to pay more! But we were afraid of shooting ourselves in the foot, so to speak.

So we settled down to a rather disturbed night.

"I think that we're doing alright really as we are, don't you?" Tony said sleepily.

"Yes, and we've still got quite a lot of videos already made, so we can relax during the day and just go and sell them at night!" I replied.

Secretly we both felt torn between the two options.

"Maybe we will never even see him again anyway!" And laughing into his pillow he added, "Maybe he's just the local idiot!"

"I wouldn't be a bit surprised! You can never be sure of anything around here!" I replied with a chuckle.

As if in agreement, we heard the sound of a quiet bleating from the remaining lamb and Tony expressed both our thoughts.

"Yes! You know the feeling don't you mate! It's a bloody uncertain life!"

⁎

It was Friday morning the 14th August and I had just finished writing my letters so that I could post them in Nidri that night. Tony was beginning to feel fed up waiting around in the heat and gave a sigh of relief when I stuck down the last envelope.

"Thank God for that!" he sighed. "Now let's go for a swim I'm beginning to melt in this heat!"

We had not seen our new neighbors as they had already gone out by the time we had emerged that day.

I was keeping a very close eye on the lamb since we had become quite accustomed to its sad little face watching us, and I felt vaguely responsible for it, since it had lost its companion; and the goat seemed quite detached, and at times rather hostile. So I threw some bread and pieces of red cool melon to brighten up its' sad little existence if only for a brief spell. Unfortunately this kindness sometimes had the adverse effect as the food sometimes fell just out of its reach and it was even more distressing to see it struggling desperately to try to reach it!

"Come on!" Tony called, "The old woman will give it the other pieces when she comes back later to collect the eggs from the hens!"

We found another small bay; it was more of a strip of stones and large jagged rocks that fringed the rather choppy sea. It was such a short distance from our camp site that we could walk there.

"Shall we spend the day there, for a change?" I asked.

"Why not, don't think there will be many people there as it is a bit difficult to reach." There was actually nobody there except us. We had to walk very carefully over slippery smooth rocks, before we found a place where we could settle down. The water there was very clear and because there was such a wide outlet to the sea, there was a breeze, which we found particularly pleasant.

We struggled against the sharp stones to fall with indescribable pleasure into the cooling, embrace of the sea.

Tony spoke between sighs of relief. "It was worth the effort for the breeze and the peace and quiet here."

We sat on a large flat rock and gazed across the wide expanse of blue. The day was exceptionally hot, and the sun beat down with unmerciful heat on two worlds, the sea and air, and where both worlds met, the ocean birds swept down and dived with avid determination to pluck their bounty from beneath the surface of the sea. Gulls competed in daring displays of noisy battle cries. We gazed at the dazzling patterns caused by the swell, where the sun danced upon the blue. Underneath silver fish moved silently and playfully, in corresponding movements, darting one way and then the other, as one mass.

The brilliance of the day passed into dusky splendor as we watched the sun go down behind the green pine clad hills, and in the distance, mountains cloaked in purple, towered up towards the sky.

A small green lizard was scurrying across the sandy rock, disappearing into a crevice, leaving a trail of tiny footprints behind it. Then suddenly a bird noticeably smaller and thinner than a sparrow settled on a rock nearby, looking at us with sharp quick gleaming eyes. Then fluttering onto one of the tall dry grasses nearby it sang proclaiming happiness to the world.

Tony smiled at me." I think that he is telling us that it is time for us to go!"

I laughed in answer as I gathered up our things. "Hasn't this been lovely!"

We were beginning to adopt the Greek philosophy of life, taking everything in our own time, and appreciating our surroundings. We were noticing things that would previously not have been important to us. We had survived our disasters and tragedies and now we treasured and savored all our experiences.

Back at our camp site, having eaten a sandwich under the tree I wondered what we would do that evening and I could sense that Tony was also pondering on some thoughts.

"Well Di, lets go and find this German bloke's house then, we might as well see what he has to say." He was feeling more adventurous now.

His house was brightly lit and it hadn't been as difficult to find as we had thought. A narrow winding road led us up one hill and down another, then up again until we found the land mark, two big green bins, he had mentioned where we should turn where the road forked.

We found the man sitting with his wife outside on the terrace drinking wine. Candles flickered prettily on the table and on the walls around them.

They got up to welcome us. He spoke first, "This is my wife, Anna, I am Max, and come let us have some wine."

His pleasant looking wife added with a smile. "Please help yourselves to some nibbles." Her hair was shoulder length and blonde, swept up and held at the sides with two slides. She was wearing a long pink dress which suited her complexion. Max smiled and I noticed that he was better looking than I had remembered. His eyes were dark and although he had very little white hair he had such a nice sun tan giving him a pleasing look; and his demeanor was likeable. I felt relaxed in their company, and I felt that Tony did too.

The house looked very grand with white archways at both sides and we could see that the interior looked very luxurious.

Tony spoke tentatively. "About the price of this video Max, since it will mean taking so much of our time, would 500 pounds be agreeable to you?"

"That seems reasonable enough." He was smiling and Tony and I were wondering if he would have agreed to pay more.

The evening passed pleasantly and by the time we were leaving after discussing what aspects of the film Max wanted us to feature, we felt that we had made new friends.

∞∞

The next morning we met him at his yacht.

When we stepped on board, we noticed that the deck was gleaming and when we walked down some steps to the galley, we felt as though we had entered another world. It was so plush!

I turned to Tony when Max had gone up on deck whispering, "I feel a bit uncomfortable, I didn't expect anything like this."

"Neither did I, he must be loaded!"

"Well he did say he had five yachts, but I thought they were just ordinary ones, not like this. It's huge!"

Max came back. "Can you film the inside first?"

"Yes," Tony grinned at him positioning the tripod and beginning to do a pan of the lounge area. While he was filming and I was helping with the lighting, a large Greek man came noisily down the stairs to join us. There was a curious expression on his face. Then I saw that he was scowling at us both. With a loud gruff voice, he spoke to Max in Greek. *"I do not like this! It is not necessary to do this. I want us to leave now quickly!"*

Max answered him compellingly also in Greek. *"No, It is better this way. I tell you, they are English and just making a film, we will leave in a few minutes. Do not worry Akis."*

I was surprised, as I had not thought that Max spoke Greek and I thought about saying something, but decided not to. Maybe it was better to be able to understand what they were saying. I was not sure why, except that I was aware of an underlying tension between them.

Akis made some sounds of protest as he thumped one of the polished wooden walls making Tony and I feel quite alarmed. At this Max threw us a strange smile, but said more sternly now, in Greek to Akis, *"Untie the rope we will leave now."*

"Can you film the harbor as we leave?" he said hurriedly turning to Tony.

"Certainly," Tony quickly picked up the equipment while I helped him to carry the tripod up the steps.

It was a lovely sight to see Nidri from this angle as the yacht moved steadily out to sea, cutting through the clear blue sea leaving a white trail behind. Two or three hundred yards out at sea there were a few small fishing boats.

I was beginning to enjoy the experience, when Akis called gruffly to Max. *"Tell them to go down now; we have left the harbor."* He was completely unaware that I understood what he was saying and so was Max.

"No, we'll let them carry on. It is better this way."

I felt a bit uncomfortable and wanted to tell Tony what they were saying but I couldn't because I knew that they would hear me. We had been at sea for about an hour. Tony continued to film, directing the camera towards an island in the distance and continued filming as we drew closer to it. Then we approached a little harbor, much smaller than Nidri and I was surprised when Max suddenly called in Greek again to Akis. *"Tie up here."*

Then he turned to Tony and then to me. He was speaking pleasantly in English.

"Have a break and sit on the deck, have a drink."

We noticed that he hadn't taken much interest at all in our filming since we had left Nidri. I felt aware that this superb, yacht seemed completely out of place among the fishing boats and Glass Bottom Boats, in the sleepy, little harbor.

"Do you want me to film this harbor?" Tony asked.

"Only as we leave." He seemed to be in a hurry. Then he opened a cupboard, took something from it and placed it into a sports bag, zipping it closed.

"I have to go to see someone, I will be back soon." He threw the bag over his shoulder, then he was gone.

Akis sat watching us the whole time that he was away while he inhaled the smoke from his cigarettes before blowing it out into the warm air.

It was nice to be sitting on the deck of a superb yacht like this one. We had envied people doing this so often as we sat in our van at the harbor.

A white car stopped suddenly and only for a moment, Max got out and as he did so, Akis got to his feet shouting. **"Now you...film... NOW!"**

Tony jumped up immediately and switched on the camera as Max came on board.

He glanced in Tony's direction as he disappeared down the steps. "Film the harbor as we leave."

Tony began filming but I sensed that he was a bit concerned. Akis was still watching us as he untied the rope and we were soon heading out to sea again.

I threw Tony one of my 'looks' my mouth drooped at the corners and my eyebrows furrowed. But Tony merely shrugged.

Another hour passed, Max and Akis had been talking quietly so I could not hear what they were saying but they were watching us. Tony was engrossed in filming and checking the equipment and then we were heading for a much bigger harbor. As Max steered the yacht into a space between two equally grand yachts he told us to go up on the deck again. This was a busy harbor full of restaurants where many tourists were either eating or walking around. It was even bigger than Nidri. We sat on the deck feeling like movie stars, except that we were making the movie. Max followed us up the stairs onto the deck as Akis tied the yacht up securely. He was looking all around; I thought he was admiring the place. Maybe he hadn't been here before; he seemed to be scanning every detail. Max stepped off the boat carrying the same sports bag and as he did so he called to us. "I'll be back soon. Please be ready to film the harbor when I come back again, as we leave."

It was only a few minutes before Max arrived back, this time he was walking. He jumped aboard and immediately Tony took his signal to start filming. I wondered where he had gone to be back so quickly. Akis untied the rope and Max started the motor. We were moving quickly again through the blue sea and through the entrance of the harbor. Max called abruptly to us. "Okay, stop now; go down please to the cabin."

As we were stepping down I managed to speak quietly to Tony. "It seems a bit weird to me, to just film harbors as we leave!"

No sooner had I got the words out when Max called something I didn't understand to Akis and his huge body came lumbering down into the cabin, opening and closing cupboards. He was out of breath and I could hear him panting and wheezing.

Max yelled to us. **"Sit down! Get out of the way! Start filming the inside again!"**

"I've done that already," Tony was replying, when Akis almost knocked him over by rushing up the steps again, with his arms full of cardboard boxes.

Then we heard a siren and a loud whistle. All of a sudden the cabin seemed to be full of policemen all shouting and rushing around. There was complete pandemonium. They were pulling cushions off the lovely sofas and generally creating a terrible mess. One policeman forced Akis down the stairs; the boxes were still in his arms, but not for long. They were taken off him by another very formidable policeman.

Another stern policeman looked at us, we wondered what to say. I looked at Tony who was now ashen, the nerve in his jaw was twitching as he spoke with a tremor.

"We were just making a video for the owner, Max. He asked us to."

"Yes," I added not even thinking of attempting to speak Greek now.

176

"You must come with me." He looked very austere.

"Where to?" I was beginning to tremble, although my voice sounded calm.

"To the police station, we have to test you for drugs."

"**Drugs**!" We both exclaimed in horror. It wasn't what we had expected to hear.

We were bundled into the port police launch with Max, who was looking a little bit sorry, and Akis who showed no sign of any kind of emotion except his usual annoyance.

When we got off at the harbor escorted by the police, people had gathered to see what was going on and it seemed that they were all staring at us in disgust. I hung my head in an effort to hide my face in shame. I imagined them all rolling their eyes, wondering what crime we had committed.

The port police station was a grey stone building, of which we were hurriedly pushed through the doorway. Then we were detained by a nasty looking policeman and an arrogant young policewoman, who otherwise would have been quite attractive.

She hardly looked at me. "You must come with me, and your husband will go with him."

Tony was taken away and it was then that I went completely to pieces.

I sat on the chair she indicated to before she left me in a dark grimy room. It was at that moment that I began shivering quite uncontrollably; my mind was a conglomeration of fear and panic.

The door was opened by a woman wearing a white coat who walked towards me, with all the stealth of a hyena, holding a syringe.

"I have to take a blood sample." She did not look at me while she spoke but just took my trembling arm and roughly stuck the needle in it. I could not feel a thing! I was numb with shock.

"Wait here," she said as she went out closing the door with a bang behind her.

I wondered how long I would be there. Did they get the results quickly or would it take some time. Surely we would soon be free as the results would be negative. I wondered what was happening to Tony.

After a short while the policewoman came back and sat down at a desk opposite me. This time her eyes were peering into mine.

"How you get to be on this boat?"

"We were asked to make a film of the cruises by the owner Max."

"How you know this man?"

"We don't, we only met him a few days ago…We went to his house to arrange…"

"What you arrange?"

"To make the video!" My panic was evident. "We have not done anything wrong, really!"

She sat back in her chair, her hands clasped in her lap. All of a sudden she leaned forward and scribbled on some paper then pushed it towards me. "Read this and sign."

I could hardly see the writing I was so distressed, but with a trembling hand I managed to sign my name.

She picked it up with a swift movement, and promptly stood up and walked out of the room.

It seemed like an age before she returned and I was so relieved to see Tony with her that my eyes flooded with tears.

He held me close. "Don't worry, it will be alright!"

"How do you know that?"

"I explained everything to the police we just have to wait now for my statement to be proved." I was too numb to question him or even to speak at all.

We were brought two cups of tea and some biscuits. I hadn't realized how hungry I was until then. We hadn't eaten all day.

After that I leaned my head against Tony's shoulder and I must have dozed off: I was so mentally exhausted.

When I opened my eyes and looked at the grey walls around me, a cold wash of dread crept through me as I recalled the horror of our situation. I was half asleep and half awake trying to piece together the fleeting memories of the day.

"How long have I been asleep?" I was looking into Tony's tired eyes.

"Quite a while." He was smiling but he still looked anxious.

It was then that the door opened and the same policewoman, who had spoken to me, came into the room again. "Come this way." She looked at us both in turn and we got to our feet and followed her.

We were in another room now and the light from the large doorway made it difficult for us to see who was standing facing us. Then we heard a familiar voice speaking Greek rapidly and sternly and we recognized that it was Demetrious.

"These are good people, they make lovely videos of our island" This was all I could understand as the rest was so fast, but I wanted to run to him and hug him, I was so relieved; but that would not have been the right thing to do.

"You can go now." The policewoman said dismissing us with one wave of her immaculately manicured hand.

We sat in silence during the journey home in Demetrious' car for two reasons. Mainly I could not begin to start explaining in Greek what had happened and Tony was unable to. However Demetrious seemed to understand.

He nodded his head saying quietly, "No problem!"

"Efharisto para poly," (Thank you very much) was all I could manage to say when he dropped us off at our camp site.

The next two days and nights lingered by, we were both still recovering from our ordeal. I was lying under the shade of our umbrella thinking. Perhaps it had been a hallucination, some false memory. But then I knew really, that it had actually happened. I had to accept it; I nodded. "Do you remember when we were traveling here and we didn't declare all our equipment and we thought we might get into trouble with the police?" I was looking at Tony. "Well when we were in that station I was thinking all sorts! Like what if they asked us about the camera and all our stuff. I was so scared, were you?"

"I was terrified! But when they asked me if I knew anyone who could guarantee our honesty, I remembered that I had Demetrious' address in our diary. They looked it up and rang him."

"Good job you had that!" For once again I was glad of Tony's little quirks of being meticulous.

We avoided any unnecessary activity and exertion, as every day seemed to be hotter than the last. In the mornings we remained in the camp-site in the shade of our tree, after everyone else had left. In the early morning the sound of adult voices and children's happy laughter filled the air. And the clanging of dishes and utensils could be heard as the women traded information, talking loudly and somewhat excitedly as they prepared the evening meals. Large round metal containers were filled with a wide assortment of food. Some were lined with fish, scrubbed at the nearby sinks, leaving a pungent odor for quite some time, and others were filled with meat and an assortment of vegetables. Later they would take these huge containers in the boot of their cars to a cooking place called, 'To Furnos, ' (The Oven) which was a couple of miles away. It was mainly used by families, and it was very inexpensive. Everyone put their meals in some massive ovens and they were all cooked together.

We didn't bother to go there since our amount of cooking could easily be done in the van. But during the evening the aroma coming from the tables where the families gathered, gossiping, was quite mouth-watering.

Back in our 'spot' at Nidri again we sold four videos on Friday night and five on Saturday night, so we were reasonably happy. I was thinking if anyone had missed us: because so much had happened since last time we were there.

"I wonder what happened to Max, do you think he is in Jail?" I was speaking my thoughts while I gazed at the yachts in the harbor, while we were driving away.

"I suppose so, after all, he was smuggling drugs. I could hear the police talking about cannabis when they were interviewing me. That is what was in those boxes Akis was trying to get rid of."

"Really?"

"Heavens yes, I saw the boxes on the table and you could smell it. He must have been going to throw it overboard." Then he spoke with a subdued voice. "You know I don't think we should talk about it. It was just a horrible experience that we have got over now and we should put it behind us and move on."

179

"I agree I don't even want to think about it any more. We came for an adventure and we got one...and a half." I laughed.

"You're not kidding!" he was smiling and shaking his head.

ಬಿಂಬ

Sunday morning arrived and we sat at our table. Tony spoke as I poured the coffee. "Let's go to Agios Nikitas today. But if the Tseticas family is there I do not want to talk about the horrid experience with Max."

"No, I'll explain," I said. "I'm sure they will understand.

We parked the van at the top of the street and began walking down on the smooth cobbles. I was thrilled to be back again and many of the locals waved cheerily to us and smiled as we passed. We entered the Car Hire office where Liana looked up. She was surprised to see us and she smiled warmly. When she spoke her words were precise, but there was a tremble of excitement in her voice. "I have... sold... three videos! So...maybe you leave some more...for me to sell. I have missed you; we all have, here in Agios Nikitas." She admitted, blushing a little. Then she opened a small drawer and took out some drachma notes and handed them to us.

"You really must take something for your trouble!" Tony offered her two of the thousand drachma notes.

"Ohi!" She shook her head from side to side and appeared slightly agitated. "I wish that I could help you more, but not many people look at the television in my small hotel."

"Thank you so much," Tony said, leaving another three videos with her.

"Efharisto!" I added feeling genuinely grateful for her help and her friendship.

As we approached the Poseidon we were bombarded with hollers and shouts, one particularly loud voice rang out, **"Hallo Tonic!"**

We looked up at all their smiling faces and felt an overwhelming appreciation as we both waved back with enthusiasm.

"Isn't it nice?" I laughed. "It's a bit like coming home!"

When we reached the beach we heard another loud cry.

"Mr. Tony! Mrs. Diana!" George came running to meet us. his handsome features beaming with pleasure at seeing us again. He led us towards the big red umbrella, under which Mata and Demetrious were sitting. They both tapped on the sand with their hands inviting us to join them.

Fotis was splashing about in the sea with some other boys; his skin now was so dark that it appeared almost black against his brilliant cotton shorts that hung on his slender young hips. On seeing us, his handsome face broke into a dazzling smile jumping high out of the crystal water, to wave to us. His hair was wet and black, curling onto his shoulders. Antigony was playing nearby. She looked up with the same delight in her soft brown eyes and soon her little arms were enfolding my neck. Within minutes I was persuaded to play the game with her boat and pebbles again. George joined Fotis and some other Greek children, swimming around talking in loud voices to each other as they played. I wondered why no one mentioned our horrible incident.

I looked at Demetrious questioningly and he understood the unspoken word. He put both hands up and closed his eyes momentarily before making a small movement with his head. I took that to mean that he had not spoken about it to anyone.

Mata had been engrossed with sorting out some towels and did not see this action. So we all sat, simply looking, interested in the activity and noise. I must say that we were both relieved. Evidently he knew that the boys would have gone on and on about it if they had known and he knew that it had been far too upsetting for us.

I felt so much respect for him and so much gratitude.

Then one of the children, a little girl pointed directly at Fotis and spoke in Greek to George. "Is that a girl or a boy?"

George looked at us all, to see if we were listening before answering in Greek.

"It's a cucumber!" Then he hollered with laughter and we all shared in the joke.

Mata told me that people were always mistaking Fotis for a girl, but they had decided that he should keep his hair long, as on the one occasion when he had his hair cut short none of them had liked it. Somehow he hadn't looked like Fotis at all!

After a while George suddenly spoke seriously.

"You would maybe like for me to take you to a very, very nice walk, yes?"

"Yes." We answered quickly, whereupon George immediately jumped to his feet.

We climbed a steep hill, our feet slipping on short course brown turf studded with wild flowers of amazing colors. Then we stood panting in the blazing heat at the top.

George had much to tell us, so we sat down, perched on a craggy peak, listening and looking all around. He spoke quite eloquently as he explained the history.

He began. "A very, very long time ago... it has been a most turbulent time in the history of the island... It was from 1797 to 1809 when the island suffered... different occupations. This caused extreme trouble to the lives of the people. In 1797 the French occupied the island until 1798, then for the... following two years it was occupied by the Russian Turks who in 1802 established a federal state of the seven islands. But this was...how you say...abolished five years later when it fell into the hands of the French again until 1810.

He smiled broadly, revealing large dimples as he continued. "But the last... sovereigns ...of Lefkas were the British, who... re-established the state of the Ionian Islands." He looked into our interested faces and ended with, "In May 1864 Lefkas and the rest of the seven islands....were united with Greece."

Then a short while later, as we were making our way down the hill again he told us that the Greek name for the island, 'Lefkada' came from the word 'lefkos' meaning white. It had originally been called 'Lefkas Petra' (White Stone) and later abbreviated to 'Lefkas'.

He smiled at our appreciation of this information and so encouraged he continued.

"It is thought that this is the island of Ulysses!"

He sucked in some air before going on. "Yes...Er...the...German....er... archaeologist, Wilhelm Dorpfield, started excavations...everywhere on the island, and after he studied the passages of Homer's Odyssey, he...concluded...that ancient Ithaca was...er...identical to to-days Lefkas!"

We were filled with wonder. We were surrounded by so much natural beauty, as far as the eye could see, yet at the same time, we knew that there was so much stark neglect. We looked at the ruined castle and felt that everywhere there were the ghosts of long past civilizations and we were aware of the mythology that encompassed everything!

As though he sensed our feelings George paused momentarily, then spoke thoughtfully.

"There is a saying in Greek, that... in such a place no one can feel lonely, for all the rest... is by his side!"

We glanced at each other and we knew instinctively what he meant.

When we reached the beach again we threw ourselves into the embracing sea, a little more enlightened from our walk with George.

Tony swam up to me. "He really is an amazing kid!" He laughed as he continued; "I don't think you'd find many kids in our country being able to tell us the history of England like that!"

"And he seems to be so interested and so proud of his heritage." I agreed.

As we came out of the water Mata called to us and George interpreted what she wanted to say. "My mother and father say, please will you come and eat with us at my father's friend's taverna?" Then seeing our hesitation he added quickly, "It is a very, very good taverna!"

"Oh! I'm sure that it is!" I agreed. "But we insist on paying."

George spoke quickly to Demetrious, who merely waved his hand in one solitary movement to dismiss the subject as he beckoned to us to follow him.

We all sat around a long table and Demetrious ordered quickly and decisively. Soon we were surrounded by waiters carrying small dishes of assortments of food along with bowls of Greek salad and baskets of fresh bread. These were accompanied by bottles of water and a large glazed terra-cotta jug of wine. We hadn't realized how hungry we were until we saw the food. It was difficult to control our enthusiasm, but we tried to eat less vigorously than we really wanted to.

We chatted amongst ourselves, but only in Greek. Unfortunately Tony sat in almost total silence only able to exchange an occasional nod and smile with Demetrious. It appeared that George had exhausted his capabilities at speaking the English language with his stories to us, and that now he wanted to relax and enjoy his meal. So there was hardly any English spoken.

I was preoccupied with the delight at having the opportunity to speak so much Greek, and to have so much Greek spoken to me. It was something that I had been missing of late.

The waiters brought some hot cheese pies and crispy fried squid along with more assorted drinks. Finally we were given a sticky honey and nut cake and a cup of Greek coffee, neither of which Tony liked at all, but he was far too polite to say.

He ate his cake and swallowed the coffee and when Mata asked if it was good, by smiling broadly and indicating to them both, he answered eagerly. "Yes! It's very good! Auraia!" Now everybody laughed.

At the end of the meal Demetrious called for the bill and Tony took out his wallet to pay, but was instantly stopped by a movement of Demetrious' hand raised in protest. Then he spoke rapidly to George, who quickly stood up and addressed us rather formally.

"My father ... say, you are our guests and our friends and it is our... pleasure to take you for a meal."

Then Mata spoke quickly and George smilingly added. "Ah! Yes, my mother say, Er...that you must not ever be lonely here... in Greece because you have us! And... We are your friends!"

&ᴑ&

We drove back rather late that afternoon and reached the camp-site just as darkness was approaching.

"I don't want to go to Nidri tonight." Tony said. "I don't feel that it is so important to earn more money. We have enough for the time being and somehow the thought of spending a nice quiet night here at the campsite seems very tempting."

We felt that we were adopting more and more of the Greek habits and we were benefiting from them. We didn't feel strangers in a foreign land now, we felt that we belonged there, and that we were beginning to get to know the island, and learn some of its secrets.

We pulled into the camp and stopped under our tree.

A family was sitting around a table outside the brown tent. It was the first time that we had seen them. The man was tall and thin with a mop of thick, black, curly hair and a thick black matching beard. His face was gaunt and sallow and his eyes were dark and strangely haunting. The woman sitting across the table to him was quite the opposite. She was very large with brown hair swept severely back into a long plait. She was wearing a colorful caftan. Nearby there were two young boys aged about seven and ten kicking a soft ball to each other. They all looked up and smiled at us as we stepped out of the van.

We sat on our chairs and couldn't help noticing that the parents didn't appear to be speaking Greek to each other, but only to the boys, warning them to be careful!

Then the younger boy kicked his ball hard and it came near to our table, so he came over to retrieve it saying, "Signomy!" (Excuse me!) or (I'm sorry)

The parents scolded him for annoying us, so I immediately responded with, "Endaxi!" (It's Okay!)

That soon drew us into a conversation with them. I mentioned that I was puzzled as to what language they were speaking. They both laughed and the woman replied in English. "It is Russian."

The man stood up and spoke softly. "Would you care to come and sit with us and talk for a while?" His manner was so gentle, so courteous, that we had no hesitation in accepting his offer.

Tony took our bottle of wine. "This 'Boutari' is very good. You're more than welcome to share it."

The man began to talk effortlessly about Russia, and Athens, and it turned out that they were in fact Russians who had lived in Athens for the last fifteen years.

We told him about our part of the world and during our idle chatter we started discussing our respective lives. The man spoke quite good English, although at times he broke off to think of a word, and so the conversation was somewhat stilted. His eyes were serious, as though he had experienced a great sadness in his life and it had lingered on in his expression. He told us that he was a computer programmer and Tony smiled in recognition of this fact.

The man caught Tony's eager response and raised a quizzical eyebrow.

"You know much about computers?"

"Quite a lot!" Tony responded. "I used to be a computer operations manager in a large company in Liverpool, England until I was made redundant last year after twenty-four years."

Those dark eyes of his opened wide. "So, we have a lot in common eh?"

"Seems so!" Tony filled the man's glass again.

The man held his glass to the moonlight observing the tawny wine. "To us! And to the little pleasures of life, because in the end it is these that matter the very most!" Then he set it down again.

Soon he and Tony were talking about things that were only understandable to each other, while I glowed inwardly, because I knew that for this brief time, Tony was feeling wholly in tune with another human being. The woman had taken the boys to prepare them for bed.

It was growing dark and long eerie shadows of the trees fell on the ground.

A thought came into my mind like a picture or a photograph that one suddenly remembers from long ago. Always in after-years, I felt that I would recall that one particular day, and this one memorable night, as though it was all part of some glorious plan. We had been brought together from such different worlds and yet we had so much in common. This surely was an experience so rare as to be precious and memorable.

As we lay in the van that night Tony looked relaxed and at ease.

"Who'd have thought it eh? That I would be sitting with a Russian Greek, under a tree in the middle of nowhere, on a little Greek island talking about the latest Computer technology and hardware!" he smiled contentedly as he turned on his side on the bed, feeling a faint trickle of cool air from the open doorway. "I don't know! It's a funny old world!"

"It is indeed!" I agreed. "It is indeed."

"But at least he has a job to go back to, not like me, I'm on the scrap heap."

ଚଡର

The morning sun awoke us first, and then we became aware of the cockerel, was he more noisy than usual, we wondered as we gradually became fully awake. A bird was singing somewhere nearby; then it stopped and the silence it left was almost tangible. We both listened for a while, hoping it would continue.

Life at Episkepos had began to settle into a rather bizarre routine, but we were quite happy and feeling curiously light-hearted and free. We were satisfied to wander from one bay of crystal sea to the next and relax during the heat of the day. And every day was definitely hotter than the last, of that we were certain. Then at night, now that we had learnt to maneuver the difficult road to Nidri, which by now was so familiar that, we knew every inch of the way, and more importantly every pot-hole, we quite enjoyed being part of the lively night life.

We were now also familiar with some of the local people, or maybe they had just grown used to our continual appearances, but at least we were on nodding terms with them. We found the locals at Nidri not as warm-hearted as the people at Agios Nikitas. Sometimes their manner was curt, but it was not unfriendly. It was their way, and we had come to know and accept it. They were simply too busy in their pursuit of enticing tourists to eat at their bars, take a trip in their boat, or to simply buy something from them, be it only a corn-on-the-cob, or a hot pancake, covered in sugar, wrapped in a paper napkin. But we felt that somehow we fell somewhere in the same category and at least nobody resented us having a go!

This, it has to be said, was rather hospitable of them. Especially since we were, after all foreigners, and tourism was to most of them, their only livelihood. And at that point of time it was also ours!

But for no particular reason we felt as though we were at ease there. There are some places that you simply feel 'at home' in, and I think this was such a place.

I had by now grown accustomed to the nightly loud chattering in the toilet block. New people came and went, and I wondered if this was a ritual that was learnt and carried on from one set of campers to another. But now I was joining in with them. Every night we all stood in our 'knickers and vests' or nightdresses at the wash bowls, laughing, brushing our teeth, combing our hair, and always talking, talking, talking. I myself actually didn't say very much since it was all far too rapid for my ears, and there were far too many conversations going on at the same time, but I was able to follow the gist of what they were saying and even understand the odd joke! So I was content to throw in an occasional word, here and there. But nevertheless it was fun, and I have to admit that I enjoyed it all. Maybe it reminded me of school days, or maybe it was the thrill of being on such intimate terms with people of such a different culture. I really do not know. But I had a happy feeling inside and sometimes it welled up so that when all around me were laughing and spluttering, I also laughed out loud, although at times I wasn't quite sure about what. It was simply nice to be included, and to be having a bit of a laugh.

It had only been a short walk to the stretch of beach, if it could be called that, but in the scorching heat it was quite far enough. We wondered how the young people with huge back-packs managed to walk for miles in this sort of heat! And we knew that they did, because we had seen them.

So we lazed on the rocky bay, and gazed at the spectacular cliffs all around us and the great unending stretch of azure, open sea. We were happy to be on our own, away from the noise of children screaming, even though it was usually only excited playful screaming it was nice to enjoy the peace and simply listen to the sound of gentle splashes around our waterside setting.

We were off the beaten track and the air was heavy with the smell of sea mingled with pine, since we chose to seek some shade among the dense trees that lined the rocks. As we felt ourselves drifting in and out of slumbering thoughts we felt aware of a wonderful sense of peace enfolding us.

℘ℭ

That night we were back in our routine and heading along the road to Nidri again.

In a short time we entered the narrow street that led onto the harbor-front. We were to say the least surprised and rather miffed, to find that there was a lot of noise and hammering and banging going on. Men of all ages were almost hurrying. I say almost, because unless they are in their cars, Greek men seem to be quite incapable of hurrying anywhere. But their usual strutting and swaggering had acquired a more purposeful manner. They were also carrying long planks of wood and some young lads were erecting a massive sign. This task seemed to require the help or interference, whichever way you looked at it, or rather listened to it, of almost every young man in the vicinity. Whether it really was an all out row, or merely another excited discussion about where exactly the sign would go and who would do what, we will never know. But no blood was spilled and no blows were thrown, so perhaps our first fearful impressions were quite unnecessary, if not unfounded.

Surprisingly amid all the chaos, the motorbike was still maintaining our parking position. And as soon as the van purred noisily towards it, Yiorgos appeared, as if by magic and moved it, smiling as usual as he ran back to the bar to continue serving a customer that he had left waiting. "**Okay Mate!**"

Tony switched the engine off and leaned back in his seat. His eyes were closed but his expression showed some slight amusement. He was shaking his head in a downward sweeping movement. "I wonder what the hell is going on here now!"

I read the sign and understood most of it.

"I think they are having some sort of dance festival."

The dates were clear enough. It was starting the following day, Tuesday the 18th of August, until Sunday the 23rd.

"Well that has well and truly botched things up for us!" Tony remarked.

"So, seeing as we're here now anyway, why don't we still have a go at showing the video?"

Tony's initial reaction was to disagree, but when he saw the hopeful look on my face, he quickly changed his mind.

"Oh! Alright, I suppose it wouldn't do any harm." Then he added with some exasperation. "We have still got quite a few copies made, and God only knows when we will be able to sell them now."

"Not for a week anyway."

We spent a rather discouraging evening sitting in the van while the video played and all around us was loud shouting and banging and some extremely loud thuds, as trucks unloaded heaps of wood and large pieces of metal.

An old man kept wandering past us and hovered near the door of the van. I looked out from my seat at the doorway. He acknowledged me with a customary nod of his head, and a brief movement of his grimy hand touching the brim of his black peaked cap. These caps seemed the common headgear for most men, particularly those who were in some way connected with the sea.

After a few minutes he spoke abruptly, but in English. "How much?"

"Four thousand drachmas," I smiled and pointed to the sign clearly visible.

"No. Not for video!" He was shaking his head from side to side,

I was confused. "How much for what?"

He walked around to the other side of the van. I jumped out of the doorway and followed him. He was standing with his hands thrust deep in his pockets and he was pointing with his foot to our generator.

"Oh! No. That is not for sale." At this he shrugged his shoulders and walked slowly away to watch the workmen.

They had by this time built a stage and were evidently very pleased with their achievements. This fact was apparent by the loud cheers and general happy mood that had now prevailed. But we were not feeling happy.

In fact Tony looked decidedly troubled and after some time he said, "This is hopeless, we're not going to sell any tonight, not with this racket going on."

As he finished speaking a woman's face appeared in the doorway. "You remember us?" How could we forget? It was the middle aged English woman who had asked us if we had videos of other islands. Her husband had by now followed her and was grinning by her side.

She spoke with such excitement. "I can't tell you how glad we are to have found you!" We looked everywhere for you last night."

"We didn't come last night," I replied; I tried to sound as though we were not that eager, since she had not bought a video from us. And she had made us feel a bit humble, like beggars, or street performers, who depended on people's generosity.

"Well, anyway we have found you now!" she said with some relief.

Her husband continued. "The thing is we would like a video for ourselves, and we would also like four more for some people who are staying in our hotel."

"We mentioned your video of Lefkas to them over breakfast and word has spread. And now four couples asked us to buy them a copy."

We looked at each other in complete surprise.

As they left us the woman said, and she sounded as though she meant it. "It really is a good idea that you have had, doing this!"

Tony smiled at me and now the worried expression had left his face, he looked so much younger as the smile slipped into laughter. "Well, what a turn up for the books!"

We studied the twenty thousand drachma notes for a moment. Then Tony lifted the bundle to his lips briefly before tucking them away in his wallet. "That will do for us, thank you very much."

He switched the television off and began putting the equipment away.

"That's about sixty pounds isn't it?" I felt so happy.

"Certainly is!" He gave me a wink as he started the engine.

"Perhaps it wasn't entirely hopeless after all!"

Later that night I swallowed the last of our red wine; and stood up, "I think we should go to Kathisma for a week!"

"And do what?"

"Oh! Just enjoy ourselves for a while." The wine had made me giddy and I began to laugh as I climbed into the van.

I remembered a tune from a television series, called, 'Auf Wiedersehn Pet,' and began singing except with different words. "Oh! You just have to muck it... and you pee in a bucket... That's living alright!"

Tony started laughing too as he followed me inside. "Somehow making money isn't all that important any more. As long as we've got food for the day and a roof over our heads, that's all that really matters." He lifted my hand to his lips and kissed it. "Yes, we'll just 'opt out' for a spell, and have a really good time!"

So we left the bright lights of Nidri harbor behind.

Chapter Ten

We awoke simultaneously, to the sound of loud clacking from a jackdaw in the nearby branches. There was an empty space where the Russian/Greek family's tent had been. Strangely, we hadn't met them again after that Sunday evening; our paths had simply just not crossed. This fact made that one occasion even more poignant somehow.

Within an hour we were sitting at our table having a breakfast, cooked by Tony.

I mention this because it is a very rare occasion when he attempts any form of cooking whatsoever. It was only boiled eggs, and bread and butter. But it was very nice and much appreciated; because I had been busy from the moment I awoke, washing all our clothes and our sheets. I wanted to start our week at Kathisma, 'all nice and clean' so I took full advantage of the washing facilities while I still had some. I wasn't sure when I would be able to wash the sheets again, or indeed anything else, but the sheets, and Tony's cut-down jeans, were the most difficult items, without a proper sink.

Anyway the line was full, and I knew that before long they would all be dry.

The air was hot and sultry, and we spent a lot of our time swatting flies, that persistently landed on our arms and legs, tickling us just enough so that we could not ignore them.

"Is the breakfast alright?"

"The eggs are delicious!" I replied, before plunging my spoon into my second one, and my sigh of delight convinced him. It wasn't that he refused to cook, it was simply the fact that I had always 'just done it'! I suppose I preferred to be a housewife, and enjoyed all the 'womanly' tasks that seemed to go with that role. I have always felt rather guilty about the fact that I must be letting 'women's rights' down, but it is something that perhaps many women of my age feel. And anyway it is too late now for either me or Tony to change. It would take far too long to train him into a 'new man'. So we stuck to our own particular rolls in life and it worked very well for us.

He had also cleaned the van out and washed it, somewhat roughly, with a bowl of water and a sponge, since we didn't have access to a hose pipe. But the old van looked a lot cleaner, now that the dust had been removed. So he had, in fact, 'done his bit'!

We did, of course, feel a bit sad at leaving the camp-site. We both said 'Goodbye' to the lamb, and I threw some melon to it, for the last time. We both wondered how long it would remain there. Surely its days were numbered, and we really didn't want to be around when it met the man with the knife!

So we drove on, along the road towards Lefkas town. We parked near the harbor and I made my way to the supermarket, while Tony made his way for a pint. There was something nice about browsing through the familiar store again. Tony was thoroughly enjoying sitting in his usual chair at the little cafe bar. Especially since the little plump lady who ran the place had welcomed him so very warmly. Also, many of the regulars nodded their greetings, as though they were saying, "Nice to see you again."

Tony likewise made a motion with his head.

I returned with my shopping. "Right then, off we go to Kathisma."

When we reached Aghios Nikitas, we resisted the temptation to turn down the street because we could see at a glance that both sides as far as the Poseidon were jam-packed with dusty cars and trucks. Instead we wound our way along the rough road, until we turned a bend and saw the bay of Kathisma.

Oh! How lovely it looked! All was blue, glistening blue, as far as the eye could see, and gold, shades of gold, from burnished ochre to dazzling white. We were so stirred that we caught our breath.

Tony spoke without taking his eyes off the road. "It's so good to see it again?"

"It's wonderful!" I replied, and I couldn't contain my delight, there was a leaping happiness in my heart, and I knew that Tony felt the same.

"Yippee! We're back again!" I shouted and laughed out loud.

We pulled up in our usual spot, near the big white stone, and jumped out. The ground was hot and baked hard, by the constant sun. We stood for a moment to absorb the familiarity of our surroundings. It was exactly the same; just as we had expected. So we began to make ourselves at home!

The beach was relatively empty of people, and those that were on the beach were evidently Greeks, since hardly any of Yiorgos sun chairs were being used.

Our first priority was to have a swim. The sand was so hot that I felt that at any minute it would burst into flames, like a volcano. We walked delicately to the waters edge, delicately because even though we wore flip-flops, our feet were still burning.

The minor triumph of conquering the journey from the van to the sea accomplished, we dived deliriously into the coolness of the blue. I think that I will always remember that moment of insurmountable relief and pleasure.

It was nice to be away from the bright lights and roaring car-and-scooter-packed streets of Nidri. But there were other factors that made our stay at Kathisma a happy one. And they were consistent. They involved the people that we shared the whole experience with. It was so refreshing to live in a setting where there was no hint of violence, or greed, or wanton destruction.

We began to listen more, and to think more, and be absorbed in another dimension of life. It was something that we had never had the time to do before.

August the 20th was a special day. It was Tony's fiftieth birthday. There were no birthday cards, except a funny one that I had made for him.

We decided to stay on the beach since it was too hot to do anything else

Then after sunset we went to Agios Nikitas, and when we entered the Poseidon it was empty. I felt dissatisfied because Tony's special birthday had not been any different from all the other days. I wanted to celebrate it! So I broke my promise to Tony, and mentioned the fact to Sylvia.

Kostas came to greet us, speaking in his usual funny voice that he kept especially for the occasions when he spoke English. "You have very...happy birthday time. I wish you many years!"

Immediately the word spread round the taverna and Vassilis danced towards us singing a sort of crying dirge that was presumably a birthday-type song! Anyway the accompanying wine was very nice!

We ordered souvlaki for our main course and mousakas for starters. Both were delicious, especially after a week of tinned ham and tinned tuna with salad.

∞∞∞

Vassilis continued to dance around us for most of the night singing and smiling cheerfully. The children all sang to us and even Thanai joined in, although from under one of the red and white plastic, table-clothed tables that stood in the white walled taverna.

Finally Sylvia brought us two big slices of red melon with sparklers stuck in them, dazzling merrily. "We do not have a birthday cake! So maybe you will like this."

We were actually very full, but we did our best to eat it so that we would appear to be grateful which, of course, we were!

When we called for the bill, Sylvia came to our table, with a mock stern expression. "No bill on birthdays." Then she laughed. "Yes, it is a rule."

We both insisted on paying, but she shook her head adamantly saying with a laugh. "You not argue!"

Then Kostas appeared from the kitchen. "What… ees the matter? You not... upset me.... Aye aye aye!"

So Tony had a memorable birthday, after all, even if a bit unusual.

⁊ɆΨ

The long hot days had made us languid, so we spent the time, in peaceful idleness. We spent hours transfixed by the tranquility of our surroundings, and by the beauty of it all. This mood prevented us from doing anything which required more than the least possible effort. So for the majority of the time we were immersed in the ever-welcoming embrace of the beautiful sea. Sometimes it was rough, but it was always beautiful. And we grew to enjoy its' varying moods, from calm serenity, to furious rage, as though we were tuning in to nature; on a colossal four dimensional screen!

We swam in the turquoise water, sometimes with only the company of silver fishes that seemed to constantly dance spasmodically in rhythm with the music of the sea.

We observed the crowds of happy people, and occasionally joined in with their merriment. But mostly we just sat and watched.

At night we basked in the coolness of the kind nights, when the entire world was asleep. We lay and gazed up at the Milky Way, and felt as though it was becoming nearer. We explored in detail the twinkling stars, and listened to the gentle lapping of the silver sea, until as though to a lullaby, we drifted off to sleep. To dream of pleasant things and wake enlightened to another glorious day.

One evening a group of children, girl-guides and scouts, sat around an open bonfire singing with the same enthusiasm as young blackbirds have at dawn.

I lay in our bed listening and looking out across the distant silver gleam, and wondered about it all. People from all over the world, were coming to Greek islands, and buying an illusion, in a package holiday. Were they trying to buy romance? I wondered how they thought that they could! To travel from their homes in about three hours, well, I suppose there was something good, and exciting in that. But to just stay in expensive hotels, to eat at fine restaurants, to sail around the Aristotle island and wonder at the irony of having so much wealth, and not be alive to enjoy any of it. To drift on splendid yachts, and sip champagne, was this defined as romance? Maybe it was! But surely a beauty such as this beach, and the sound of children's voices, sweet and vibrant drifting across the sand and over the sea, yes, this surely could be defined as romance.

So we lived in a kind of euphoric haze, a dream-like lotus land. And we enjoyed ourselves!

We awoke to golden mornings when small birds twittered in the long dry pampas grass, and twisted branches of nearby trees. A silver mist sometimes rose from the distant sea, and glistened like frost stars on pebbles at the water's edge, and the sand dazzled with sun sparkle. Sunbeams spread their warmth and filled the day with expectancy and light. And in the fiery dazzle of the sunset, small birds shook their feathers and swished on whirring wings, into some tiny refuge away from the mighty blast-like furnace of the sun.

After the fiery sun had made it's nightly awe-inspiring decent, some evenings we would make our way up the winding road to Agios Nikitas, to wander around and enjoy a drink, usually at Zak's bar.

This particular morning we were sitting in the fast diminishing shadow of the van, sipping our coffee, in a race against the sun's powerful rays. Soon all the shade would have gone and we would be exposed, and vulnerable. The only place in which to hide was the sea. We gazed trance-like at a long line of ants, marching in a single line from one side of the roadway to the other, carrying bits of leaves and orange peel. Their sheer determination had to be admired, since it appeared to be a task that had, and would, go on for ever. A green lizard came sneaking out of the dried grass and ran with darting movements and disappeared into a crevice in the rock-hard ground. And nearby on a yellow daisy flower, a Red Admiral rested while it drank. All the while there was the sad crying of the curlews as they staged their displays of fighting over the vast expanse of sea.

We had decided that this nomadic life, wonderful though it was, did lack a certain commodity that well-brought-up, respectable people needed from time to time. And that was simply the use of a decent bathroom. So we planned on visiting Iro again.

Tony stood up straightening his back. He was acting like a man who had suddenly and surprisingly come into a fortune. He felt young again, and full of vital life. There was a suspicion of moisture in his eyes. "Oh! Di, I could stay here like this forever!"

"Yes, well you had better start packing everything up." I laughed back, "because we really must set off and see if we can find a room."

We left the van at the entrance to the street and walked down on the slippery cobbles. Iro smiled and waved her hand to us from where she was sitting under the large tree, with her sister and the old man, who we later discovered was not as old as we thought; but that he had suffered a stroke. He was not their father; he was the husband of Iro's sister.

We walked up to Iro and I asked if she had a room. She said nothing, but she bobbed her head and laughed. Then she touched my face, stroking my cheek, as though I was a child, and she smiled into my eyes. She beckoned to us to follow her. "Ella!"

We walked up the steps and through the doorway along the short corridor and stopped outside our old room. She unlocked the door and threw it wide open, then with a laugh she said. "Einai to eithio!"(It is the same!)

We asked how much she would charge us to stay for three weeks. I hastened to add, that I would make the beds up, and that she needn't bother cleaning our room, as I would be happy to do it myself for the duration of our stay.

At this, she smiled. "Yia sas, mono 1,000 drachmes yia mia nickta."

I turned to Tony. "For us it is only 1,000 drachmas a night."

We thanked her warmly and I turned to Tony with a smile saying. "That's only about three pounds a night."

She looked happy as she indicated to us to sit in the shade of the tree which we were grateful to do, while she brought clean sheets for our beds. Within a minute she had returned and placed before us two big glasses of cold orange juice.

It was a lovely feeling being back in our room again, and the most wonderful thing of all was that it was cool. We finished drinking our orange, while we sat on our balcony. The air was pleasant, out of the sun. All of a sudden there was a movement in the nearby tent among the chaos, and fat Yiani emerged. He was both surprised and pleased to see us; he began waving frenziedly. His voice was as loud as ever. "**Yia**!" Then he walked towards us. "**Tonic! Yiasou**!"

Tony answered. "Yiasou Yiani, my old mate!" This pleased him enormously.

"Maiol maiet!" He murmured as he plodded noisily in loose fitting flip-flops, down the side street.

"That's your Liverpool accent!" I said, as we tried to stifle our laughter.

We were both so glad to be back.

In this place there was a pleasant camaraderie, among the inhabitants, whether they were the handful of elder citizens who remained all year round, or the majority who came from the mainland, to open the tavernas, and to let rooms, for the holiday period. They all shared naturalness in the simple wish to be content. So the best in others was sought, and not the worst. We felt privileged to be allowed to join in with their way of life. We were accepted. No, it was even more, we were welcomed. We experienced a rare friendship like we have never known before, or since. And there was this barter...meals were provided at various tavernas, in exchange for us doing some kindness. Sometimes it was some shopping for one of the tavernas. Whenever we went into town we would have a strange shopping list, from postage stamps to kilos of lettuce, and five kilos of lettuce is an awful lot! Other times we would simply lend someone our generator to enable them to keep their fridge going, when for no good reason that we could see, the electricity company would go on strike. But even this, in itself, proved to establish more of a bond of comradeship, and was always a cause for laughter, and much joviality. It was something akin to an air-raid scene that I have seen in old 1940 films, when people helped each other, simply because they wanted to. There was a simple aim to be friendly, without self-conscious effort, it came in the form of enthusiasm, sympathy and general cheerfulness.

Now and again we were asked to collect a prescription for one of the old folk, and in return we would be given some fresh eggs, or a freshly baked cake. But we were always given something. Even though we didn't want payment, that was simply the way it was, and we had to accept it; and the gift, whatever it may be.

These were the customs that had lasted for generation after generation, and we respected them.

Two days had passed, and we were feeling quite respectable again, having acquired the use of a bathroom.

There was however an even worse parking problem.

A police patrol called intermittently, without warning, and caused quite a commotion. Two policemen with leather holsters draped causally around their hips, guns gleaming, hats strategically placed on the side of their dark heads, and a cigarette dangling from their lips, would arrive in the middle of the street abandoning their car, or motorbikes dramatically, and strut around blowing whistles extremely loudly.

This brought an almost immediate response.

Cars and trucks of all descriptions were moved with a resounding clatter. Engines were revved, doors banged, brakes screeched, alarms went off, and horns hooted. All accompanied by an assortment of dialogue, from calls of mock alarm to friendly exchange of greetings, and a considerable amount of hollers of laughter. The street was suddenly empty of vehicles. The policemen sometimes stopped for a drink in the shade of the Poseidon, and admired the passing female tourists, and they themselves, were frequently admired in return. Then they left with a loud tooting on their horn, and a revving of their engine. And as soon as they had departed, all the vehicles returned. It was like something from the 'Keystone Cops'! There was the same hullabaloo as before, except that there was even more laughter. So whatever the reason was for this display of law and order, we never found out. But it made us weary of leaving the van in the street so that we could claim our position for the evening, while we spent the day on the beach. We didn't want to run the risk of getting another parking ticket. But, the children were constantly pleading with us to show the video in the street again.

Liana suggested that we should go and speak to the 'Gaithouros.' "He is the President of the village," she said. "And he will be able to give you permission to park wherever you want to...then you will have no problem."

We heard that he was holding a weekly meeting in his office on Wednesday at 11am. So off we went to have a word with him, and hopefully obtain his permission to leave the van outside the Poseidon so that we could show the film there in the evenings.

His house was some way along the main road that ran across the top of the street. We were both sweating and panting from the heat and the excursion of the walk by the time we reached the building. We entered through a series of shabby brown painted doors. The passageway was dark and dreary. A small old man showed us into a room that was equally dismal. Once we were inside, we wished heartily that we had not come. Behind a large dark desk sat a man. He didn't look up when we first walked in, but finished writing. Then slowly he lifted his head and made two imperceptible nodding motions, towards both of us. He indicated to two chairs, so we both sat down. When we were seated he said something in Greek, but his voice was gruff and his words were fast, and what he said was lost on me. So I just stared rather stupidly. Then I ventured. "Milate Anglika Kirie?"(Do you speak English Sir?)

"Ohi." He replied. So there was nothing else but to try to explain what we wanted as best as I could in Greek. I hoped that he would not interrupt my flow with questions, because although I knew what **I** was saying, I sometimes found it hard to know what **they** were saying; Particularly when the atmosphere was authoritative, or tense. I became nervous and lost my concentration. Anyway I babbled on and thankfully he didn't interrupt me, but listened intently to what I was saying. I think that I actually noticed an indication of admiration in his dark eyes. I do know that he noted the fact that I used the polite form of address, and the customary acknowledgements that are respectful to a person of high regard. And he was suitably impressed by this and nodded appreciatively at the appropriate moments of my speech. I finished by assuring him of our gratitude if he would give us his permission, and I smiled hopefully into his face. He nodded briefly at us both then got to his feet and went out of the room.

Tony and I looked at each other in bewilderment. Then the man came back into the room accompanied by a particularly eccentric character that we had already had the misfortune to meet on a few occasions in the village, and had, I am ashamed to admit, tried to avoid meeting him again.

His name was Patros. He was middle-aged, but wore ridiculous floral shorts with a checked shirt, and was always bare-footed. He shaved his head, but sported a long thick black beard. This combined with a large sombrero hanging on his back and a walking cane made a rather bizarre image. But he could speak English very well, except that his tone never varied. He spoke as though he was announcing a dreadfully sad event, as though breaking the news of a death. And never did he smile or laugh, but remained permanently in this awful state of despair. He told us once, that he had lived his life without hope! And that he was a depressive. We sympathized, but we did not want to become too involved, so we usually avoided meeting him.

The President introduced him to us briefly. "This ...Patros."

Tony and I immediately felt embarrassed, but smiled. "Hello."

On seeing us Patros spoke to the President telling him that he had already made our acquaintances. I hoped that he wouldn't also tell him that we had deliberately avoided him.

Patros spoke slowly and drearily. "The President says that you want to show a video in the street, is this right?"

"Yes." We both answered.

"And you will charge for this video, is this right?"

"Yes." We answered again.

He then turned to the President and there followed a long loud verbal exchange that I found very difficult to understand.

Then Patros turned to me again. "How much money will you charge people?"

"Four thousand drachmas," I was beginning to feel a little uneasy, would he consider this too much.

Again there was a somewhat heated dialogue between the two men and the President threw his arms in the air a few times and shook his head from side to side. Did they think that this was too expensive, I wondered. I thought about offering him a percentage, but I was unsure if this might be considered bribery, so I hesitated.

Then eventually both men turned towards me and the President peered directly into my eyes, as Patros posed the question. "The President wants to know why you charge so much money just for people to look at the video?"

"Oh! No!" I cried. "We don't charge them anything to look at the video, only if they want to **buy** a video."

At my alarmed, but amused response, the President appeared confused, until Patros explained what I had said. Then the President burst into laughter and Tony and I joined his joviality. We all saw the funny side of the misunderstanding. But Patros remained straight faced as ever, and completely unstirred.

The President said something to Patros, who made a polite bowing gesture before leaving the room, and then he sat down. Still smiling, he wrote something in a large black book before closing it and with one wave of his arm he dismissed us from the room. Our meeting was over; but we were none the wiser.

As we emerged through the doorway again into the brilliance of the day we saw Patros outside with the old man who had shown us in.

We went over to him and I spoke. "Excuse me Patros but could you tell us if we have been given permission or not. I'm afraid we are not quite sure since the President didn't give us anything in writing."

Patros stared at me for a long moment in silence then he glanced at Tony, before he droned. "The President will decide and give you his deliberations accordingly." Then he turned away abruptly and walked off.

Tony and I looked at each other and Tony said. "Well, I suppose that is that!"

"Yes and at least he didn't say no!" I replied. So feeling quite optimistic about the whole business we walked back to our room.

೮ం೧౩

By Friday morning we still hadn't heard any news from the President, and we learnt that he lived in Lefkas town so we might have to wait until his next visit before we heard anything. We wanted to please the children and let them see the video, and we were not averse to earning a bit of money either, if it was only enough to pay for the room and our food.

So on the evening of Friday the 28th we prepared to show the film.

The children were so delighted that they ran excitedly up and down the street shouting at the top of their voices, "**Video! Video!**" Then they stood around excitedly waiting near to the van. When Tony and I stepped out there was a resounding cheer. People passing by were completely baffled by it all. We had noticed quite a few people stopping to look at our van with the GB sticker and English registration.

"It must have cost you a few bob to fly that over!" One man said to me. I don't think he quite believed that we had driven there. But I suppose when you are so far away from home, and in such diverse surroundings, England does appear to be in another world.

We had set everything up, and were just about to start the video, when suddenly darkness fell, that was as black as pitch. All the lights in Agios Nikitas had gone out. There was loud laughter coming from the Poseidon, as the staff ran around lighting candles and sticking them into empty bottles. People on their way back to their rooms walked carefully, carrying a lighted candle, and before long the street had taken on the appearance of some religious ceremony.

The video began, and a rapturous applause rang out. Then as the music started, the crowd fell silent, entranced and completely captivated. It was as though some miracle had fallen out of the sky, old people and children alike stood gazing as though they were watching flickering pictures in a magic lantern.

The old lady, who always wore the traditional brown costume, was standing right in the front. "Auraia!" She murmured as though she was observing some amazing phenomenon. And children echoed her exclamations, with wide-eyed interest. Liana's two little girls were ecstatic, and Constantino was almost delirious with excitement!

When the street appeared on the screen the children cheered so loudly that holiday-makers came to see what was going on. And when they saw the children all swaying and singing along with the video they were all over the moon. Maybe the magical atmosphere was accentuated by the candle-lit ambience, since their spirits were already jubilant. The enthusiasm of the children was such that the mood was definitely infectious.

A lady who had been watching the children's happy faces with interest, suddenly pushed her way to the front and asked for four copies. She told us that she was part of a large group from Lancashire. "Eh! We all want one of them to take home with us!" she said smiling. "Eh! It's the best thing I have seen in a long while!"

That was it then; everybody wanted one. Hands were appearing holding out drachma notes. Some people were writing cheques, with some difficulty, since the children were shouting and pushing so much.

"To Gaithouros!" The children suddenly started shouting with some alarm.

I looked up to see the figure of the President looming above me. I was instantly filled with dread, and I looked beseechingly at Tony.

"What are we going to do?"

Tony looked utterly helpless. We were like two children caught in the act of doing something wrong. We waited for retribution. But we were surprised to witness sheer delight on the face of this rather austere man, as he watched the video with the same fascination as the children.

"Auraia!" he muttered.

We knew then that he was impressed, and this was confirmed by the fact that he held out four-thousand drachma notes to me smiling. "Parakalo Video!"

"The President wants to buy a video!" I whispered to Tony, handing him the money as he handed a cassette to me, which I gave to the President.

He held it high in the air and spoke loudly to the people all around. I wasn't sure of his words, but I knew that they were complimentary by the applause that they received and by the broad smile that he gave me as he departed.

"Efharisto para poly!" (Thank you very much!) Then he added in Greek that we were doing a very fine thing for his village, and showing everybody how beautiful Lefkas is, so that many more people will come to see the island and visit Agios Nikitas.

I seized the opportunity to mention our parking permit, whereupon he burst into fits of laughter saying that we could park anywhere that we wanted to.

I again suggested that he would write that down for us, but he merely said. "No problem!" Then he walked away.

Maybe his approval encouraged more people to buy a video, I don't know, but by the end of our first showing we had sold twenty copies. Tony had been sweating profusely again, causing me to become almost hysterical with laughter.

He wiped his streaming face with a towel and looked into my eyes.

"We've already made two-hundred and forty pounds so far!"

We showed the video again. But it was solely because we wanted to keep the happy mood going; it would have been shameful to have denied everyone so much enjoyment.

It was as though the night had been touched by a magic wand.

We did however sell another fourteen videos! This was also wonderful, but less important somehow.

"How much money did we earn?" I asked Tony as he prepared to close down until the following evening.

"Just over four-hundred pounds," he answered with a laugh. "But wasn't it great?"

"It certainly was! But I wish that the President had given us some sort of parking permit."

As we walked into the Poseidon Tony gave me a wink. "I don't think we need to worry about anything any more! I really think that we will be alright!" I glanced into his face and he smiled. "No problem!" Then added with a laugh, "I'm only just beginning to learn the Greek ways!"

The Poseidon was glowing brightly. Small lanterns had been placed on all the tables and inside the kitchen.

I looked about me and remarked, blinking against the brightness, "Doesn't it all look welcoming!"

"The paraffin lamps, they look very nice!" Tony said as Sylvia came to take our order.

"They are not paraffin; they are petrol."

Tony almost gagged on his beer. "Isn't that rather dangerous?"

"Yes," she answered, with a light-hearted shake of her head. "Yes, one day there will be a big BOOM!" Then she added, "paraffin...we call...kerosene...is very hard to get. So Kostas he use...petrol."

We looked inside the kitchen and noticed one lamp almost alongside the barbecue! Tony shook his head. "Well here's a potential catastrophe, if ever I saw one!"

We ate our meal quickly and decided not to go to the Poseidon again during an electricity strike. On our way out we saw Vassilis, with his pet canary that never flew far away, looking very relaxed.

However, regarding our parking problems, we didn't need to worry about anything. The following day we waited until the police patrol arrived and all the vehicles left the street. We watched to see if we would get a ticket, Tony was ready to rush up and explain about the President giving us permission, but he would move the van if necessary. However, there was no need. It was as though our van was invisible; It was the only vehicle in the street. As the two young policemen strolled past, resplendent in pale blue short-sleeve shirts and dark blue trousers and peaked hats, I heard one mutter something about the video, and his companion answered. "Auraia!"

Was our fame spreading? I wondered.

The days and evenings passed, each with its own special moments that we were to remember in the months and years ahead.

We were indulging in what we wanted to do in our environment which was, to say the least, very pleasant and we were enjoying ourselves. We wondered how many others would have enjoyed living the way that we were. We had our problems, yes, but we had learnt to adapt. We were not being forced to conform to a set of rules or conditions set out by employers. Nobody demanded anything from us. We were alone, but not alone, for as George had put it, that day on the hill-top, "In such a place no-one is lonely, for all the rest is by his side."

We felt that we had friends all around us, but above all, we had each other. We were together in everything we did. Our relationship had never been deterred by passing fancies or conventional standards. What we had was true friendship plus a continual unselfish love.

There were other factors that made that time of our lives so special, and they were constant. They were the people that we associated with during the last period of our stay in Greece. Locals of all ages, old people, young people, from strutting young bucks to attractive giggling girls, and children, everywhere the children, waving to us good-humouredly and smiling. This is the picture that will spring to my mind when I recall our stay in Lefkas.

One day we were planning to go into town for a few items, as well as a container of petrol for the generator.

We called up the steps of the Poseidon, "Do you want anything from town?"

"Yes, some lettuce, tomatoes and twenty stamps from the Post Office," Sylvia replied.

I asked how much lettuce and tomatoes? She deliberated for a moment before coming back with, "Er...about five kilos of each."

Suddenly fat Yiani remembered that the old lady needed some ointment, so he ran down the steps to her humble home. He was soon back again clutching a prescription shouting, "Appo pharmacio!" (From the pharmacy!)

We assured him that we would find the chemist shop.

We set off up the street and felt a queer little thrill, a feeling that seems to come from somewhere deep inside your being, only remotely described by words. It must have been love! Yes, that is what it was. It was love, and it was gratitude, for allowing us to become, 'part of it all'.

As we drove back from town, with the van full to bursting with tomatoes and lettuce, Tony merrily declared. "When I was a computer manager in Liverpool, I never thought I'd finish up as a green-grocers errand boy in Greece!" This made us both laugh out loud.

ഓരു

On Friday the 11th September we were sitting on an ancient stone wall gazing across the shimmering blue, when the old lady in the brown traditional costume strolled towards us. She said nothing, but she smiled affectionately, placing five almonds in my hand. It was a simple gesture, but it was significant. I have kept the almonds to this day.

I telephoned my mother and heard that our house would be vacated on the 22nd of the month. Iro was planning to close down the rooms within a week, intending to go back to Athens. All the tavernas were preparing to close down for the winter. The old folk who stayed behind were preparing for the cold spell, and everyone who was able, was collecting wood for them. Our old friend in brown, walked about now with an additional shawl wrapped around her arms saying with a smile that was permanent. "Hirmona erthi!" (Winter is coming!)

"Einai krio!"(It's cold!) Iro was now wearing a black cardigan on top of her black dress, or jumper, and she rubbed her hands together.

We however, found the temperature was very pleasant and far from cold. In the evenings we needed some covering on our arms, but that was all.

So we spent our last Sunday, the 6th.September, with the Tsetikas family, at Agios Nikitas, playing in and out of the water. Demetrious again insisted on taking us for lunch at one of the tavernas, he was still adamant that we must not offer to pay. We chose the cheapest meal, but were scolded by Mata who ordered us something else in addition, so defeating the whole object. But we thoroughly enjoyed being in their company. They had become like family to us in a strange and wonderful way. George spoke English to us almost all the time, while Demetrious and Mata nodded their approval. So, it seemed that we were providing George with a rare opportunity of improving his English, so they were showing us their gratitude.

The evening ended with a lot of hugs and kisses, even Demetrious hesitantly kissed me on both cheeks, and then shook Tony's hand warmly. We exchanged addresses and I promised to write in Greek to George, while he would write to us in English. We would correct each others letters. This seemed an agreeable arrangement.

George spoke on behalf of the whole family, "We have had wonderful time with you...Er my mother and father say that you must come any time to stay with us. Yes, we have very big flat. You must come!" Then he added with a smile, "You must remember that we will always be your friends."

We both thanked them all, but somehow words were not enough!

Unexpectedly George stood up to make an announcement.

"My brother Fotis is... going to say... something now... in English to you." Then he promptly sat down again.

Fotis shyly got to his feet; he glanced towards us, and then looked all around, diverting his big, dark, shining eyes. There was a hint of pink flooding over his face, while he swayed in time with the rhythm of his much practiced words.

"We all will... miss you … and we hope... to one day... meet again."

"Auraia!" Antigony shouted, and everyone clapped.

At that moment the little girl slid down from her chair and walked slowly up to my side. She put her small hand to her mouth and she whispered in my ear. "Se agapo!"(I love you!)

₧₨

The following week passed pleasantly.

We showed the video most evenings and the children never seemed to tire of seeing it. Business was quite good. We usually sold anything between one to twenty videos. So we were happy to realize that our idea had been a success, but more importantly it had brought so much happiness to the village.

One evening, our aged friend came up to the door of our van. Her face was lined as always, but there was a twinkle in her black eyes. She frowned and gnawed at her lip. Then she told me that she had really enjoyed watching the video. I thanked her for telling us that, whereupon she began to chuckle, saying that she would prefer to see another video next year, because she was getting a bit bored with the same one.

₧₨

One evening towards the end of the week, Tony and I were strolling up the street. The children of the village had positioned themselves in small groups at appropriate places along the way. In front of them they had an upturned cardboard box, with a lighted candle in a jar. All around the candle was an assortment of stones, picked from the beach, but painted with various designs, flowers, animals, spots and stripes. There was also another jar for people to place a few coins, if they wished to buy a decorated stone. But the children didn't ask anybody to buy one. They simply sat and waited and hoped! And we knew how they felt! But if somebody did select a stone and place a coin or two in the jar, there was such jubilation! Again we identified with their delight. But there was this wonderful first impression that was pleasing to behold, a lovely vision of children being absorbed in their own work; feeling exhilarated by their own achievements. Maybe they were unaware of the fact that each painted pebble sold, would give pleasure to people, reminding them of this little street and of the children that they had come to know. Even so, there was a pride and satisfaction that went beyond words. We also knew this feeling. So we felt an affinity with these children.

On the bottom step of the 'Korrali', Constantino was sitting alongside Katrina and Louisa, who were Lianas' little girls. In front of them was their box, complete with candle, jar, and various sized stones. They were probably not as expertly painted as some, but the children were every-bit as proud of their labor and craftsmanship.

Tony and I stopped to admire the stones, seeing three elated little faces gazing up at us. I selected a stone with pink and blue flowers. "Poso cani?" (How much is it?"

"Yia sou, teepota!" (For you, nothing!) Constantino immediately replied, Wrapping it carefully in a paper serviette and enclosing a card from the restaurant, he spoke with a shy little smile. "Eene thoro, appo to Korrali!" (It's a present from the Korrali!)

This picture of children happily occupied in the pursuit of simple pleasures will remain with me, as will all the other reflections, far too numerous to mention.

At the time we were part of it all, so we did not perceive any of it as outsiders, so maybe our involvement prohibited us from appreciating fully the implications. It is often the case that it is only on reflection that one realizes how important certain seemingly trivial events really are. In this age of computerized living, life can sometimes become dull. Daily routine becomes boring, we lose the motivation, and we don't stop to take the time to dream.

Children lose the ability to amuse themselves, to find pleasure in simple things, they are so pre-occupied in obtaining possessions, but what is the saddest thing of all, they forget how to play.

Maybe all our lives are destined by luck! Who really knows? I certainly don't. But I do believe that in the great scheme of things there must be a reason for everything. Maybe we were lucky to recognize the fact that this was our chance to achieve our dream. It is not always easy to know when an opportunity comes along. Sometimes we are too involved with more important issues, because that is the way we live; in a pre-planned society. So rare opportunities become obscure, so they are often missed. It is only when one looks back we wonder why we lost the chance of doing something. But at that particular moment of time maybe we were muddled by conflicting ideas and circumstances. They were probably terribly important at the time, yet when we look back to question, they are so insignificant that they cannot even be recalled. And ironically the missed opportunity remains crystal clear in our minds, and we wonder why we never saw it at the time. Maybe fear of risking failure is contributory, or we decide to play safe, so we lose our spirit of adventure.

But undoubtedly we all look back at some time or other and wonder why we didn't listen to our instincts. Why did we hesitate? Why did we lose our dreams?

I believe that everyone should have a dream and try to catch it before it fades away.

For us, this sojourn in Greece was a way out of a depression and in achieving 'our dream' of making holiday videos in Lefkas: for many other people, we were also catching dreams for them. We had captured the atmosphere of the island, and its' beauties, so providing them with a vivid memory of their holiday. We had gained joy from the knowledge that not only had we given pleasure to the locals, who we came in contact with, but that our videos would bring eternal happy memories in homes all over the world.

We had learnt so much from our varied experiences.

Greece had brought us some odd adventures, cherished friendships, but most importantly a valuable lesson in morality.

It was like the dawning of a new day, in a new world, vibrant and alive and Oh! So very beautiful!

We felt that we had left a part of ourselves there, a part that we would never get back. Some people search all their lives, but never find true happiness.

Maybe we had been blessed, because from our sadness we found a certain happiness that we had never known before. Maybe when you have lost everything material, you have nothing left to lose. Then, if you are lucky and determined, you can overcome all obstacles. But you have to have a dream!

On our last day, Saturday 12th September we climbed a winding path that led to the top of a hill that overlooked Lefkas town and harbor.

The air was now considerably cooler, so much so that it had been very comfortable to walk on daisy studded turf, with only the company of crickets, unseen but always heard.

We had grown to recognize the sound of a scolding jackdaw and the cheerful chirruping of sparrows in the safety of the sweet-smelling pine behind us. In the distance, perched on crevices in the white cliffs, the mournful cries of kitty hawks came drifting on the breeze. While butterflies of unexplainable brilliance danced among the myriads of wild flowers.

In the valley below, nightingales sang sweetly and the glade echoed with birdsong. When we reached the summit we stood for a long moment, somewhat unsteadily. The climb had taken its' toll, the path had been steep. I felt as though we were standing on the edge of the world. Around us the ground was carpeted with wild thyme, so we sat down on a craggy rock in the shade of a grotesquely-twisted old citrus tree. The view from there was spectacular. It exceeded anything that I had ever seen.

To the right of us some little way away were some ancient ruined walls. Maybe at one time it had been someone's home. It could have been the ideal scholar's retreat, somewhere where one could live in seclusion with one's thoughts. Where you could watch the days unfold and feel man's relation with the environment... Past and present seemed an illusion.

Now the ruins were covered with rambling creepers, and what had been an ancient tiled roof, was interspersed with purple vines. Among the broken walls flowers bloomed in abundance. Even in such a dreary place, it somehow looked charming. It must have been there for about two thousand years. I wondered what secrets it held. Like the island itself.

Tony spoke suddenly, interrupting my daydreams.

"What will we do to earn our living when we go home?"

"I suppose we'll think of something!" I replied with a sigh. Then still looking out over the distant bay, I added, "Maybe we could start making wedding videos."

"Yes, I think I'd like to do that. It would be nice to feel that we could capture the magic and excitement of a very special day for people."

"We could make them really special!" I was suddenly filled with an intensity of feeling.

"Yes." Tony nodded his head. His voice was unexpectedly gentle. "We'll be alright, Di." His hand reached across the grass and covered mine. In that brief moment I knew that everything would turn out well for us, because we had the most important thing of all. We had an emotional safety that came from knowing that we could share our joys and sorrows with each other. No-matter what life threw at us, together we could face the world.

₧₨

After a while the thought of leaving this beautiful island didn't seem so daunting. We had found a reason to go home. Apart from seeing our family, of course! We had a new dream, something else to aim for. And what was more, we believed that we would be successful.

Sometimes the path of life is not clear before us, sometimes darkness surrounds us and we feel lost and vulnerable. Our spirits become weak, so we can't be bothered to dream and let our thoughts flow like a rushing, flowing stream. We lose the ability to recognize the elusive, magical, enchanting elements of life that are with us every day, but we don't take the time to stop and look.

We all have our memories, pictures vivid in our minds. But do we have visions of the future? Do we know how to enjoy the moment? For the future may not even exist! Life hangs in a fine balance of yesterday...today. and forever.

The way of our dreams had called; and we had heard and followed.

Later, when we slowly made our way down the winding path beneath the pines, we knew that we had done far more than climb a hill that day. We had decided which way our future lay. So far as anyone can plan ahead, for no-one knows for sure, 'what is around the next bend'? But we no longer felt lost, or vulnerable. We had confidence in our own abilities.

Our last night at the Poseidon was something very special. We were treated to Kostas' mousaka, for starters. After that we had pork kebabs and chips, with two bottles of beer. The children always waited until we had finished eating before they joined us.

First fat Yiani came to our table and gave Tony a rather hefty pat on the back; he made a pointing gesture with his entire hand towards the top of the road.

"Avrio, tha pate?"(Tomorrow you will go?)

"Neh, prepi Na pame!"(Yes, we have to go!") I replied sadly.

He studied our faces for some time then nodded and with a questioning look in his dark eyes asked. "Alla, tha yierisete?"(But, you will return?)

"Elpiso! Ena mera."(I hope so! One day.) I answered.

Vassilis danced towards us with a bottle of 'Ouzo' balanced on his head. "For you!" He placed it on the table with such a dramatic gesture that we were quite overcome.

Then Sylvia brought us a bottle of 'Retsina.' "This is to remember your friends at the Poseidon." As if we could ever forget them!

Kostas came out of the kitchen. "Have good journey home! And our best weeshes are going with you." Then we saw Thanai smiling from the tent, where she was playing.

She walked bashfully up to our table and placed a little gift wrapped in brown paper in front of me. I opened it, while she wriggled about with embarrassment, before she ran back inside the tent again.

I unwrapped the present to find a small clay pot.

Sylvia told us that Thanai had made it at school and that she was particularly proud of her achievement. She was very surprised that she had wanted to part with it.

So we felt doubly honored. We called. "Efharisto poly!" And Thanai smiled sweetly back.

At this point of time, fat Yiani suddenly disappeared inside the tent while little Yiani his cousin and Demetrious his brother, gave me a kiss and Tony a handshake.

When he came out again he was holding a small plastic carrier bag. With delight, as well as his usual self-esteem, he presented us with a collection of unusual shells. Some had been touched-up with colored pens, but we pretended that we believed them to be genuine, for we knew that the sentiments that went with them certainly were. It was all that he had to give!

He took one large cone shaped shell out of the bag and placed it to his own ear, before handing it to me.

"Akouies!"(You listen!)

I put the shell to my ear and listened to the echoing sound.

"Einai y thallassa!"(It is the sea!) He was smiling broadly.

And I replied, "Tha sas thimomaste panta!" (We will remember you all, always!)

We felt sorrier to say goodbye to him, than to anyone! And we both hugged him with such affection.

When we walked out of the Poseidon that night all the staff waved good-humoredly and applauded us.

Kostas shouted. **"You not... forget us!"** When we waved back, he pointed as he had done on the video laughing. "Aye... aye... aye!"

കരു

The morning sun shone brightly outside our balcony. We were feeling a mixture of emotions. Suddenly fat Yiani emerged from the tent and stretching his arms in the air called to us, "Kalimera!"

We would miss his friendly greetings. We would miss so many things. We had grown accustomed to our surroundings, even fond of the strange view from our balcony. The half dead bushes, the wiry scrub, the bare zigzag of track that wound its way over the headland, and up to the old ruins.

Iro was running around fussing over us and repeatedly told us to come back again the following year.

We were feeling quite sad when we walked out of our room and down the steps for the last time. Placing our suitcase in the van we prepared to take our leave. Just as Iro was hugging us again, our ancient friend came up to us and carefully handed us a brown paper bag. Today she had a deeply worried look and seemed slightly more subdued than usual, but the sparkle was still evident in her eyes when she spoke.

"Partei afta!" (Take these!) she said. "Yia taxidi sas."(For your journey.)

I peeped inside to find about a dozen large brown eggs. Thanking her warmly we wondered if we would ever see her again, because she was so very old.

It seemed a long time before we were driving slowly up the street. The children were all standing along the side of the road waving and smiling at us. Thanai and Constantino had climbed up onto a high wall with Liana's two little girls, who were almost in tears, but they were smiling just the same. As did all of the locals who saw us leave. They left whatever they were doing to smile and wave to us. That is what we will remember above all else.

Words cannot describe how we felt as we left Agios Nikitas.

കരു

On reaching the wide bend in the road where the bay of Yiro lay, with Lefkas town and causeway in the distance, Tony stopped the van and we sat and gazed at the view.

"Well here it is!" Tony said. "And we are leaving again! I wonder if we will ever come back!"

"I wonder!" I answered, and held my hand out to him.

He squeezed it gently. "We did it though Di didn't we?"

"Yes, we did!""

We drove on through the town, now strangely quiet because it was Sunday; Then across the noisy metal bridge.

I glanced at Tony and spoke casually, but from my heart. "I wish that I could share all this with other people. There must be dreamers out there who would enjoy sharing our experiences."

"Well you could always write a book!"

I smiled and wondered was this one of those opportunities? Would I look back and wonder why I hadn't? If so, then what we had learnt from this whole venture would have been in vain.

"You know, I think I might just do that!" I felt that I could do anything that I set my heart to; As though I had been blessed, and I had been given a special gift.

৳০৪

The road ahead was very long, but we were filled with excitement. Our dreams were calling! This was not the end, it was only the beginning... We had a new goal! We had a hope! We had a dream!

"Now Lefkas was behind us, and I looked back sadly thinking, Lefkas, you are not unique, but as magical as all Greek islands are! Here in the land of the ancient Gods, and on the island of Ulysses, did we really find the secret of true happiness...Or were we merely... "Chasing Dreams?"

৳০৪

Four days later after a long and tiring journey we eventually parked our van back onto our driveway at home in West Kirby, Cheshire, UK, It felt very strange. We walked inside our house and immediately felt like intruders. The house seemed so big and luxurious.

Tony picked up a note that was lying on the carpet behind our front door.

"It's from Cliff!" he said. "It says ring me as soon as you get home. It's very important."

"Well you had better ring him then." I was beginning to feel nervous wondering if anything awful had happened to Maureen. I also felt guilty at not keeping in touch with her, since she had been such a good friend to me for a long time. But we were forced to leave their kind of lifestyle and get on with our own.

"Hi Cliff," I heard Tony say. "Yes we had quite an experience."

"How is Mo?" I interrupted.

"Cliff heard you, and she's fine except she wonders what you have been up to?" Then he was listening intently and I could hardly contain my curiosity.

"You need what?" He looked at me and his smile spread from ear to ear, every trace of fatigue from the journey was gone.

"I'll be there at nine on the dot tomorrow," he said before adding, "Thanks Cliff Thanks ever so much."

"What was all that about?" I was completely puzzled.

"They need an IT manager at Montgomery's," he went on with a bemused expression. "The managing director wants to meet me tomorrow. Cliff has been waiting for me to get back and the company agreed to wait for me. Cliff has convinced them that I am the man for the job." Happiness was welling up in him. "I start on double the salary that I earned before!"

My jaw fell and my mouth opened. "That's amazing!"

"I know and there is a new company car of my choice."

"Gosh!" Was all I could say.

Then he remembered something else. "Oh, yes and we can use the villa in Portugal!" He winked saying, "It's what they call benefit in kind."

I was walking into our lounge to sit down. Tony followed me and sat beside me. "Apparently when he told the Managing Director, Graham, about what we had done, he was very impressed. He said to Cliff, 'that is the sort of bloke we need in this company, someone who is not afraid of a challenge.' Imagine that!"

"I bet he doesn't know that it was really **my** idea!" I replied with a smile.

"Anyway now all our worries are over, we have a brand new life ahead." Tony laughed and his face was flushed with happiness.

I was speaking through tears of joy now. "Oh Tony I am so happy! I love you!"

"I love you too!" He replied.

We had taken a risk to try to reach our dreams, and by doing so, we had found success and the true meaning of happiness.

Printed in the United Kingdom by
Lightning Source UK Ltd., Milton Keynes
141156UK00001B/22/P